Landlo

Landlord and Tenant

J M Male
Barrister

SECOND EDITION

Pitman Publishing Limited
128 Long Acre, London WC2E 9AN

A Longman Group Company

© Pitman Publishing Ltd 1984

First published 1982
Second edition 1984
Reprinted 1986

British Library Cataloguing in Publication Data

Male, J. M.
    Landlord and tenant.—2nd ed.—(The
    M & E HANDBOOK series)
    1. Rental housing—Law and legislation—
    England
    I. Title
    344.2064'344   KD899

ISBN 0-7121-0500-X

Filmset in Great Britain by Northumberland Press Ltd,
Gateshead, Tyne and Wear
and printed by Richard Clay (The Chaucer Press) Ltd,
Bungay, Suffolk

Preface

I first thought of writing this book in about November 1977. At that time it seemed to me that there was a lack of a very basic book on landlord and tenant setting out the main general principles without the detailed analysis of the more learned textbooks. I think that there still is, to a certain extent, such a lack in what is a very complicated field of the law and I hope that this book goes a small way towards filling the gap.

The book will be suitable for those studying for law degrees, for the Bar, solicitors' and legal executives' professional examinations, and for courses in estate management and surveying.

It must be stressed that the chapters on statutory protection only give an outline of the various codes. Accordingly, if any question of detail arises, rather than one of general principle, on one of the statutory codes, reference may have to be made to some more learned text. This is particularly so of the chapters on long leases, leasehold enfranchisement, agricultural tenancies and the Rent (Agriculture) Act 1977. At the end of the book there are chapters dealing with the main effects of the Housing Act 1980. This extensively revised second edition covers the provisions of the Housing and Building Control Act 1984, the County Courts Act 1984, the Housing Defects Act 1984 and the Agricultural Holdings Act 1984.

My thanks must go to Mr. Michael Barnes, Q.C., for reading through the first draft and making so many helpful comments and pointing out the errors. Any errors that remain are entirely mine. My thanks also go to my father and mother for their encouragement and active assistance in the preparation of the book.

October 1984   JMM

Contents

Table of Cases

PART ONE
LANDLORD AND TENANT
AT COMMON LAW

CHAPTER I

Introduction

THE LAW

1. The relationship of landlord and tenant. This book is concerned with the legal effect of the relationship between landlord and tenant. The law on the subject falls conveniently into two parts. They are:

(*a*) the general principles governing the relationship of landlord and tenant; and

(*b*) the statutory control of the relationship.

The purpose of this chapter is to provide a brief, general introduction and to define basic terms.

2. History. The relationship of landlord and tenant confers on the tenant an estate in land. This has not always been, so, for in medieval land law the relationship was regarded as a matter of contract only. It gave rise to a purely personal right and not to any right of property. This meant that it bound only the two parties to the agreement and did not, as is the case today, create rights and obligations binding upon third parties. It was not until the end of the fifteenth century that the law treated the relationship as conferring on the tenant a right in property which was binding on other people.

The more recent history of the law of landlord and tenant is concerned with the various statutes enacted to regulate and control the relationship. Such statutes started to appear in the mid-nineteenth century and there has since been a steady flow of them. They first dealt with agricultural lettings in the nineteenth century. Since the 1914–18 War, however, there have been Acts dealing with residential lettings, business lettings and, more recently, leasehold enfranchisement as well as others dealing with agricultural lettings.

1

Most recently there has been statutory regulation of local authority lettings.

TENANCY

3. The essential attributes of a tenancy. In the following chapter there is a detailed consideration of what constitutes a tenancy. At this stage it will be convenient to outline the two essential attributes of a tenancy. They are:

(*a*) that the tenant has exclusive possession of land;

(*b*) that the possession is for a period subject to a definite time limit or which can be made subject to a definite limit by either party.

Unless these two elements are present, there will be no tenancy.

4. The creation of a tenancy. A tenancy may arise in one of two ways. First, it may be created by an express or implied agreement between the two parties. This may be either the simplest of oral agreements with the most elementary terms—parties, property, rent and period—or it may be a formal document running to many pages and dealing with every possible eventuality from responsibility for cleaning the windows to liability in the event of destruction by fire or other similar disaster. Second, it may be created by statute. This is a method of recent origin but which is now a fundamental and well-established part of English law.

5. The subject matter of a tenancy. The relationship of landlord and tenant may arise in relation to an infinite variety of property. The central factor is that there must always be a letting of *land*. Consequently a tenancy may be created in relation to a farm, a funeral parlour, a department store, a mews house, a stately home, a mine, a lake, a road or simply a hole in the ground. The possible situations in which it may arise are limitless and the reported cases on landlord and tenant bear witness to this fact as will be seen throughout this book.

APPROACH TO PROBLEMS

6. The proper approach to a landlord and tenant problem. It has already been stated that the law falls into two broad parts (*see* **1**). In any problem which arises in this field, whether it is an examination question or a point which arises in everyday practice, the best approach is first to apply the general principles and then to consider the statutory controls. Whilst this may appear an obvious approach, it is one which will bear rewards when considering the later parts of this book which concern statutory controls.

OTHER MATTERS

7. Terminology. The following is a selection of some of the basic terms which are used in this book.

(*a*) *Assignment:* the transfer of an interest; it may be the landlord's interest or the tenant's interest which is assigned.

(*b*) *Covenants:* the terms contained in a lease which cast obligations on the landlord and tenant.

(*c*) *Deed:* a formal document which normally has to be signed, sealed and delivered to be effective.

(*d*) *Demise:* another term for to let or to lease (also sometimes means a lease).

(*e*) *Demised premises:* the land or building which is the subject of the lease.

(*f*) *Distress:* the lawful taking of goods to enforce the payment of rent.

(*g*) *Fine/premium:* a sum of money or other consideration paid normally by the tenant to the landlord on the grant or assignment of a lease.

(*h*) *Head lease:* a lease out of which lesser interests (called sub-leases) have been granted.

(*i*) *Holding over:* where a tenant continues to occupy the demised premises after the end of his lease.

(*j*) *Lease/tenancy:* (*i*) a tenant's interest in the land; and (*ii*) a document creating the interest and recording the terms.

(*k*) *Lessee/tenant:* the person to whom the lease is granted.

(*l*) *Lessor/landlord:* the person who grants the lease.

(*m*) *Licence:*—(*i*) a permission to do an act; and (*ii*) a contractual right to use or occupy land.

(*n*) *Parol:* oral, not in writing.

(*o*) *Reversion:* the interest retained by the lessor on the grant of a lease.

(*p*) *Right of re-entry/forfeiture:* a right for the landlord to determine the lease and re-enter the land in the event of a breach of covenant by the tenant.

(*q*) *Sub-lease:* a lease granted by a person who is himself a lessee and which is necessarily for a period shorter than the lease out of which it is derived.

8. Specimen lease. At the end of this book (*see* Appendix I) there is a short lease containing some typical terms encountered in practice. It is not intended as a precedent but as an illustration of typical terms. Reference should be made to the lease when mention is made in the text of terms contained in a lease.

PROGRESS TEST 1

1. What are the two essential attributes of a tenancy?   **(3)**
2. In what ways may a tenancy be created?   **(4)**
3. When were the first statutory restrictions on the relationship of landlord and tenant? What form of letting did they concern? **(2)**
4. What do the following terms mean: (*a*) covenant; (*b*) premium; (*c*) sub-lease; (*d*) lessor?   **(7)**

CHAPTER II

Creation of Leases

INTRODUCTION

1. Creation. There are normally two stages to the creation of a lease. They are:

    (*a*) an agreement for a lease;
    (*b*) the grant of a lease.

By an agreement for a lease the parties agree that one will grant and the other will take a lease. By the lease that agreement is carried out and the lease is actually granted. It is not necessary that there be both an agreement for a lease and then a lease; sometimes the parties will proceed straight to the second stage and a lease will be granted without a prior agreement for it. Sometimes the parties may not proceed beyond the first stage. As appears later (*see* **27**), the legal effects at each stage are different. Short lettings of residential premises are sometimes entitled "tenancy agreements"; despite the words used these are usually leases not agreements for a lease.

THE AGREEMENT

2. Agreement for a lease. Whether there is a binding agreement for a lease must be decided by reference to the ordinary rules of the law of contract. These rules require that there be an offer by one party and an acceptance of that offer by the other party. In the case of an agreement for a lease, the offer will be to let land at a certain rent for a certain period from a certain date. Whether there has been an offer and an acceptance will depend on the circumstances of each case. A formal written agreement is not necessary to bind the parties, and the agreement may be formed equally by word of mouth or by exchange of correspondence or by whatever method is convenient to the parties. Whilst a formal written agreement is not necessary it has the practical advantage of reducing possible disputes between the parties because it will be clear that there is an agreement upon specified terms. Where the parties do not for the moment wish to commit or bind themselves it is often the practice to add the words "subject to contract" to their negotiations and correspondence. By this means they will normally prevent a binding agreement from arising.

3. Law of Property Act 1925, s. 40. As appears from above, there is no requirement that an agreement for a lease be in writing or any specific form. A requirement of form, however, may be introduced in an indirect way by the Law of Property Act 1925, s. 40, which provides that:

> "40 (1) No action may be brought upon any contract for the sale or other disposition of land or any interest in land, unless the agreement upon which such action is brought, or some memorandum or note thereof, is in writing, and signed by the party to be charged or by some other person thereunto by him lawfully authorised.
>
> (2) This section .... does not affect the law relating to part performance...."

An agreement for a lease is, of course, within this provision because it is a contract for the sale of land. The origin of the provision is the Statute of Frauds 1677, whose object was to prevent fraudulent practices in relation to various sales including the sale of land. The difficulty facing the courts was that, in the absence of evidence such as a document, parties might perjure themselves in order to establish, or get out of, an agreement. The solution was to require the party seeking to enforce the agreement to produce some evidence in writing of the agreement signed by the other party; this removed the necessity to rely upon oral evidence. At first the requirement of a memorandum under the Statute of Frauds 1677 was strictly enforced by the courts of law. The courts of equity, however, developed an exception to the statutory requirement of writing in favour of a party who could show that he had carried out acts in performance of the contract. In such a case equity considered it unfair to allow one party to rely on the lack of writing if the other party had by his conduct committed himself to the contract. This is known as the doctrine of part performance. The exception is specifically preserved by the Law of Property Act 1925, s. 40(2).

In summary, the effect of s. 40 is that while an agreement for a lease may be made orally, unless there is an act of part performance or a sufficient memorandum in writing, it will be unenforceable. In the absence of part performance there will, in effect, be a requirement of form.

NOTE: The effect of s. 40(1) is not to render an agreement void but simply to make it unenforceable by action. The distinction is of importance. If the agreement were void because of an absence of writing there could be no question of it being enforced where there was part performance.

4. Sufficient memorandum in writing. The essentials of a sufficient memorandum are:

(a) it must be in writing;

(b) it must contain the material terms of the agreement, which are:

(i) the parties;

(ii) the price, i.e. the rent, and the premium if there is to be one;

(iii) the property;

(iv) the period of the tenancy;

(c) it must be signed by the party "to be charged", i.e. by the person against whom it is desired to enforce the agreement.

In practice, a memorandum may be derived from a letter setting out the terms, or perhaps a receipt, or a note of a conversation. It is possible to derive a memorandum from several documents provided there is some reference linking one document to another: *Timmins* v. *Moreland Street Property Co. Ltd.* (1958). Where an agreement for a lease is derived from correspondence, as may often occur, the various letters have to be linked to form the memorandum.

5. Doctrine of part performance. Where there is an oral agreement for a lease but there is no memorandum, the agreement may still be enforceable if there is part performance of the agreement. In order to establish this, the party seeking to enforce the agreement must show that:

(a) there is a binding agreement; and

(b) there have been sufficient acts of part performance by him; and

(c) those acts point to the existence of an agreement and are consistent with the agreement alleged.

If the party can show these matters the court will normally give effect to the agreement by means of the equitable remedy of specific performance.

The principle underlying the doctrine of part performance is that, where one party to the agreement has carried out the contract (whether in part or to completion), it would be inequitable to allow the other party to rely on the Law of Property Act 1925, s. 40(1): *see Maddison* v. *Alderson* (1883) per Selbourne L.C.

6. What are sufficient acts of part performance? The following have been held to be sufficient acts of part performance:

(*a*) the taking of possession of land by one party with the consent of the other (*Caton* v. *Caton* (1867));

(*b*) the carrying out of repairs and alterations to the premises to be let (*Rawlinson* v. *Ames* (1925));

(*c*) the erection of new buildings on the land to be let;

(*d*) the giving up by a housekeeper of her former home and moving into her employer's home (*Wakeham* v. *Mackenzie* (1968)).

In contrast, the following have been held not to be sufficient acts of part performance:

(*a*) the continuing in possession by a former tenant (*Wills* v. *Stradling* (1797));

(*b*) the viewing and visiting of the land (*Clerk* v. *Wright* (1737)).

7. Payment of money. At one time it was thought that the payment of money, normally the purchase price or rent in advance, could not be a sufficient act of part performance. Recently, however, the House of Lords has said that there is no general rule that the payment of money cannot constitute an act of part performance: *Steadman* v. *Steadman* (1974).

8. Enforcement of an agreement for a lease. If either party refuses to go ahead with the agreement and grant a lease the other party has two remedies:

(*a*) specific performance;

(*b*) damages.

Specific performance is an equitable remedy by which the court orders that the party in breach shall perform his side of the bargain. As an equitable remedy, it is a matter for the discretion of the court to decide if it should or should not be decreed. In exercising its discretion the court has regard to matters which include the conduct of the parties, the effect of the order and whether it would cause hardship. If, for instance, the party seeking specific performance is guilty of bad conduct or has delayed unreasonably in enforcing his rights he may not obtain the decree. The right to specific performance will also, of course, depend upon satisfying the Law of Property Act 1925, s. 40. Thus in order to obtain specific performance of an agreement there must be either a sufficient memorandum or sufficient acts of part performance (*see* **3, 5**).

Damages are the ordinary common law remedy for breach of contract. In addition there are what are sometimes called "equitable damages," that is damages awarded by a court in pursuance of its equitable jurisdiction in addition to or in lieu of specific performance. The power to award equitable damages was first given to the Chancery courts by the Chancery Amendment Act 1858.

GRANTING A LEASE

9. The lease. Having considered an agreement for a lease, we now go on to consider the second stage—the lease itself. As already indicated, the parties may go straight to this second stage without a prior agreement for a lease. Whether they do so will depend upon the speed with which they choose to act, the value of the property and the length and proposed terms of the tenancy. The more valuable the property and the more complicated the proposed terms, the more likely it is that the parties will first set matters out in an agreement and then proceed to the actual lease.

10. Creation of a lease. A lease is created when one of the parties grants to the other the right of exclusive possession of land or buildings for a definite period or for a period which can be made definite by either party. In the case of leases for more than three years, various formalities must be complied with. In summary, therefore, there must be:

    (*a*) exclusive possession;

    (*b*) a definite period (this is considered separately in III, **3**); and

    (*c*) (in the case of leases over three years) compliance with formalities.

11. Exclusive possession. The right of exclusive possession of land means the right to control of the land and to exclude all other persons from it. Where a person is granted the right to use the premises without the right to exclusive possession, the grant is a licence and not a lease.

12. Lease or licence? The distinction between a lease and a licence is of considerable importance nowadays. This is because of the effect of the Rent Act 1977, which protects residential tenancies, and the Landlord and Tenant Act 1954, Part II, which protects business tenancies; these Acts apply only to tenancies and do not apply to licences. In recent years the use of agreements creating licences only has grown as a means of avoiding the effect of these Acts. The following cases illustrate this.

Shell-Mex Ltd. v. *Manchester Garages Ltd.* (1971). S owned a petrol station. By a licence agreement S permitted M to occupy it for one year. When the agreement expired S asked M to leave but M refused and claimed the protection of the Landlord and Tenant Act 1954, Part II. The Court of Appeal HELD that

    (*a*) the agreement was indeed a licence; and

    (*b*) it was therefore outside the protection of the 1954 Act.

Somma v. *Hazlehurst* (1978). H and T a young unmarried couple occupied one room in a house owned by S. H and T had each signed a separate licence agreement to occupy the room. In each agreement it was provided that the licensee should share the room with such one other person as S might from time to time permit to use the room. The Court of Appeal HELD that there were separate agreements and, therefore, neither H nor T had exclusive occupation of the room and they were only licensees. It was stressed by the Court of Appeal that, if it is the intention of the owner and the occupier that only a licence should be granted, the court will not prevent them from achieving that object. The court will not take into account the fact that the licence has been granted to avoid the Rent Act.

13. How to distinguish a lease from a licence. In order to do this it is first necessary to consider whether exclusive possession has been granted to the occupier. If it has not there cannot be a lease; if it has been granted, it is then necessary to go on to consider all the relevant factors in the case and decide whether these point to a lease or not. At one time the law was that if exclusive possession had been granted, then this was conclusive of a lease. This is no longer the law and a person may now be granted exclusive possession and yet not have a lease: *Shell-Mex Ltd.* v. *Manchester Garages Ltd.* (1971) (*see* **12**).

14. The relevant factors. The relevant factors in determining the question, lease or licence, include:

(*a*) whether the terms in the agreement are such as are normally found in a lease, e.g. repairing covenants, covenants against assigning, forfeiture clauses;

(*b*) the relationship between the parties: if it is commercial this suggests a lease; if it is personal this suggests a licence;

(*c*) the more formal the agreement, the more likely it is to be a lease;

(*d*) the amount of money involved, i.e. whether a commercial rate is being paid.

The fact that an agreement is described as a lease or as a licence is not conclusive; what is important is the substance and reality of the arrangement, rather than the label applied. Nonetheless, the label used by the parties is a material factor.

15. Illustrations. The following cases illustrate the above principles.

Cobb. v. *Lane* (1952). A house was bought by a woman who allowed her brother to occupy it free of charge. The brother lived there for more than 13 years and the woman paid the rates throughout the period. The Court of Appeal HELD that the brother was only a licensee as this was a family arrangement which negatived any intention to create a lease.

Addiscombe Garden Estates Ltd. v. *Crabbe* (1958). The owner of a tennis court and clubhouse granted to a tennis club the right to use the premises for two years. The agreement contained clauses similar to those found in a lease, e.g. repairing obligations, but was described as a licence. The Court of Appeal HELD that, although described as a licence, it was in reality a lease.

Marchant v. *Charters* (1977). A house was divided into furnished service apartments which were let out to single men. A housekeeper cleaned the rooms daily and clean linen was provided. The Court of Appeal HELD that the occupation of each room gave rise to a licence and not a lease.

See also the cases set out in **12**.

16. Employees. Where an employee, such as a caretaker or shop manager, is required to occupy premises for the better performance of his duties, he is considered to be what is called a service licensee or service occupier. The requirement may be contained in his contract of employment or implied from the circumstances of his employment. If the requirement is not present the employee will be a service tenant, provided the other requirements of a tenancy are satisfied. A service licensee is not protected by the Rent Act 1977 whereas a service tenant is protected by that Act.

17. Definite period. This is the second requirement to create a valid lease; it is dealt with in III, **3**.

FORMALITIES

18. Introduction. At common law a lease could be validly created by a purely oral transaction. This was subsequently altered by statute and formalities were required in certain cases. The relevant provisions are now contained in the Law of Property Act 1925, ss. 52 and 54.

19. Law of Property Act 1925, ss. 52 and 54. So far as relevant these provide:

"52(1) All conveyances of land or of any interest therein are void for the purposes of conveying a legal estate unless made by deed.

(2) This section does not apply to:

(*d*) leases or tenancies or other assurances not required by law to be made in writing."

"54(1) All interests in land created by parol and not put in writing and signed by the persons so creating the same or by their agents thereunto lawfully authorised in writing have, notwithstanding any consideration having been given for the same, the force and effect of interests at will only.

(2) Nothing in the foregoing provisions of this Part of this Act shall affect the creation by parol of leases taking effect in possession for a term not exceeding three years (whether or not the lessee is given power to extend the term) at the best rent which can be reasonably obtained without taking a fine."

20. Effect of 1925 provisions. The combined effect of these two provisions is that:

(*a*) a lease may be made orally, or in writing, if it satisfies the conditions in s. 54(2);

(*b*) a lease for a term of more than three years must be made by deed, i.e. under seal.

NOTES: (1) Once a lease has been validly created, it must be assigned by deed in order for there to be a valid legal assignment: Law of Property Act 1925, s. 52(1). Thus even if a tenancy was created orally, it may be assigned only by deed.

(2) There is nothing to stop a term of less than three years being made by deed if the parties require it to be so made.

21. Parol leases. The leases which fall within the Law of Property Act 1925, s. 54(2), are those which:

(a) take effect in possession (i.e. start) from the date of grant;
(b) are for a term not exceeding three years; and
(c) are at a full rent.

This will include periodic tenancies although their ultimate duration may exceed three years.

ABSENCE OF FORMALITIES

22. Introduction. In order to consider the effect of failure to comply with the formalities described above, it is necessary to examine the position at common law and in equity, and then to consider the position after the Judicature Act 1873.

23. Position at common law. A lease which failed to comply with the requirement of formality was void at law. Despite this, if the tenant entered into possession with the landlord's consent, he would become what is called a tenant at will. If he then paid rent to the landlord a periodic tenancy was created. The period of the tenancy would depend upon the basis on which rent was paid.

EXAMPLE: T purports to take a seven-year lease of Blackacre from L. The transaction is oral. T enters into possession and pays rent on a monthly basis. The oral transaction would be ineffective to create a seven-year lease but T would have a monthly tenancy by reason of the payment and acceptance of rent on a monthly basis.

24. Position in equity. If the informal lease was either sufficiently evidenced in writing or supported by acts of part performance, equity would treat it as an agreement for a lease. Specific performance of the agreement could then be granted, provided the conditions for granting it were satisfied (*see* **8**). Where the tenant had the right to apply for specific performance, in equity the lease would be deemed to be granted whether or not the tenant actually sought it. The tenant's position would then be the same as if the lease had been validly granted to him. Such a lease was called an "equitable lease."

25. The Judicature Act 1873. As appears from the above paragraphs, before 1873 a tenant under an informal lease might have different rights depending on whether the matter was before the courts of law or the courts of equity. At law the tenant would have a periodic tenancy; in equity he might have a specifically enforceable agreement for a lease. There was, therefore, a conflict between the rules of law and equity and this was eventually resolved by the Judicature Act 1873, which provided that where there was a conflict between law and equity, the equitable rules should prevail. In *Walsh* v. *Lonsdale* (1882) it was confirmed that the effect of the Judicature Act was that the equitable lease should prevail over the periodic tenancy.

26. Walsh v. Lonsdale. L agreed to grant to W a lease of a mill for seven years. Under the terms of the lease it was agreed that L might at any time demand payment of one year's rent in advance. No deed was executed but W went into possession and paid rent; subsequently L demanded one year's rent in advance, which W refused to pay. L then distrained for the rent. W brought this action for damages for illegal distress and argued that he had only a yearly tenancy and that there could be no obligation to pay rent in advance implied into his yearly tenancy. HELD: That since the Judicature Act it was no longer the rule that a tenant held under a periodic tenancy but that he held under the terms of the agreement. Accordingly, the distress was lawful as it was permitted by the agreement.

27. The effect of Walsh v. Lonsdale. As a result of this case it is sometimes said that an agreement for a lease is as good as a lease. In broad terms such a proposition is correct. There are, however, certain ways in which an agreement for a lease (or equitable lease) is not as satisfactory as an actual lease. The more important are:

(*a*) An equitable lease is dependent upon the agreement being specifically enforceable. Specific performance is a discretionary remedy and is not granted in all cases: e.g. if a tenant were guilty of breaches of covenant, he might not be granted specific performance.

Coatsworth v. *Johnson* (1886). L agreed to grant T a 21-year lease of a farm. T entered into possession under the agreement without a lease being executed. Before any rent was due L gave

T notice to quit and took possession because T had failed to cultivate the farm properly. This would have been a breach of the covenants intended to be inserted in the lease. T sued L for trespass claiming that he could have obtained specific performance and was, therefore, entitled to an equitable lease. HELD: Specific performance would not have been granted because of T's breach of covenant. Therefore, T did not enjoy an equitable lease and as he had paid no rent was at most a tenant at will and L was entitled to take possession.

(*b*) An equitable lease is not always enforceable against third parties. An agreement for a lease made after 1925 can be protected by registration under the Land Charges Act 1972, and is registrable as an estate contract. Failure to register it will render it void against a purchaser for money or money's worth of a legal estate in the land.

EXAMPLE: L grants T a lease of Blackacre for a term of seven years. There is no deed and, therefore, no valid lease. T fails to register the agreement for a lease as a land charge. L sells his reversion to X. X is not bound by T's interest.

28. Significance of doctrine. The doctrine in *Walsh* v. *Lonsdale* is of practical importance in two categories of case. The first is when there is a true agreement for a lease which is specifically enforceable. It is for most purposes as good as an actual lease. The second category is where the parties have purported to create a lease but there is some formal deficiency. The courts will treat the defective lease as an agreement to create the lease, and the doctrine in *Walsh* v. *Lonsdale* will then apply to that "deemed" agreement as to a true agreement for a lease, i.e. it will for most purposes be as good as an actual lease.

29. Summary. A lease may be validly created in the following ways:

(*a*) if it is for under three years it may generally be made orally, or in writing or by deed;

(*b*) if it is for more than three years it must be by deed;

(*c*) if it is for more than three years and is made orally and there is part performance, by virtue of the doctrine in *Walsh* v. *Lonsdale*, an equitable lease will arise;

(*d*) if it is for more than three years and there is a sufficient written memorandum, by virtue of the doctrine in *Walsh* v. *Lonsdale* an equitable lease will arise;

(*e*) if it comes within (*c*) or (*d*) but the tenant has been guilty

of bad conduct or for some other reason specific performance
would not be granted, the doctrine in *Walsh* v. *Lonsdale* will not
apply and there will be no equitable lease; but if the tenant enters
and pays rent, a periodic tenancy will arise;

(*f*) if it is for more than three years and there is neither a sufficient memorandum nor part performance it will be unenforceable by specific performance and the doctrine in *Walsh* v. *Lonsdale*
will not apply. On the other hand, if the tenant enters into possession with the consent of the landlord and pays rent a periodic
tenancy will arise.

PROGRESS TEST 2

1. How is a lease created? **(1)**
2. What formalities are needed to create (*a*) a weekly tenancy;
(*b*) a tenancy for 99 years; (*c*) a tenancy for two years at no rent?
(18)
3. What is an agreement for a lease? **(2)**
4. What is a licence? **(12)**
5. How can a lease be distinguished from a licence? **(13)**
6. L permits J to occupy a flat on terms that "he shall share
it with such other person as L may designate." L designates B who
is unknown to T and who occupies on terms similar to those under
which T occupies. L now wishes to recover possession of the flat.
Advise L. **(12)**
7. What is the rule in *Walsh* v. *Lonsdale*? **(27)**
8. "An agreement for a lease is as good as a lease". Comment.
(27)
9. What leases must be under seal? **(18)**
10. L agrees orally to let Blackacre to T for 99 years. L now
refuses to go ahead with the agreement. Advise T. Would the
position be different if T had gone into possession and carried out
works to Blackacre? **(27)**
11. What is part performance? Can the payment of money constitute part performance? **(6)**
12. What is exclusive possession? **(11)**
13. C has a game-keeper, M, who has to live in a cottage on
C's estate so that he can carry out his duties. M is dismissed but
refuses to leave. Advise C. **(16)**
14. What is the effect of the Law of Property Act 1925 s. 40?
(3)
15. What are the requirements of a valid lease? **(29)**

CHAPTER III

Tenancies

TYPES OF TENANCY

1. Introduction. This chapter deals with three important matters:

(*a*) the different types of tenancy (*see* **3–21**);

(*b*) certain statutory modifications to particular classes of tenancy (*see* **22–27**);

(*c*) concurrent and future leases (*see* **28, 29**).

2. The different types. A tenancy may be:

(*a*) a tenancy for a fixed term (*see* **3–7**);

(*b*) a periodic tenancy (*see* **8–15**);

(*c*) a tenancy at will (*see* **16–18**);

(*d*) a tenancy at sufferance (*see* **19**);

(*e*) a tenancy by estoppel (*see* **20, 21**).

FIXED TERM TENANCIES

3. Tenancies for a fixed term. This is a tenancy for a fixed period of any length, be it one month, 100 years, 1000 years or any other term of years, months, weeks or days. The commencement and the duration of the period must be certain before the tenancy takes effect, otherwise the tenancy will be void.

Lace v. *Chantler* (1944). A lease "for the duration of the war" was HELD to be void at common law for uncertainty because there was no way to ascertain the duration of the period when the agreement took effect.

NOTE: To avoid the effect of this particular decision legislation was passed which converted such tenancies and agreements made during the Second World War into terms of ten years: Validation of War-time Leases Act 1944. This Act was repealed by the Statute Law (Repeals) Act 1976, but may still be relevant where there has at some stage been a tenancy of this type.

The test of certainty will be satisfied if the period is capable of being rendered certain before the agreement takes effect.

EXAMPLE: A tenancy is granted to commence on 25th December 1978 "for as many years as A shall name." If A names the period before the commencement date, the tenancy is valid. If A fails to name the period before that date then it will be void because it is not a certain term.

4. Commencement. A tenancy for a fixed term may take effect from the date of the grant, or from some past or future date. Where it takes effect from the date of the grant, e.g. a lease granted on 1st January 1978 for three years from 1st January 1978, it is said to take effect in possession. Where it takes effect in the future, e.g. a lease granted on 1st January 1978 for three years from 1st January 1979, it is sometimes called a reversionary lease but this may cause confusion and it is best to call it simply a future lease. *See also* **29**, below.

5. Law of Property Act 1925, s. 149(3). There is a limitation in law upon how far in the future a tenancy may take effect. By s. 149(3) it is provided that a term, at a rent or for a fine, to take effect more than 21 years from the date of the instrument purporting to create it, will be void, and any agreement to create such a lease will also be void. (The purpose of the above rule with its comparatively short time limit is obscure, especially when it is remembered that leases may be granted for any length of time and that options to renew leases may have effect during a much longer period.) The effect of this provision is illustrated by the following examples.

EXAMPLES: (1) By a lease dated 1st January 1978 L grants to T a lease to take effect from 1st January 1988. The lease is valid because it takes effect less than 21 years from the date of the lease.

(2) By a lease dated 1st January 1978 L grants to T a lease to take effect from 1st January 2008. The lease is void because it will take effect more than 21 years from the date of the lease.

6. Effect of s. 149(3). The conclusion in the examples above would be the same whether there was a lease or an agreement for a lease. The words "any contract to create such a term shall also be void," however only invalidate a contract to grant a lease which, *when granted*, will take effect more than 21 years after its date. They do not invalidate a contract to grant, at a date more than 21 years after the date of the *contract*, a lease which when granted will not infringe the rule in s. 149(3): *Re Strand and Savoy Properties Ltd.* (1960). This principle is best illustrated by examples.

EXAMPLES: (1) On 1st January 1978 L agrees that he will grant to T a lease on 1st January 2008 which will take effect from 1st January 2018. Although the contract will operate more than 21 years in the future, the lease when actually granted will take effect within ten years of its grant and the contract is therefore valid.

(2) On 1st January 1978 L agrees that he will grant to T a lease on 1st January 2008 which will take effect from 1st January 2058. In this case the lease when actually granted will take effect more than 21 years from the date of its grant and the contract is therefore void. If in due course the lease were actually granted as contemplated it would also be void.

7. Termination. At common law a tenancy for a fixed term automatically comes to an end at the expiration of the term without the necessity for notice to quit (*see* VII, **2**).

PERIODIC TENANCIES

8. Introduction. A periodic tenancy is one which continues automatically from period to period until it is determined by a valid notice to quit given by one party to the other. The periods are normally either a year, a quarter, a month or a week, but any period may be chosen. In one case the period was 364 days.

9. Yearly tenancy. This continues from year to year. It may be created by:

(*a*) express agreement; or
(*b*) implication; or
(*c*) statute.

Creation by statute is dealt with in relation to agricultural holdings (*see* XXII).

10. Creation by express agreement. A yearly tenancy may be created by the parties agreeing to a tenancy "from year to year" or that the tenant shall be a "yearly tenant" or by the use of any words showing a similar intent. If, however, the parties agree to a tenancy "for one year and so on from year to year" there is created a tenancy for a fixed term of one year which is followed by a yearly tenancy. It follows that such a tenancy cannot be determined during the first year.

11. Creation by implication. This is sometimes called creation by operation of law. A yearly tenancy will arise by implication whenever the following conditions are satisfied:

(*a*) a person occupies land with the owner's permission but not as a licensee and not for an agreed period; and

(*b*) rent is paid and accepted and is expressed to be, or calculated as a, yearly sum.

The requirement that there be a yearly rent is satisfied if the rent reserved is expressed as an annual sum. It does not matter by what instalments the annual sum is payable. So, for instance, where the rent is £52 per year payable weekly, that will give rise to a yearly tenancy. In contrast, where the rent is £1 per week, that will give rise to only a weekly tenancy.

The satisfaction of the two conditions just mentioned gives rise to a presumption of a yearly tenancy. The presumption can always be rebutted by any evidence that the parties did not in fact intend that a yearly tenancy should be created.

12. Examples. The following are examples of creation of a yearly tenancy by operation of law:

(*a*) L grants to T a lease of land for ten years. At the end of that lease T holds over with L's consent and pays rent on a yearly basis. In the absence of evidence to the contrary T becomes a yearly tenant.

(*b*) L allows T to occupy land; subsequently rent is paid and accepted on a yearly basis. T thereby becomes a yearly tenant.

(*c*) L agrees to grant a lease; before the agreement is completed T enters into possession and pays rent to L on a yearly basis. T thereby becomes a yearly tenant.

NOTE: If, for example, the parties had expressly agreed that L could evict T at a day's notice at any time before the grant of the lease, the agreement would be sufficient to rebut the presumption of a yearly tenancy. T would probably then occupy as a licensee only.

13. Effect of statute. As appears from the previous two paragraphs, at common law a yearly tenancy might arise from the mere acceptance of rent. In modern times statutes have given certain tenants the right to remain in occupation of premises after the termination of their lease. As a result the courts are less likely to infer a tenancy simply because rent is accepted from a person who is holding over and who may have some statutory right to occupy. The position was explained by Denning L.J. in *Marcroft Wagons Ltd.* v. *Smith* (1951):

> "If the acceptance of rent can be explained on some other footing than a contractual tenancy, or, for instance, by reason of an existing or possible statutory right to remain, then a new tenancy should not be inferred."

Marcroft Wagons Ltd. v. *Smith* (1951). A Rent Act protected tenant died in 1936. His widow was entitled to continue to live in the house as a statutory tenant, and did so with her daughter. In March 1950 the widow died. The landlord allowed the daughter to reside in the premises until September 1950 and accepted the same sum as the widow had paid as rent. The landlord brought proceedings for possession. The daughter claimed that by his conduct the landlord had granted her a periodic tenancy. The Court of Appeal HELD that a tenancy should not be inferred as the acceptance of periodical payments could be explained on a footing other than that a contractual tenancy was being created, i.e. by reference to the statutory rights. In effect the existence of a statutory right to remain is a fact which rebuts the presumption of an annual tenancy.

More recently, in *Longrigg, Burrough & Trounson* v. *Smith* (1979) C.A., Lord Scarman explained the position in the following way: "Indeed, one would have thought that today, where tenants have in one respect or another the protection of the law for possession of premises to which they would have at common law no contractual entitlement, the courts would not be as quick to infer a new tenancy as in the old days they would have been where there was nothing to explain the presence of a defendant upon the premises or upon the land other than a trespass or a contract."

14. Determination. A yearly tenancy can be determined in such manner as the parties agree. In the absence of agreement, it can be determined by the giving of at least a half-year's notice to expire at the end of a complete year of the tenancy. This is considered more fully in VII, **13**.

15. Other periodic tenancies. What has been said above in relation to yearly tenancies applies with appropriate modifications to other periodic tenancies. Quarterly, monthly and weekly tenancies can be created in the same way as a yearly tenancy. They can be created by express agreement or by implication where rent is paid and accepted on a quarterly, monthly or weekly basis. They are determinable on giving notice of at least one full period to expire at the end of a period of the tenancy, e.g. one month's notice to expire at the end of a complete month of the tenancy is required to end a monthly tenancy.

TENANCY AT WILL

16. Introduction. A tenancy at will arises when a tenant occupies land with the consent of the owner on terms that the tenancy may be determined by either party at any time. A demand for possession by the landlord will suffice to determine such a tenancy. A tenancy at will comes to an end if either party dies or parts with his interest in the land. It may be created:

(*a*) by express agreement; or
(*b*) by implication.

17. Creation by express agreement. A tenancy at will may be created by express agreement. Whilst a tenancy at will of residential premises is protected by the Rent Acts, such a tenancy of business premises is outside the scope of the Landlord and Tenant Act 1954, Part II. An express tenancy at will therefore provides a means of avoiding the effect of Part II of the 1954 Act. The creation of an express tenancy at will is a comparatively rare phenomenon. The reservation of a rent in the agreement is not necessarily inconsistent with the nature of a tenancy at will.

Hagee Ltd. v. *Erikson* (1976). L let premises to T for use as a showroom with exclusive occupation but as "tenants at will only." L purported to determine the tenancy but T refused to leave the premises and claimed the protection of Part II of the 1954 Act. HELD: A tenancy at will created by an express agreement was not within the scope of Part II of the 1954 Act.

18. Creation by implication. A tenancy at will is created by implication where a person is in possession of land with the consent of the owner, but does not possess it by virtue of any freehold estate or any tenancy for a fixed term or a periodic tenancy or any licence. The following are examples:

(*a*) occupation by permission of the landlord without payment of rent;

(*b*) where a purchaser of land has been let into possession pending completion of the sale;

(*c*) where a tenant takes possession under an informal or void lease and has not yet paid rent.

If rent is subsequently paid and accepted on a regular basis a periodic tenancy will then be created in accordance with the principles already discussed (*see* 10–13).

OTHER TENANCIES

19. Tenancy at sufferance. A tenancy at sufferance arises when a tenant holds over on the expiry of his lease without the consent or dissent of the landlord. Such a tenancy can only be created by implication and not by express agreement; it will become a tenancy at will if the landlord should give his consent to the tenant's occupation. These tenancies are of little practical importance today.

20. Tenancy by estoppel. Estoppel is often said to be a principle of the law of evidence. It operates to prevent one party from denying the existence of certain facts which he has previously represented to be true. The application of the principle to the law of landlord and tenant is as follows. If a person purports to grant a lease of land but has no legal estate in the land entitling him to grant the lease, both parties will be bound by that purported lease and they will be estopped as against each other from denying that the grant was effective. The tenancy is called a tenancy by estoppel and it binds both parties and their successors in title although no estate in land has, in fact, been granted. The tenancy and the reversion expectant on it are capable of being transferred to a successor in title.

EXAMPLE: L is under the mistaken impression that he owns certain land and lets this land to T. There arises a tenancy by estoppel.

21. The consequences of a tenancy by estoppel. The main consequences are as follows:

(*a*) the tenant is estopped from denying the title of his landlord, and the landlord cannot deny the validity of the lease on the grounds of his lack of title;

(*b*) the estoppel does not bind a third party who is not a party to the transaction;

(*c*) a tenant by estoppel may claim the protection of the Rent Act 1977;

(*d*) if the landlord later acquires the legal estate this ends the estoppel, but the tenant then acquires a legal estate himself. This is called feeding the estoppel.

EXAMPLE: Taking the facts in the example above (*see* 20), suppose that later L acquires title to the land. When he acquires it, T's tenancy becomes a true legal tenancy, just as if L had had proper title at the date of the grant.

STATUTORY MODIFICATIONS

22. Introduction. There are certain statutory provisions which deal with special kinds of leases. Of particular importance to students are:

(*a*) perpetually renewable leases (*see* **23, 24**); and
(*b*) leases for lives or until marriage (*see* **25, 26**).

23. Perpetually renewable leases. Perpetually renewable leases are rare, and the courts tend to lean against them in construing a lease. They may arise where a lease contains an option to renew the lease on the same terms and the same terms then include the option clause. The effect is that there will always be a further option and the lease could go on for ever.

Caerphilly Concrete Products Ltd. v. *Owen* (1972). A lease contained an option clause which provided: "the landlord will on the written request of the tenant made six months before the expiration of the term .... grant to him a lease .... for a further term of five years .... at the same rent and including the like covenants and provisos (including an option to renew such lease) for a further term of five years at the expiration thereof." It was HELD that this clause entitled the tenant to an option to renew at the end of each succeeding term of five years and that there was, therefore, a perpetually renewable lease.

24. The statutory provisions. Perpetually renewable leases may be both unfair and inconvenient. There are now special provisions dealing with them in the Law of Property Act 1922, s. 145, Sch. 15. Students should note the following:

(*a*) all perpetually renewable leases are converted into terms of 2,000 years;

(*b*) a perpetually renewable sub-lease is converted into a term of 2,000 years less one day;

(*c*) the 2,000 year term will be held on the same terms and conditions as the original lease with the following modifications:

(*i*) the tenant, but not the landlord, may determine the lease by giving at least ten days' written notice before any day upon which, but for the conversion by the Act, the lease would have expired if it had not been renewed;

(*ii*) the tenant must register with the landlord every assignment or devolution of the lease within six months of it taking place;

(*iii*) an original tenant who assigns the lease is not liable for breaches of covenant after the assignment. (This is an exception to the general rule (*see* VI, **21**) that despite an assignment an original tenant remains liable for all breaches occurring during the term).

25. Leases for lives or until marriage. The leases involved here are:

(*a*) leases for a life or lives, e.g. a lease for T for his own life or for the life of A;

(*b*) leases for a term of years determinable with life or lives, e.g. a lease to T for 21 years if A shall so long live;

(*c*) leases for a term of years determinable on the marriage of the lessee, e.g. a lease to T for 21 years until T marries.

26. The statutory provisions. By virtue of s. 149(6) of the Law of Property Act 1925, a lease at a rent or a fine "for life or lives or for any term of years determinable with life or lives or on the marriage of the lessee" is converted into a term of 90 years. This 90-year term may be determined by written notice given by either party upon the death or marriage of the named person as the case may be. Such notice must be in writing and must give at least one month's notice to expire on one of the quarter days applicable to the tenancy.

NOTE: It is important to note that this provision only applies to cases where the lease is at a rent or for a fine. If a person is given a life interest in land without any monetary consideration a settlement of land within the ambit of the Settled Land Act 1925 will come into existence.

27. Concurrent and future leases. The previous paragraphs have been concerned with the different types of tenancies. It is now necessary to consider two particular situations, one of which has already been touched upon. They are:

(*a*) where a landlord grants a lease to run at the same time as a pre-existing lease: this is called a concurrent lease (*see* **28**);

(*b*) where a landlord grants a lease to take effect in the future: this is called a future (or reversionary) lease (*see* **29**).

28. Concurrent leases. This is best illustrated by an example: suppose that L grants to T a lease of Blackacre for 21 years from 1st January 1969. In 1980 L grants a further lease of Blackacre to S for a term of ten years from 1st January 1980.

The lease to S operates as a lease of the reversion on T's lease. S is therefore entitled to receive the rent from T for the ten years of his term. If S's lease were for more than T's lease, at the end of T's lease S would be entitled to possession of the land. The effect of a concurrent lease is therefore that the concurrent lessee is interposed in the chain of interests between the original lessor and lessee and becomes the landlord to the original lessee. The position of the original lessee becomes in most respects that of a sub-lessee. Concurrent leases are, confusingly, sometimes called reversionary leases because they are a lease of the landlord's reversion. It is best if the expression reversionary lease is either not used at all or is confined to use as a synonym for future leases as described in the next paragraph.

29. Future leases. This is where the landlord grants to the tenant a lease which will take effect at a future date. The detailed rules regarding these leases have already been considered in **4–6** above.

PROGRESS TEST 3

1. What different types of tenancy are there? **(2)**

2. In 1940 L grants to T a lease of a dwelling-house until the end of the War. What is the effect of the lease? **(3)**

3. What is a tenancy by estoppel? **(20)**

4. How would you differentiate between a tenancy for a fixed term and a periodic tenancy? **(3, 8)**

5. What are concurrent leases? **(28)**

6. What are the normal periods of a periodic tenancy? **(8)**

7. How far in the future can (*a*) a lease and (*b*) an agreement for a lease take effect? **(5)**

8. How can a periodic tenancy be created? **(9)**

9. L allows T to occupy his land in return for a payment of £100 per year payable in monthly instalments. What sort of tenancy is created? **(11)**

10. What are the common law rules concerning the creation of periodic tenancies by operation of law? How has statute affected these rules? **(13)**

11. Is a tenancy at will protected by (a) the Rent Act; (b) Part II of the Landlord and Tenant Act of 1954? **(17)**

12. What are the differences between a tenancy at will and a tenancy at sufferance? **(19)**

13. How can a tenancy at will be created? **(16)**

14. What is the effect of the following arrangements:

(a) L agrees to sell his freehold farm to T. Before completion L lets T into possession;

(b) L mistakenly thinks he owns Blackacre and agrees to let it to T;

(c) L lets land to T with an option "to renew on the same terms including this option". **(18, 20, 23)**

15. What is feeding the estoppel? **(21)**

16. What special statutory provisions apply to: (a) perpetually renewable leases; (b) leases for lives; (c) leases until marriage? **(24, 26)**

17. What is the effect of the decision in *Re Strand and Savoy Properties*? **(6)**

CHAPTER IV

Implied Covenants

IMPLIED COVENANTS IN A LEASE

1. Generally. A landlord and tenant will generally agree expressly the terms upon which the land is to be held by the tenant. If, however, there are no express terms, the common law implies certain basic terms or covenants into the lease in order to give effect to it.

2. Implied covenants. If there is no express covenant dealing with these matters, the common law will imply the following covenants into a lease:

(*a*) by the landlord:
  (*i*) for quiet enjoyment;
  (*ii*) not to derogate from his grant;
  (*iii*) in limited circumstances, an implied condition of fitness;
(*b*) by the tenant:
  (*i*) to pay rent;
  (*ii*) to pay rates and taxes;
  (*iii*) an obligation not to commit waste;
  (*iv*) an obligation to use the premises in a tenant-like manner.

3. Limitations to implied covenants. It should be noted that no other covenants than these are implied. In particular, the law does not imply a proviso for re-entry nor any repairing covenant. If a lease is silent about a matter which does not fall within the above categories, at common law there is simply no covenant or obligation with respect to that matter. Also, if a lease deals expressly with any of these matters, the express covenant will, naturally, prevail over the implied covenants.

LANDLORD'S IMPLIED COVENANTS

4. The covenant for quiet enjoyment. This covenant protects the tenant's possession and enjoyment of the demised premises. It entitles the tenant:

(a) to be put into possession and enjoyment of the demised premises; and

(b) to enjoy possession of the demised premises without physical interruption by any person to whom the covenant extends.

If there is a breach of the covenant, the tenant will have remedies against his landlord for damages or, in certain cases, an injunction.

5. Extent of the covenant. The implied covenant for quiet enjoyment is a "qualified" covenant. This means that it only applies to the acts of the landlord and those people who derive title from him, e.g. other tenants of property owned by the same landlord. It does not extend to the acts of other people or people with a title superior to that of the landlord, e.g. a freehold owner of land which has been let on a sub-lease. Where there is disturbance of the tenant's enjoyment of the demised premises by a person with a superior title to that of the landlord it is called "disturbance by title paramount." Where this occurs the tenant has no remedy against his landlord under this covenant.

NOTE: In contrast to a qualified covenant, there is an absolute covenant which extends to disturbance by people with a title superior to that of the landlord. Express covenants for quiet enjoyment may be in the qualified or the absolute form.

6. What amounts to a breach of the covenant? There is breach of covenant if the tenant's ordinary enjoyment of the demised premises is substantially interfered with by either the landlord or by those claiming under him (*see* **5** above). It was at one time thought that there was only a breach of covenant if there was some physical interruption of the tenant's enjoyment but today mere nuisance such as excessive noise is probably enough (*see Kenny* v. *Preen* (1962), and *McCall* v. *Abelesz* (1976)). The implied covenant protects the tenant's enjoyment of the premises against any such interruption by his landlord. It also gives the tenant a remedy against his landlord in respect of lawful acts by other people claiming through the landlord and which disturb the tenant's enjoyment of the demised premises. The reason why the covenant only extends to lawful acts is that if the act is unlawful the tenant will have a remedy, normally in the law of tort, against the person who disturbs him. The following cases illustrate these principles.

Owen v. *Gadd* (1956). L erected scaffolding in front of T's shop and blocked the entrance. HELD: There was a breach of the covenant for quiet enjoyment entitling T to damages.

Sanderson v. *Berwick-upon-Tweed Corporation* (1884). L let three farms to T1, T2, T3. T1's farm suffered damage from flooding of drains on the other two farms. T2 had defective drains but he had used them properly. T3's drains were in good order but he had used them improperly. T1 sued L for breach of the covenant for quiet enjoyment. HELD: L was liable for T2's drains but not for T3's drains because T3 had acted unlawfully and therefore his acts were outside the scope of the covenant for quiet enjoyment.

7. Covenant not to derogate from grant. A landlord must not derogate from his grant. What this means is that if he lets land, he must not subsequently do anything which is inconsistent with the purpose of the letting. The remedy is an action for an injunction or damages.

Aldin v. *Latimer Clark, Muirhead & Co.* (1894). L let land to T, a timber merchant, for use as drying sheds for timber. L then let certain neighbouring buildings which impeded the flow of air to the drying sheds and interfered with the drying process. HELD: There was a breach by L of his covenant not to derogate from his grant.

8. Implied condition of fitness. Generally there is no implied warranty or condition by the landlord that the premises are fit for any particular purpose. The rule is *caveat emptor*—let the buyer beware. It is for the tenant to ensure that the condition of the premises is suitable for his purposes. There is one exception to this rule: in the case of furnished premises there is an implied condition that the premises are fit for habitation at the start of the tenancy.

Smith v. *Marrable* (1843). L let a furnished house to T. It was infested with bugs. HELD: There was an implied condition that the house should be reasonably fit for habitation. T could repudiate the tenancy and recover damages.

There is also a condition as to fitness of small dwellings implied by the Housing Act 1957, s. 6 (*see* **14**).

TENANT'S IMPLIED COVENANTS

9. Covenant to pay rent. If there is no express covenant to pay rent, there will be an implied covenant to pay rent from the time of entry by the tenant onto the demised premises.

10. Covenant to pay rates and taxes. There is an implied covenant that the tenant will pay all rates and taxes except those for which the landlord is liable. The landlord's liability will be determined by reference to the statute which imposes the rates or tax.

11. Obligation not to commit waste. If a tenant does anything to alter the premises he is said to commit waste. There are four kinds of waste:

(*a*) *voluntary waste*, namely any act causing damage to the land e.g. cutting trees, demolishing buildings;

(*b*) *ameliorating waste*, namely alterations which improve the land;

(*c*) *permissive waste*, namely waste which is due to a failure to maintain, e.g. allowing a house to fall into disrepair;

(*d*) *equitable waste*, this is an aggravated form of voluntary waste and includes extreme and serious acts of waste, e.g. cutting trees intentionally planted to shelter a house.

The landlord's remedy if the tenant commits waste is an action for damages, or an injunction to prevent apprehended waste.

12. Extent of obligation. The obligation not to commit waste varies with the nature of the tenancy:

(*a*) a tenant for a fixed term is liable for voluntary and permissive waste;

(*b*) a tenant under a yearly tenancy is liable for voluntary waste; he is not liable for permissive waste save that he must keep the premises wind- and water-tight, fair wear and tear excepted: *Warren* v. *Keen* (1954);

(*c*) a tenant under a lesser periodic tenancy is liable for voluntary waste only.

13. Tenant-like user. A tenant is under an implied obligation to use the demised premises in a tenant-like manner. In *Warren* v. *Keen* (1954), Denning L.J. said of this obligation "The tenant must take proper care of the place. He must, if he is going away for the winter, turn off the water and empty the boiler. He must clean the chimneys, when necessary, and also the windows. He must unstop the sink when it is blocked by his waste. In short, he must do the little jobs about the place which a reasonable tenant would do. But apart from such things, if the house falls into disrepair through fair wear and tear or lapse of time, or for any reason not caused by him, then the tenant is not liable to repair it."

NOTE: The tenant's duties under the law of waste and the implied obligations as to tenant-like user are very much narrower than the onerous duties created by express tenant's covenants to repair.

14. Covenants implied by law. The above covenants are implied at common law, and will apply to all tenancies unless there is an express provision dealing with the matter. In relation to certain residential tenancies, statute has intervened and imposed obligations on the parties. The main provisions are:

(a) Housing Act 1957, s. 6 (*see* **15**);
(b) Housing Act 1961, s. 32 (*see* **8, 16**);
(c) Housing Act 1980, s. 81 (*see* **17**).

15. Housing Act 1957, s. 6. Where a house is let on a tenancy at a rent not exceeding £80 per year in London, or £52 per year elsewhere, there is implied upon the part of the landlord:

(a) a condition that at the start of the tenancy the house is fit for human habitation; and

(b) an undertaking that he will keep the house fit for human habitation.

This does not apply to a tenancy of a house for a term of not less than three years on terms that the tenant is liable to put it into a condition reasonably fit for human habitation. Nor does it apply to a tenancy determinable at the option of either party before the expiration of three years.

NOTE: A landlord's liability under the undertaking is dependent upon him being given notice of the defect: *McCarrick* v. *Liverpool Corporation* (1947).

16. Housing Act 1961, s. 32. Where a dwelling-house is let for a term of less than seven years, there are implied covenants by the landlord:

(a) to keep in repair the structure and exterior of the house, including drains, gutters and external pipes.

(b) to keep in repair and proper working order the installations in the house:

(i) for the supply of water, gas and electricity and for sanitation (including basins, sinks, baths and sanitary conveniences but not other fixtures, fittings and appliances for making use of water, gas and electricity); and

(ii) for space heating or heating water.

NOTES: (1) A landlord cannot contract out of these obligations;
(2) A landlord is only liable under this Act for defects of which

he has notice: *O'Brien* v. *Robinson* (1973). However, the notice may be acquired by the landlord from a third party: *McGreal* v. *Wake* (1984);

(3) By virtue of the Housing Act 1980, s. 80, the provisions of the Act of 1961, s. 32, do not apply to leases granted after 3rd October 1980 in favour of the Crown, local authorities and certain other public bodies;

(4) If a landlord receives a registered rent (*see* XVIII) assessed on the basis that he is liable for s. 32 repairs, he may be estopped from claiming that the tenant is liable to do such repairs: *Brikom Investments Ltd.* v. *Seaford* (1981).

17. Housing Act 1980, s. 81. By virtue of s. 81 it is a term of every secure tenancy, protected tenancy and statutory tenancy (*see* XV, 3) that the tenant will not make any improvement without the written consent of the landlord. In other words such tenants are given a qualified right to carry out improvements. The consent required is not to be unreasonably withheld and, if unreasonably withheld, will be treated as given: s. 81(3). The term "improvement" means:

"any alteration in, or addition to, a dwelling-house and includes:

(*a*) any addition to, or alteration in, landlord's fixtures and fittings and any addition or alteration connected with the provision of any services to a dwelling-house;

(*b*) the erection of any wireless or television aerial; and

(*c*) the carrying out of external decoration."

Item (*c*) does not apply to a protected or statutory tenancy if the landlord is under an obligation to carry out external decorations or to keep the exterior of the dwelling-house in repair (*ibid.*).

Section 81 applies to tenancies granted before as well as after the coming into operation of the provision. In the case of some protected tenancies the provisions are modified: *see* s. 81(4).

IMPLIED COVENANTS IN AGREEMENTS FOR A LEASE

18. General note. So far this chapter has been concerned with the implication of covenants in a lease. Where there is an agreement for a lease and the agreement says nothing about what terms are to be included in the lease, there is implied into the agreement a term that the lease shall contain the "usual covenants." These are:

(*a*) by the landlord:

(*i*) a qualified covenant for quiet enjoyment;

(*b*) by the tenant:
  (*i*) to pay rent;
  (*ii*) to pay rates and taxes not payable by the landlord;
  (*iii*) to keep the premises in repair;
  (*iv*) to permit the landlord to enter and view the state of repair.

In addition to the above covenants there will be inserted whatever other covenants are usual having regard to the nature of the premises, their situation, the purposes for which they are being let, the length of the term, the evidence of conveyancers and the books of precedents: *see* for example, *Chester* v. *Buckingham Travel Ltd.* (1981).

These "usual" covenants are only implied into an agreement for a lease which is open, i.e. where the agreement is silent as to the terms of the lease agreed to be granted. They will become express terms in the lease when it is actually executed. They do not concern or affect the implied covenants in a lease.

PROGRESS TEST 4

1. What is the covenant for quiet enjoyment? **(4)**
2. What is the difference between an absolute and a qualified covenant for quiet enjoyment? **(5)**
3. What are the "usual covenants"? In what situation are they relevant? **(17)**
4. L grants a tenancy of a factory to T. L then obstructs the access to the factory. What remedies does T have against L? **(6, 7)**
5. What are the covenants implied into a lease by (*a*) the landlord, and (*b*) the tenant? **(2)**
6. Can a landlord forfeit a lease if there is no express forfeiture clause? **(3)**
7. What is the scope of the covenant not to derogate from grant? **(7)**
8. T rents a buildings from L for use as a shop. In fact the shop is not fit for such use. Does T have any remedy against L? **(8)**
9. What is waste? **(11)**
10. What are the different types of waste? **(11)**
11. How does liability for waste vary with the type of tenancy? **(12)**
12. What is the effect on the terms of a tenancy of: (*a*) the Housing Act 1957; and (*b*) the Housing Act 1961; and (*c*) the Housing Act 1980? **(14, 17)**
13. When does liability under the implied covenants under the 1957 and 1961 Acts arise? **(17)**

CHAPTER V

Express Covenants

INTRODUCTION

1. Generally. The covenants in a lease govern and regulate the relationship between landlord and tenant. They are the terms of the contract between the two parties and they allocate the responsibility for matters arising out of the lease e.g. the amount of rent payable, the liability for repairs, the responsibility for insurance. If a lease is silent about some matter it means that, unless a term is implied by law (*see* IV), neither party is responsible for it. So, if a lease says nothing about the question of repairs neither party will be responsible.

2. Types of covenant. The covenants considered in this chapter are those relating to:

   (*a*) rent (*see* **3–13**);
   (*b*) repairs (*see* **14–31**);
   (*c*) alterations and improvements (*see* **32–35**);
   (*d*) user (*see* **36–38**);
   (*e*) insurance (*see* **39–40**);
   (*f*) options (*see* **41–47**); and
   (*g*) service charges (*see* **48**).

These are the covenants most frequently encountered in leases. It needs hardly be said that there is no limit to the variety of other covenants which may be found.

RENT

3. Introduction. Rent is the compensation or consideration which the tenant pays to the landlord for the exclusive possession of land under a lease. The following points should be noted:

   (*a*) rent does not have to be money, it may be the performance of services or payment in kind;
   (*b*) rent must be certain or capable of being ascertained with certainty; if it is not certain the tenancy will be of no effect;

(c) rent is payable by the tenant to the landlord or to his authorised agent; it must be paid in the manner specified in the lease;

(d) if the lease is silent about the manner of payment, rent is payable at the end of each period of a periodic tenancy, or at the end of each year of a term of years;

(e) rent is payable without deduction unless the lease authorises the making of deductions or the tenant has paid sums which the landlord has a duty to pay.

4. The obligation to pay rent. In the absence of an express provision, the tenant's obligation to pay rent will normally continue unaffected by any changes in the nature of the demised premises. The doctrine of frustration, however, applies in principle to leases and the obligation to pay rent may therefore be ended by a frustrating event, although such events are likely to be rare: *National Carriers Ltd.* v. *Panalpina (Northern) Ltd.* (1981) H.L.

It is sometimes the practice to insert in a lease a term suspending the obligation to pay rent in the event of an occurrence such as destruction of the demised premises by fire or some other similar serious event.

Where a tenant is evicted from the demised premises by his landlord or by a person with title paramount, the obligation to pay rent ceases.

5. Rent books. Where residential property is let and the rent is payable weekly, the landlord is obliged to provide a rent book: Landlord and Tenant Act 1962, s. 1. The book must contain the name and address of the landlord and various detailed matters which are prescribed by regulation. The current regulations are the Rent Books (Forms of Notice) Regulations 1976. The matters prescribed include:

(a) a statement of the tenant's rights under the Rent Act 1977 in relation to:
   (i) security of tenure, and
   (ii) rent regulation;
(b) the amount of rent and rates,
(c) an explanation of any rent allowance schemes.

6. Rent review clauses. In recent years it has become common to include in leases, and particularly in leases of commercial property, a rent review clause to counter the effect of inflation. Such a clause usually provides for the rent to be reviewed at fixed intervals during the term. At each review date the market rent then current for the demised premises will be assessed and substituted for the rent previously payable. The form of these clauses varies from lease to lease. A properly drafted clause should make clear:

(a) the review period;

(b) the time for taking steps in having the rent reviewed;

(c) whether timē is, or is not, of the essence;

(d) the procedure for determining the reviewed rent by agreement or, in default of agreement, by an independent expert or by arbitration;

(e) the basis of valuation, i.e. what is and what is not to be taken into account in fixing the rent;

(f) the effect of a late review, i.e. from when rent is payable and whether interest is payable thereon;

(g) whether the rent can go down.

7. Time limits in rent review clauses. A rent review clause will normally contain a timetable for taking the steps which lead to the rent being reviewed. In recent years the courts have had to consider the effect of a failure to comply with such a timetable. For instance, if the landlord should fail to serve a notice requiring the rent to be reviewed at the specified time, does this deprive him of the right to have the rent reviewed and of the right to receive a reviewed rent during the period until the next review date? In legal terms the question is whether "time is of the essence". Prior to 1977 there were several conflicting cases on this question. In *United Scientific Holdings* v. *Burnley Borough Council* (1977), the House of Lords considered this problem and overruled certain earlier cases.

The principle of law now applied is that in time stipulations in rent review clauses there is a presumption that time is not of the essence. Time will only be of the essence

(a) if it is expressly so provided by the terms of the lease; or

(b) if there is some indication in the lease that time is to be of the essence, e.g. where the rent review is linked to an option to determine the lease and time is of the essence as regards that option; or

(c) if there is some indication in the surrounding circumstances that time is to be of the essence.

8. Decisions on time limits since United Scientific. Since 1977 cases on time limits in rent review clauses have continued unabated. In some it has been held that time was of the essence notwithstanding the general rule in **7** above.

Drebbond v. *Horsham District Council* (1979). A clause requiring the landlord to give notice requiring arbitration within a certain time limit "but not otherwise" was HELD to make time of the essence because of those quoted words.

Al Saloom v. *Shirley James Travel Services Ltd.* (1981). Where the time limits of a rent review clause were closely linked to those of a break clause, time was held to be of the essence. This was because time was clearly of the essence of the break clause and that clause was linked to the rent review time limits to give the tenant a way out if the reviewed rent was too high. Therefore, if the landlord had been allowed to give a late rent review notice, the tenant would have lost his way out.

Lewis v. *Barnett* (1982). The review clause provided that the landlord's rent review notice would be void if served late. HELD time was of the essence in view of this clear provision.

Trustees of Henry Smith's Charity v. *A.W.A.D.A. Trading and Promotion Services* (1984). Complicated provisions in a review clause which meant that failure to give notice in time gave rise to a deemed reviewed rent were HELD to make time of the essence.

It will be appreciated from the above that a rent review clause must be carefully scrutinised because, notwithstanding the general principle above, time may still be of the essence in complying with the time limits in the machinery. However, where time is not of the essence a lengthy delay will not deprive the landlord of his right to a review unless there is such a combination of delay by the landlord and such hardship to the tenant as will cause an estoppel to arise: *Amherst* v. *James Walker Goldsmith and Silversmith* (1983).

9. Other cases on rent review clauses. Rent review clauses have continued to prove a fruitful source of litigation. Some of the cases have concerned the procedural aspects of a rent review clause; others have concerned the actual process of valuation. The following are some of the more important valuation cases.

Ponsford v. *HMS Aerosols Ltd.* (1978). A rent review clause provided that the reviewed rent was to be "assessed as a reasonable rent for the demised premises". The premises were burnt down and rebuilt by the landlords with substantial improvements which were paid for by the tenants. On review, the question arose whether in assessing a "reasonable rent" account should be taken of the improvements paid for by the tenants. The landlords argued that as the improvements were incorporated in the premises they must be taken into account. The tenants argued that a "reasonable rent" meant a rent which was reasonable between the parties. It was HELD (by the House of Lords (3 : 2)): On a true construction of the lease the rent was payable for the demised premises and this meant the premises as improved. An independent surveyor would have to assess a reasonable rent for the premises and not a reasonable rent between the parties.

Plinth Property Investments v. *Mott, Hay & Anderson* (1981). Where there was a very strict user clause the Court of Appeal HELD that no account should be taken of the possibility that the landlords might relax the covenant; the valuer had to look at the legal position of the parties only.

Pivot Properties Ltd. v. *Secretary of State for the Environment* (1979). The Court of Appeal HELD that in assessing the rent under a rent review clause rights under the Landlord and Tenant Act 1954 are to be taken into account.

Beer v. *Bowden* (1981). Where a review clause failed to provide machinery for assessing the rent if the parties failed to agree it was HELD by the Court of Appeal that the rent must be a fair rent representing what the premises were reasonably worth at the review date.

10. Non-payment of rent. If a tenant fails to pay rent, the landlord may seek to recover it by,

(*a*) levying distress; or

(*b*) an action on the covenant to pay rent; or

(*c*) if there is a forfeiture clause, an action for forfeiture of the lease.

11. Distress. Distress is the taking of goods by one person from another, without legal process, in order to hold the goods as a pledge for the satisfaction of a debt or the performance of a duty. A landlord may secure the payment of rent by seizing goods found on the premises in respect of which rent is due. The right to distrain arises as soon as any rent is due and unpaid. The landlord may then enter and take goods to the value of the rent owed. In general the landlord may distrain on all goods on the demised premises, but certain articles are privileged against distress, e.g. property of the Crown. After the goods are seized, the tenant then has time within which he can pay the arrears and recover the goods. If the tenant fails to pay, the landlord may sell the goods and keep so much of the proceeds as covers the arrears.

NOTE: The subject of distress for rent is very complicated. In *Abingdon R.D.C.* v. *O'Gorman* (1968), Lord Denning M.R. described it as "an archaic remedy which has largely fallen into disuse." The Law Commission has recommended its abolition. It is a subject replete with ancient technicalities. Accordingly in this book it is dealt with in this single paragraph. Where a tenancy is protected by the Rent Act 1977 the leave of the court is needed before the landlord may levy distress.

12. An action for rent. This action is based on the express or implied covenant in the lease by the tenant to pay rent. The action must be brought within six years from when the rent fell due, otherwise it will be barred by the Limitation Act 1980. s. 19.

13. Forfeiture for non-payment of rent. This is dealt with in VIII.

REPAIRS

14. Generally. If there is no express covenant to repair by either party, subject to the law of waste, (*see* IV, **11**) and to the Housing Acts 1957 and 1961 (*see* IV, **15**, **16**), neither party is obliged to repair the demised premises and neither party can require the other to carry out repairs. It is, however, normal to make express provision for one party to repair, or for one party to repair part of the demised premises and for the other party to repair the rest. In short leases the landlord will often be responsible, while in long leases the tenant will be responsible. In leases of flats or offices which form part of a larger building it is frequently the practice to require the tenant to keep the interior in repair while the landlord is responsible for the exterior. The landlord will often seek to recover the cost of fulfilling his obligations from the tenant by way of a service charge.

15. The meaning of "repair." The word "repair" in this context means "making good damage so as to leave the subject as far as possible as though it had not been damaged. It involves renewal of subsisting parts": *Calthorpe* v. *McOscar* (1924). It does not mean the replacement or renewal of the whole or substantially the whole of the demised premises: *see Lurcott* v. *Wakely* (1911). The modern tendency is to see whether on a common sense approach the work required is within the ambit of the word repair: *see Brew Brothers* v. *Snax Ltd.* (1970).

It was sometimes considered that work to remedy an inherent defect could not be a repair although there was never any real support for such a proposition. In *Ravenseft Properties Ltd.* v. *Davstone (Holdings) Ltd.* (1979), Forbes J. expressly rejected the submission that there was any rule of law to that effect. The judge adopted a test that it was always a question of degree whether what the tenant was being asked to do could properly be described as repair, or whether it would involve giving back to the landlord a wholly different thing from that which he demised.

16. Illustrations. The following cases illustrate the scope of repairs.

Lister v. *Lane* (1893). A house was built on poor ground. In order to put the house in good condition it was necessary to underpin it to a great depth. The Court of Appeal HELD: The tenant was not liable to do these works as they would produce a new house and not a repaired house. The works were not repairs and they were outside the scope of his covenant to repair.

Lurcott v. *Wakely* (1911). The front wall of an old house had to be rebuilt because it had become dangerous. The Court of Appeal HELD: This was a repair and the tenant was liable to do it. The works were the renewal of a defective part rather than the replacement of the whole.

Collins v. *Flynn* (1963). L let a house to T. A structure supporting part of the back and side wall of the house collapsed and it was necessary to rebuild the structure and the walls with new foundations. HELD: This was an important improvement which would require the tenant to give up the premises in a different condition from that which they were let in and therefore it was not a repair.

Brew Brothers v. *Snax Ltd.* (1970). The putting in of entirely different foundations was HELD not to be a repair within the tenant's repairing covenant.

17. The standard of repair. The standard of repair required under a repairing covenant will vary from property to property. The general rule as described by Lord Esher M.R. in *Proudfoot* v. *Hart* (1890), requires: "such repair as having regard to the age, character, and locality of the house would make it reasonably fit for the occupation of a reasonably-minded tenant of the class who would be likely to take it."

In determining the standard required by a particular covenant these matters must be considered as at the beginning of the lease and not as at the end of it, as in the following case.

Calthorpe v. *McOscar* (1924). A house was let on a 95-year lease in 1825 in what was then a fashionable area of London but which by 1920 had deteriorated. HELD: The standard of repair must be determined by reference to the character of the premises at the beginning of the lease rather than at the end.

18. Particular covenants. The following are some typical repairing covenants and their effect:

(*a*) *to keep in repair*; this requires the landlord or tenant to repair the premises up to the standard described in it and carries with it an implied obligation to put and to leave in repair: *Payne* v. *Haine* (1847); *Proudfoot* v. *Hart* (1890). It is obvious that where a tenant takes a lease of run-down premises and enters into an ordinary covenant to repair he may assume a very onerous burden since he will not be required merely to keep the premises in the poor state in which he takes them but to put them into a proper state of repair;

(*b*) *to leave, deliver or yield up in repair*; the liability under this covenant only arises at the end of the lease;

(*c*) *to repair and renew*; this is in fact the same as in (*a*) above; the word "renew" adds nothing to an ordinary covenant: *Collins* v. *Flynn* (1963);

(*d*) *to carry out structural repairs*; this requires repairs to the main structure of the building i.e. walls, floors, roofs.

19. The landlord's remedies for tenant's breach of covenant. Where a tenant is in breach of a repairing covenant, the landlord may

(*a*) sue for damages for breach of covenant; or

(*b*) if there is a forfeiture clause, forfeit the lease (*see* VIII).

In the case of certain leases, the landlord cannot start proceedings for either damages or forfeiture without the leave of the court under the Leasehold Property (Repairs) Act 1938.

20. The Leasehold Property (Repairs) Act 1938, s. 1. This Act applies where the lease was granted for a term of seven or more years and there are at least three years of the term unexpired. Where the Act applies, the landlord cannot proceed to forfeit the lease or to sue for damages for breach of repairing covenant without first giving a notice under the Law of Property Act 1925, s. 146 (*see* VIII, **21**) informing the tenant of his right to serve a counter-notice claiming the benefit of the Act. If the tenant serves such a counter-notice within 28 days no further proceedings (by action or otherwise) may be taken unless the court gives leave. The court may give leave if the landlord establishes that one of the grounds specified in s. 1(5) is satisfied. These grounds are that:

(a) the value of the reversion has been substantially diminished;

(b) immediate repair is necessary to comply with any Act;

(c) immediate repair is necessary to protect another occupier;

(d) the cost of immediate repair would be small compared to the cost of future repair;

(e) special circumstances render it just and equitable to grant leave.

On an application for leave under the 1938 Act, the landlord need only make out a prima facie case, in the sense of a case made out by the landlord, without the need to go into any rebutting evidence put forward by the tenant: *Land Securities PLC* v. *Metropolitan Police Receiver* (1983).

Where a term in a lease enables a landlord to enter and do repairs in default of the tenant doing them under his obligations and provides for the recovery by the landlord of the cost of those repairs, an action for the cost is not subject to the 1938 Act: *Hamilton* v. *Martell Securities Ltd* (1984).

21. An action for damages. The procedure is that the landlord will start proceedings in the High Court or the county court claiming damages from the tenant for his failure to perform his repairing covenants. The damages which a landlord may recover for breach of a repairing covenant are subject to special statutory rules. In order to understand these rules it is first necessary to consider the position at common law (*see* **22**) and then to consider the changes effected by statute (*see* **23, 24**).

22. The measure of damages at common law. Where the action is brought during the term, the landlord is entitled to damages representing the diminution in the value of the reversion which has resulted from the breach. This means the amount by which the market value of the landlord's interest is reduced by the disrepair. Accordingly the longer the residue of the term, the less this diminution should be.

Where the action is brought after the lease has ended, it is based on the tenant's covenant to yield up the premises in repair. At common law the measure of damages was the actual cost of carrying out the repairs necessary to put the premises into the state of repair required by the covenant: *Joyner* v. *Weeks* (1891). This was the measure even if the premises were to be demolished so that the repairs were useless. A landlord could also recover for the loss of rent during the period the repairs were being carried out: *Woods* v. *Pope* (1835).

23. Landlord and Tenant Act 1927, s. 18(1). It is provided by this section that damages for breach of a covenant to keep or put premises in repair during the currency of a lease or to put premises in repair at the end of a lease may in no case exceed the amount, if any, by which the value of the reversion in the premises is diminished owing to the breach, and in particular no damages will be recoverable for any such breach of a covenant to leave or put in repair if it is shown that the premises would at or shortly after the end of the lease have been or be pulled down, or such structural alterations would have been made as would render valueless the repairs covered by the covenant.

24. The effect of s. 18(1). The provision has the following effects:

(*a*) the tenant is no longer liable for damages on his covenant to yield up in repair where the premises have been or are to be demolished or structurally altered;

(*b*) there is now an upper limit on the amount of damages recoverable whether the action is brought during the term or at its end: the limit is the diminution in value of the reversion caused by the breach;

(*c*) the proper approach to assessing damages is to ascertain the amount recoverable at common law (*see* **22**) and to ascertain the diminution in value of the reversion. The lesser of the two sums will be the recoverable damages.

25. Tenant's remedies for landlord's breach of repairing covenant. The extent of a landlord's liability to repair will, like a tenant's covenant, depend upon the exact wording of the covenant. Also, the landlord's liability to repair will not arise until he is given notice of the defect or he has knowledge of it: *McCarrick* v. *Liverpool Corpn.* (1947). Where the landlord is in breach of his repairing covenant and the tenant has given notice of the disrepair, the tenant has the following remedies:

(*a*) an action for damages for breach of covenant (*see* **26**);

(*b*) an action for specific performance of the landlord's covenant (*see* **27**);

(c) self-help, i.e. do the work himself and then recoup the expenditure from his landlord (*see* **28**);

(d) the appointment of a receiver (*see* **29**).

26. Action for damages. The measure of damages in an action by the tenant is such pecuniary compensation as will restore the tenant to the position he would have been in if there had been no breach; this may include

(a) the cost of alternative accommodation,

(b) the cost of any repairs paid for by the tenant, and

(c) compensation for living in unpleasant premises: *Calabar Properties Ltd.* v. *Stitcher* (1983). The tenant may start proceedings for recovering such damages. Alternatively, he may withhold his rent and then if he is sued by the landlord for arrears of rent, may set off against the landlord's claim for arrears of rent the damages to which he is entitled: *see British Anzani (Felixstowe) Ltd.* v. *International Marine Management (UK) Ltd.* (1979).

27. Action for specific performance. In a suitable case, the court will compel a landlord to perform his repairing covenants if he is clearly in breach and if there is no doubt about what is required to remedy the breach.

Jeune v. *Queens Cross Properties Ltd.* (1973). L let a flat to T and covenanted to repair. L failed to repair a balcony so that it collapsed. T sought an order compelling L to do the necessary repairs. HELD: In an appropriate case where there was a clear breach and it was clear what had to be done, the court would compel a landlord to perform his repairing obligations. This was an appropriate case.

Since the decision of the court in that case, it has been provided by the Housing Act 1974, s. 125, that in any proceedings in which a tenant of a dwelling-house alleges a breach on the part of the landlord of a repairing covenant relating to any part of the premises in which the dwelling is comprised, the court may in its discretion order specific performance of that covenant. This power is in addition to the power of the court to order specific performance in accordance with ordinary equitable principles as was done in *Jeune* v. *Queens Cross Properties Ltd.*

NOTE: There is old authority that a landlord cannot get specific performance of a tenant's repairing covenant against the tenant: *Hill* v. *Barclay* (1810).

28. Self-help. Where a landlord is in breach of his repairing covenant and he has notice of the defect, at common law a tenant who carries out the repairs may recoup himself out of future rents for the money expended on the repairs: *Lee-Parker* v. *Izzet* (1971). This means that a tenant can do the repairs himself and then deduct the cost from future rents to be paid to the landlord. If the landlord should sue the tenant for such rents, the tenant will have a good defence to the claim. It must be remembered that this can only be done where the repairs fall within the scope of the landlord's repairing covenant and he has notice of the breach.

29. Appointment of a receiver. Where the landlord refuses or neglects to perform the covenants in the lease to repair and to insure, the Court may appoint a receiver to manage the property in accordance with the rights and obligations of the reversioner: *Hart* v. *Emelkirk* (1983).

30. Landlord's right to enter and execute repairs. Where a landlord has covenanted to repair, in the absence of an express provision relating to entry on the premises, the law implies a licence by the tenant so that the landlord may enter and carry out repairs within his covenant: *Saner* v. *Bilton* (1878). In practice a lease will usually contain an express provision to enter to view the state of repair and, if necessary, carry out repairs. Where the express provision enables the landlord to recover costs incurred on repairs for which the tenant is liable, the sum recoverable is a debt, not damages, and is not therefore subject to the 1938 Act (*see* **20**).

31. Defective Premises Act 1972, s. 4. Where a landlord is under an obligation to repair or maintain the premises, or he has the right to enter the premises to maintain or repair them, s. 4 of the 1972 Act provides that the landlord owes a duty of care to all who might reasonably be expected to be affected by defects in the premises, e.g. the tenant, his family, his visitors. The duty is to take reasonable care to see that the people to whom the duty is owed are reasonably safe. The duty is only owed if the defects fall within the landlord's repairing obligation and he knows or ought reasonably to have known of the defect. If the landlord is in breach of his duty, a person to whom the duty is owed and who is injured by reason of the breach may recover damages from the landlord.

ALTERATIONS AND IMPROVEMENTS

32. Generally. We now turn from the liability to repair to the question of altering or improving the premises. A lease usually contains a covenant by the tenant not to make any alterations to the demised premises. In this context an alteration occurs when the actual fabric of the demised premises is altered. Such a covenant may be qualified by words such as "not without the consent of the landlord," alternatively, it may be an absolute prohibition on the making of alterations. The former covenant is referred to as a "qualified covenant" and the latter as an "absolute covenant".

A lease does not usually contain a covenant against the making of improvements. The reason is that the making of improvements will normally be an alteration which will fall within the covenant against alterations. The word "improvement", however, is used in the Landlord and Tenant Act 1927, and it is therefore important to consider its meaning.

33. What is an improvement? This can be a difficult question to answer. In considering the question, the following points must be borne in mind:

(a) the question has to be considered from the tenant's point of view, not from the landlord's;

(b) an improvement need not necessarily increase the value of the demised premises.

The above points are derived from *Woolworth & Co. Ltd.* v. *Lambert* (1937). In that case the tenant wished to convert two shops held under separate leases into one shop. The Court of Appeal HELD that the proposed alterations were improvements even though the letting value would be reduced.

34. Landlord and Tenant Act 1927, s. 19(2). This provides that a covenant against the making of improvements without the consent of the landlord (i.e. a qualified covenant) is deemed to be subject to a proviso that consent will not be unreasonably withheld. It also provides that the landlord is not precluded from requiring, as a condition of his licence or consent:

(a) the payment of a reasonable sum in respect of any damage to or diminution in the value of the premises or of any neighbouring premises belonging to the landlord;

(b) the payment of any legal or other expenses properly incurred in connection with such licence or consent;

(c) in the case of an improvement which does not add to the letting value, an undertaking by the tenant to re-instate the premises to the condition in which they were before the improvement was executed.

NOTE: Section 19(2) does not apply to tenancies of dwelling-houses which are either secure tenancies or protected tenancies or statutory tenancies; instead there is special provision in the Housing Act 1980, s. 81 (*see* IV, **17**).

35. Effect of s. 19(2). In summary therefore, the effect of s. 19(2) on a covenant against making alterations is as follows:

(*a*) if the covenant is absolute, s. 19(2) does not apply and no alterations or improvements can be made unless the landlord, in his absolute discretion, permits it;

(*b*) if the covenant is qualified *but* the alteration is not an improvement, s. 19(2) does not apply and so the tenant can only carry out the alteration if the landlord gives his consent;

(*c*) if the covenant is qualified and the alteration is an improvement, the landlord cannot unreasonably withhold his consent, but he can require as a condition of his consent certain payments and an undertaking (*see* **34** (*a*)–(*c*)).

THE USE OF PREMISES

36. Introduction. Unless the lease contains an express restriction on the use of the demised premises, subject to compliance with planning and similar restrictions, the tenant may use the premises for any purpose provided it is not illegal or immoral. Most leases contain a covenant by the tenant restricting the use of the premises to one particular use, or prohibiting the use of the premises for certain specific uses. Such covenants will vary from lease to lease and their effect will depend upon their precise terms.

37. Landlord and Tenant Act 1927, s. 19(3). It is provided that a covenant against the alteration of the use of the demised premises without licence or consent (i.e. a qualified covenant) is, if the alteration does not involve any structural alteration, deemed to be subject to a proviso that no fine or sum of money in the nature of a fine will be payable for or in respect of such licence or consent. This provision, however, does not stop a landlord requiring the payment of a reasonable sum in respect of any damage to or diminution in the value of the premises or any neighbouring premises belonging to him and of any legal or other expenses incurred in connection with such licence or consent. It is further provided that where a dispute as to the reasonableness of any sum has been determined by a court, the landlord is bound to grant the licence on payment of the sum determined to be reasonable.

38. Effect of s. 19(3). In summary, therefore, the effect of s. 19(3) on a user covenant is as follows:

(a) if the covenant is absolute, s. 19(3) does not apply and the use cannot be altered unless the landlord in his absolute discretion consents;

(b) if the covenant is qualified *but* the change of use involves structural alterations to the demised premises, s. 19(3) does not apply;

(c) if the covenant is qualified and the change of use does not involve structural alteration, s. 19(3) applies and the landlord cannot take a fine for his consent to a change of use;

(d) s. 19(3) does not, *however*, make the covenant subject to the proviso that the landlord may not unreasonably withhold his consent.

INSURANCE

39. Introduction. In leases other than short leases it is the normal practice to place the liability for insurance on one party. If the covenant to insure is by the tenant, he must arrange the insurance and pay the premium. There will be a breach of covenant if the property is uninsured at any time, even though the property is not damaged. If the covenant to insure is by the landlord, normally there will be a further term which will enable him to recover the premium from the tenant by way of additional rent. The following points should be noted:

(a) if the covenant is to insure with a specified company or other company approved by the landlord, the landlord can refuse to approve any company other than that specified without giving his reasons: *Viscount Tredegar* v. *Harwood* (1929);

(b) if the covenant is to insure with a specific company and the tenant takes from that company what is their usual policy which excepts certain risks, the tenant is not liable under this covenant if the house is destroyed in one of the excepted ways: *Upjohn* v. *Hitchins* (1918);

(c) if the landlord covenants to insure the premises, the court will not normally imply a term that he should place the insurance so as not to put an unnecessarily high burden on the tenant who is obliged to pay the premium by way of additional rent: *Bandar Holdings Ltd.* v. *Darwen* (1968).

40. Insurance money. When insurance money is received following the destruction of the premises, the position is as follows:

(*a*) if the landlord or tenant takes out a policy without being obliged to do so, he is not liable to spend the insurance money on re-instatement of the premises;

(*b*) where there is an express term providing for re-instatement, as is normally the case, the insurance money must be applied in accordance with that term;

(*c*) where a landlord covenanted to insure at the tenant's expense, but there was no covenant to re-instate, the landlord was held liable to apply the policy money on re-instatement because the insurance covenant was intended to benefit both landlord and tenant: *Mumford Hotels Ltd.* v. *Wheeler* (1964);

(*d*) where a tenant covenanted to insure in the joint names of landlord and tenant and when the money was paid re-instatement was impossible because of legislation, it was held that the money belonged to the tenant alone because it was he who had paid the premiums: *Re King* (1963).

OPTIONS

41. Introduction. A lease may give to the tenant three kinds of option:

(*a*) an option to purchase (*see* **42–44**);

(*b*) an option to renew (*see* **45–46**);

(*c*) an option to determine (*see* **47**).

42. Option to purchase. An option to purchase is a term which gives the tenant the opportunity to buy the landlord's interest in the demised premises. The normal form of such an option is a covenant by the landlord that, if the tenant at a specified time gives notice to the landlord of his desire to exercise the option, the landlord will sell his interest to the tenant for a specified sum. An option to purchase is not a contract because until it is exercised neither party is obliged to purchase or to sell. An option to purchase is in the nature of an offer to sell which cannot be revoked. Upon exercise of the option a binding contract for sale arises. Contracts which create options are sometimes called unilateral contracts (in the sense that they impose obligations on one party only) as distinct from ordinary contracts (which impose mutual obligations).

43. Effect of assignment of the lease on an option to purchase. If the lease is assigned the benefit of an option to purchase will normally pass with the lease to the assignee, unless the option is limited in its terms to the original lessee.

44. Effect of assignment of the reversion on an option to purchase. Whether an assignee of the reversion will be bound by an option to purchase will vary depending on whether the land has registered title.

(*a*) If the land has unregistered title, the validity of the option depends on whether it (the option) was registered under the Land Charges Act 1972. Under s. 2(4) of that Act, an option to purchase is registrable as a Class C land charge as an estate contract. The Act provides that failure to register the option will make it void against a purchaser of the legal estate for money or money's worth.

(*b*) If the land has registered title, an option exercisable by a tenant in occupation has been held to be an "overriding interest" under the Land Registration Act 1925, s. 70(1), which is binding on an assignee of the reversion without the need for any sort of registration under the Act: *Webb* v. *Pollmount* (1966). Where the tenant is not in occupation the option must be protected by an entry on the register.

45. Option to renew. This gives the tenant the option to take a lease for a further term. Such an option will normally be worded so that the new lease excludes the option itself. If the option is in fact worded so as to include all the clauses of the original lease including the option itself, the lease may be perpetually renewable (*see* III, **23**). An option to renew is usually made expressly dependent upon the tenant complying with all the covenants in the lease. Thus, if the tenant is in breach of any of his obligations, then however trivial the breach, the tenant will be unable to exercise the option.

West Country Cleaners (Falmouth) Ltd. v. *Saly* (1966). T was entitled to an option to renew. He failed to observe a covenant to repaint at fixed intervals. *Held* by the Court of Appeal: The breach disentitled T from exercising the option.

46. Effect of assignment on the option to renew. The rules set out at **43** and **44** above apply to an option to renew.

47. Option to determine. A lease for a term of years may give either party the right to determine the lease at a specified time or when a specified event occurs. For instance the landlord may wish to redevelop the premises when economic conditions permit or the tenant may wish to re-locate his business at a specific time in the future.

An option to determine is often called a "break-clause." The exercise of such a clause will depend on its precise terms. Frequently it is made a pre-condition of its exercise by the tenant that the tenant must have performed all his obligations under the lease.

If the lease is assigned, the clause becomes exercisable by the assignee, if the reversion is assigned, the new lessor is bound by the clause. The validity of an option to determine is not dependent on any form of registration.

SERVICE CHARGES

48. Service charges. It is now common in leases of flats to provide for the recovery by the landlord from the tenant of service charges in respect of heating, lighting, porterage and other services provided by the landlord. The recovery of such sums is subject to regulation by the Housing Act 1980, s. 136 and Sched. 19, the effect of those provisions being:

(*a*) to limit the landlord's right to recover a service charge to reasonable sums reasonably incurred or to be incurred; and

(*b*) to require the landlord to obtain estimates for work costing more than a specified sum; and

(*c*) to require the landlord to inform the tenant of the costs; and

(*d*) to require the landlord in certain cases to consult the tenant.

PROGRESS TEST 5

1. What are the essential attributes of rent? **(3)**

2. When is rent payable under (*a*) a periodic tenancy; and (*b*) a term of years? **(3)**

3. What is the effect of frustration on the obligation to pay rent? **(4)**

4. In what circumstances must a landlord give a tenant a rent book? What information must it contain? **(5)**

5. L lets land to T on a 21-year lease with rent reviews every seven years. There is a procedure for carrying out the review with time limits at various stages. Time is expressed to be of the essence.

L fails to initiate the rent review by the first time limit. Advise L. **(7)**

6. What is a rent review clause? **(6)**

7. What is the effect of the decision in *Ponsford* v. *HMS Aerosols Ltd.*? **(9)**

8. Outline the steps available to a landlord to recover unpaid rent. **(10)**

9. In the absence of an express covenant to repair who is liable to repair property let under a lease? **(14)**

10. What standard of repair is required under a repairing covenant? **(17)**

11. What remedies does a landlord have against a tenant who is in breach of his repairing obligations? How do these remedies differ from those available to a tenant for breach of landlord's repairing obligations? **(19)**

12. What is the measure of damages at common law for breach of a tenant's repairing covenant? How has statute affected the measure? **(22)**

13. When is leave needed under the Leasehold Property (Repairs) Act 1938? To what actions does the Act apply? On what grounds may leave be granted? **(20)**

14. What is the difference in the measure of damages (1) before 1927, and (2) today, in an action brought during the term and at the end of the term for breach of repairing covenants? **(21–24)**

15. What does s. 4 of the Defective Premises Act 1972 provide? **(31)**

16. L is obliged to repair T's roof under the terms of the lease to T. T refuses to permit L to enter. Advise L. **(30)**

17. What constitutes an improvement for the purposes of the Landlord and Tenant Act 1927? **(33)**

18. What is the effect of s. 19(2) of the 1927 Act on

(a) an absolute covenant against making improvements;

(b) a qualified covenant against making improvements? **(35)**

19. L lets a house to T with no user clause. To which of the following uses may T put the premises: (a) residential use; (b) a brothel; (c) light industrial use? **(36)**

20. What is the effect of s. 19(3) of the 1927 Act on user covenants? **(38)**

21. Who is normally responsible for insuring premises let under a lease? What arrangements do the parties normally make regarding insurance? **(39)**

22. L lets property to T and covenants to insure, T being obliged to repay the premium to L. The premises are burnt down and L refuses to use the insurance money to rebuild the premises. Advise T. **(40)**

23. What are the three different kinds of option that may be given to a tenant? **(41)**

24. What is the effect of (*a*) an assignment of the lease, and (*b*) an assignment of the reversion on the three kinds of option mentioned in Question 23? **(43, 44)**

25. What is a "break clause"? **(47)**

CHAPTER VI

Assigning and Sub-letting

INTRODUCTION

1. Generally. This chapter is concerned with the different ways in which a landlord and tenant may deal with their respective interests and the effect of such dealings. The major topics dealt with in the chapter are:

(*a*) assignments and sub-lettings generally (*see* **2–7**);

(*b*) the requisite formalities;

(*c*) covenants against assigning and sub-letting (*see* **8–18**);

(*d*) the enforceability of covenants upon assignment (*see* **19–30**);

(*e*) devolution of leases (*see* **31–33**).

ASSIGNMENTS AND SUB-LETTINGS

2. Assignment of the lease. An assignment of the lease takes place when the tenant transfers to another person his entire interest in the property for the whole of the residue of the term of the lease.

3. Formalities of an assignment. In order to effect a valid assignment, the following formalities must be satisfied.

(*a*) An agreement to assign a lease will not be enforceable unless the agreement is in writing, or there is a memorandum or note of it signed by the party to be charged: Law of Property Act 1925, s. 40. The doctrine of part performance may remedy the lack of writing. (*See* II, **3**, **22** *et seq.*)

(*b*) The assignment must be by deed if the legal estate is to pass to the assignee: Law of Property Act 1925, s. 52(1). This rule applies to any tenancy. It produces the result that while a periodic tenancy or some other tenancy for a period less than three years can be created orally (*see* II, **19**), an assignment of it must be by deed in order to be effective.

(*c*) If (*b*) is not complied with but there is an agreement to assign for value, this may be effective to pass an equitable interest to the assignee.

4. Sub-letting. A sub-letting takes place where a tenant of property lets it or part of it to another person for a period less than the residue of his own term. This period of the sub-lease must be at least one day less than the unexpired period of the lease. If a tenant tries to sub-let the property for a period equal to, or more than, the unexpired period of his own lease this operates as an assignment of the term, not as a sub-letting.

EXAMPLE: L lets land to T for seven years from 1st January 1975. Later T purports to grant a sub-lease to S for three years from 1st January 1979. Three years equals the residue of the lease and the purported sub-lease therefore operates as an assignment, not as a sub-lease.

5. Sub-letting by a periodic tenant. A periodic tenancy, whether it be weekly, monthly or yearly, is regarded in law as continuing until it is actually determined. Accordingly a tenant under a periodic tenancy can validly grant a sub-lease for a term of years without infringing the rule described in **4** above. The sub-letting will not operate as an assignment. This can produce unusual results, as shown by an example.

EXAMPLE: L lets land to T on a yearly tenancy. T sub-lets the land to S for a term of ten years. This operates as a valid sub-letting, not as an assignment.

Thus in theory a weekly tenant can create a valid sub-lease of, say 99 years or more. Of course, at common law, the sub-lease will end with the determination of the interest out of which it is carved. The 99-year sub-lease will, therefore, end if the weekly head-lease is validly ended by notice to quit.

6. Formalities for sub-letting. The same rules apply to the creation of a sub-lease as apply to the creation of a lease: *see* II, **18**.

7. The right to assign and sub-let. In the absence of any provision to the contrary, the tenant has the right to deal with his interest as he wishes; he may assign or sub-let freely. In practice, however, many leases contain a covenant by the tenant not to assign or sub-let. A common form is that the tenant covenants not to assign, sub-let or part with possession of the demised premises or any part thereof. If the tenant assigns or sub-lets in breach of such a covenant the result is as follows: the assignment or sub-letting will be effective to vest a legal estate in the assignee or sub-lessee, but the landlord will have the right to forfeit the lease (provided there is a proviso for re-entry) and will in any event have a right to damages for breach of covenant.

NOTE: Where a tenant assigns his lease in breach of covenant the assignment is, as stated above, effective and any notice of forfeiture of the lease under the Law of Property Act 1925, s. 146 (*see* VIII, **20** *et seq.*) must be served on the assignee, who is the person concerned to avoid forfeiture, not on the original tenant (who is no longer the tenant): *see Old Grovebury Manor Farm Ltd.* v. *W. Seymour Plant Sales & Hire Ltd. (No. 2)* (1979).

COVENANTS AGAINST ASSIGNING OR SUB-LETTING

8. Introduction. The operation of these covenants depends on their precise wording. There are many cases dealing with this topic. In each case it is necessary to look at the words of the covenant in the lease and consider if what the tenant wishes to do falls within the restriction imposed by the covenant. The courts tend to construe such covenants against the landlord in accordance with the general rule of construction of contracts that terms are construed *contra proferentem*, i.e. against the person who has inserted the term for his benefit. The following cases illustrate the approach that the courts have adopted in construing these covenants.

Cook v. *Shoesmith* (1951). L let land to T who agreed "not to sub-let." T sub-let a part of the premises. HELD: The sub-letting of part was no breach unless the covenant expressly extended to "the demised premises or any part thereof." This covenant did not so extend and therefore there was no breach.

Crusoe d. Blencowe v. *Bugby* (1771). A covenant against assigning was not broken by an underletting of the premises.

Lam Kee Ying v. *Lam Shes Tong* (1974). T covenanted not to assign, underlet or part with possession of the demised premises or any part thereof. The Privy Council said that a covenant against parting with possession was not broken by a tenant who, in law, retained possession even though he allowed another to use and occupy the premises. Accordingly, a tenant who grants a licence to another to use the demised premises does not commit a breach of covenant unless the agreement with the licensee ousts the tenant entirely from the legal possession.

Marks v. *Warren* (1979). T covenanted not to underlet or part with possession of the demised premises, without the landlord's consent. T assigned without getting the landlord's consent. In proceedings between the assignee and T, the question arose whether an assignment fell foul of the covenant. HELD: The assignment by T necessarily involved a parting with possession and was therefore a breach of the covenant.

The effect of the penultimate case above is that the restrictive effect of a covenant against assigning, sub-letting or parting with possession may be evaded by the tenant granting a licence to the occupier provided the tenant is not entirely ousted from the legal possession. In consequence landlords are well advised to insist upon covenants not to allow any other person to *occupy* the demised premises.

9. Involuntary assignments. A covenant against assigning is not broken by an involuntary assignment, i.e. an assignment which takes place by operation of law rather than by the act of the parties. The following are examples of involuntary assignments:

(*a*) when the lease passes on the death of the tenant (*see* **32**);

(*b*) when the lease passes on the bankruptcy of the tenant to his trustee in bankruptcy (*see* **33**);

(*c*) when the lease is acquired by a public body exercising compulsory purchase powers.

10. Absolute and qualified covenants. There are two different types of covenant against assigning and sub-letting:

(*a*) an absolute covenant, i.e. the tenant covenants not to assign or sub-let;

(*b*) a qualified covenant, e.g. the tenant covenants not to assign or sub-let without the landlord's consent.

Under the first type the tenant is absolutely prohibited from assigning or sub-letting. If the tenant wishes to assign he will have to cast himself on the landlord's mercy and the landlord will be entitled either to refuse his consent or to impose onerous conditions on the grant of his consent. Under the second type, the tenant may assign or sub-let if the landlord gives his consent. There are statutory provisions which restrict the grounds upon which a landlord may withhold his consent and the conditions which he may attach to his consent (*see* II). These provisions only apply to qualified covenants; they do not apply to absolute covenants.

11. Statutory provisions relating to qualified covenants. The provisions are contained in

(*a*) the Law of Property Act 1925, s. 144; and

(*b*) the Landlord and Tenant Act 1927, s. 19(1).

12. Law of Property Act 1925, s. 144. This provides that where a lease contains a covenant against assigning or sub-letting without licence or consent (i.e. a qualified covenant), except where the lease contains an express provision to the contrary, the covenant is deemed to be subject to a proviso that no fine or sum of money in the nature of a fine will be payable for such licence or consent. The landlord is not, however, precluded from requiring payment in respect of any legal or other expenses in relation to the licence or consent.

13. Landlord and Tenant Act 1927, s. 19(1). Where a lease contains a covenant against assigning or sub-letting without licence or consent, notwithstanding any express provision to the contrary, the covenant is deemed to be subject to a proviso that the licence or consent is not to be unreasonably withheld. The effect of this is as follows.

(*a*) Before the tenant assigns, he must seek the landlord's consent even though consent could not reasonably be withheld. If the tenant fails to seek the landlord's consent, and proceeds with the assignment, the lease will be liable to forfeiture by the landlord: *Eastern Telegraph Co.* v. *Dent* (1899).

(*b*) If the tenant seeks the landlord's consent but the landlord unreasonably withholds his consent, the tenant is free to assign without the landlord's consent: *Treloar* v. *Bigge* (1874). Thereafter the landlord cannot rely on different grounds to justify his withholding: *Bromley Park Garden Estates Ltd.* v. *Moss* (1982).

(*c*) Alternatively, and more prudently, if the landlord unreasonably withholds his consent, the tenant may apply to the court for a declaration that consent has been unreasonably withheld. Upon the granting of the declaration, the tenant can go ahead and assign the lease.

NOTES: 1. Leases frequently provide in express terms that consent to an assignment or sub-letting will not be unreasonably withheld; if this is the case, there is no need to invoke the statutory proviso.

2. Where a qualified covenant is subject to a proviso that the tenant should first offer a surrender of the lease to the landlord, the proviso is lawful and is *not* invalidated by s. 19(1): *see Bocardo S. A.* v. *S & M Hotels Ltd.* (1979).

14. Unreasonable withholding of consent. The following are examples of an unreasonable withholding of consent to an assignment or sub-letting. They apply to both the statutory and express proviso.

Parker v. *Boggan* (1947). L withheld consent because the proposed assignee had diplomatic immunity against legal proceedings.

Bates v. *Donaldson* (1896). L withheld his consent because he wanted to gain possession for himself.

Houlder Bros. v. *Gibbs* (1925). L withheld consent because the proposed assignee already held premises from L and if the assignment went through, the assignee would give up those premises which would then prove difficult to re-let.

Bromley Park Garden Estates Ltd. v. *Moss* (1982). L withheld consent so as to obtain a surrender of the lease and another lease in the same building.

NOTE: By virtue of the Race Relations Act 1965, s. 5(1), where consent is withheld on the ground of colour, race or ethnic or national origins, it is deemed to be unreasonably withheld. This does not apply to a tenancy of part of a dwelling-house of which the remainder, or part of the remainder, is occupied by the person whose licence or consent is required and if the tenant is entitled in common with that person to the use of any accommodation other than the means of access.

15. Reasonable withholding of consent. The following are examples of a reasonable withholding of consent.

Pimms Ltd. v. *Tallow Chandlers Company* (1964). L withheld his consent because the assignee wished to profit from redevelopment plans by means of the nuisance value of the remainder of the lease.

Bridewell Hospital (Governors) v. *Faulkner and Rogers* (1892). L withheld his consent because other property owned by him would be injured by the use to which the proposed assignee wished to put the demised premises.

16. Reasonableness and statutory protection. There are many cases which deal with the difficult question whether a landlord may reasonably refuse his consent to an assignment on the grounds that an assignee will gain a statutory protection that the assignor did not enjoy. The cases fall into two broad groups. First, there is a line of cases which concern the Rent Act. In these it was held that the landlord acted reasonably in refusing his consent to an "abnormal" assignment. By this is meant an assignment, usually at or near the end of the lease, designed to gain for the assignee some protection under the Rent Act which the assignor did not have. The cases in this group include:

Lee v. *K. Carter Ltd.* (1949). The assignor was a company which could not enjoy full Rent-Act protection. The assignee was a director of the company who could enjoy that protection. HELD: The landlord could reasonably withhold his consent to the assignment where the term has only a short time to run.

Swanson v. *Forton* (1949). The assignor was not actually occupying the premises and sought to assign the lease to someone who would occupy them and thereby gain the protection of the Rent Act. HELD: The landlord could reasonably withhold his consent as the term only had a short time to run and the assignee would gain a protection the assignor did not enjoy.

It was thought as a result of these cases that there was a general principle that a landlord could reasonably refuse his consent to an abnormal assignment but not to one which was otherwise normal. Doubt has now been cast on there being such a general principle by the second line of cases. These are two recent decisions of the Court of Appeal.

Norfolk Capital Ltd. v. *Kitway* and *Bickel* v. *Duke of Westminster* (1976). The landlords in these cases refused their consent to assignments by tenants who would not be entitled to the benefit of the Leasehold Reform Act 1967 to assignees who would be so entitled. The assignments were otherwise perfectly normal and were not devised in order to secure the statutory protection. HELD by the Court of Appeal: The landlords acted reasonably in refusing their consent because the assignments would adversely affect the value of the landlords' interest and it could not therefore be said that they were being unreasonable in refusing their consent.

Following the two above cases it is doubtful whether there is any doctrine of normal and abnormal assignments left even in Rent Act cases. This appears from a recent case on the topic.

West Layton Ltd. v. *Ford* (1979). L let to T a butcher's shop with residential accommodation above. T covenanted not to let the living accommodation except as a furnished tenancy for which L's consent was not to be unreasonably withheld. At the time the lease was granted a furnished tenant had no security of

tenure. In 1977 when a furnished tenant had Rent-Act protection
T wished to let the living accommodation separately to sub-
tenants who would have full Rent Act protection. L refused to
give his consent and T sought a declaration that this was unreasonable. HELD by the Court of Appeal: It was not unreasonable for L to refuse his consent as the effect of the sub-letting
would be to alter the nature of the property from a commercial
property to a property let on multiple occupancy of a shop and
separate residential accommodation, and this was not the purpose of the covenant.

**17. Applications to the court for a declaration that consent has been
unreasonably withheld.** As has already been noted, (*see* **13** (*c*)), a
tenant may apply to the court for a declaration that consent has
been unreasonable withheld. If the court makes such a declaration
the tenant may assign his lease. On such an application, the
burden of proof is on the tenant to show that consent has been
unreasonably withheld: *Shanly* v. *Ward* (1913).

By virtue of the Landlord and Tenant Act 1954, s. 53(1), the
county court has jurisdiction to make a declaration that consent
has been unreasonably withheld. The county court has jurisdiction
irrespective of the rateable value of the demised premises. The
High Court also has jurisdiction, but the county court will normally
be a quicker and cheaper forum.

18. Building leases. Where a lease is granted for more than 40 years
and is made in consideration of the erection of buildings (i.e. is a
building lease), if it contains a qualified covenant against assigning etc., the following special provision applies. The landlord and
Tenant Act 1927, s. 19(1)(*b*) provides that in such a lease, there
is implied a proviso that no consent is required to an assignment
made more than seven years before the end of the term provided
written notice is given to the landlord within six months after the
assignment. This is therefore a special case where no consent is
required. It does not apply, however, where the landlord is a public
or statutory authority. The value of s. 19(1)(*b*) as a statutory rule
today is doubtful.

EFFECT OF ASSIGNMENT ON COVENANTS AND THEIR
ENFORCEABILITY

19. Introduction. It is now necessary to consider the extent to
which an assignee of either the lease or the reversion is bound by

the covenants contained in the lease. This subject is dealt with in the following way:

(a) enforceability generally (see **20**);
(b) between the original parties (see **21–22**);
(c) against and by an assignee of the lease (see **23–24**);
(d) against and by an assignee of the reversion (see **25–26**);
(e) liability between assignor and assignee of the lease (see **27**);
(f) underlessees (see **28–29**).

20. The enforceability of covenants generally. Between the original landlord and the original tenant, there is what is called "privity of contract"; what is meant is simply that there is a contractual relationship between them. So long as the lease and the reversion upon it are vested in the original parties, there is also another relationship between them, "privity of estate." This subsists so long as they own their respective interests. If the landlord sells his reversion or the tenant sells his lease there is no longer privity of estate between them. There is then privity of estate between the new landlord and the old tenant or between the old landlord and the new tenant. There is, however, no privity of contract between these parties for there is, of course, no contract between them. It can be seen therefore that the original landlord and tenant are in a special position, and the enforceability of covenants between them is therefore considered separately before considering the position of assignees.

21. Enforceability of covenants between the original parties. As has already been said, privity of estate lasts only as long as the reversion and the lease remain vested in the original parties. When the privity of estate ceases, either because the reversion or the lease has been assigned, there continues to be privity of contract between the original parties. Privity of contract continues between them until the lease ends. It means that the original tenant continues to be liable to the original landlord on the covenants in the lease even though he no longer holds the lease.

EXAMPLE: L lets land to T who covenants to repair the property. T assigns his interest to A who fails to repair the property. L may sue both A and T: he may sue A because there is privity of estate between them; he may sue T because there is privity of contract between them because of the original contract whereby L let the land to T.

Consequently an original tenant must be wary about any person to whom he assigns his interest for if he assigns it to a person who proves to be an irresponsible tenant, the original tenant may find himself bearing the responsibility for the assignee's breaches of covenant. Normally the landlord will pursue his remedies against the assignee of the lease (with whom he has privity of estate) rather than suing the original tenant. If, however, the assignee has no assets the landlord may prefer to sue the original tenant.

22. Exceptions. There are only two exceptions to the rule concerning the liability of the original tenant. They are:

(*a*) where the original landlord and tenant agree that the tenant shall not be liable:

(*b*) where there is an assignment of a perpetually renewable lease (*see* III, **23**).

23. The enforceability of covenants against and by an assignee. The problem to be considered here is as follows. Suppose a tenant assigns his lease to an assignee, can the landlord enforce the tenant's covenants against the assignee? Can the assignee enforce the landlord's covenants against the landlord? The rule is that if the relevant covenant "touches and concerns" the land, it runs with the land and is enforceable by or against an assignee of the lease: *Spencer's Case* (1583).

EXAMPLE: L lets land to T who assigns his lease to A. Whether A can sue or be sued on the covenants in T's lease will depend on whether the relevant covenant touches and concerns the land.

The assignee's liability depends upon there being privity of estate between him and the landlord. This means that if the assignee should assign his interest his liability will cease, unless he has entered into a separate agreement with the landlord.

It is often the practice on an assignment for the assignee to enter into a direct agreement with the landlord that he will observe the covenants, the object being that there should be privity of contract between the assignee and the landlord. On account of this privity the assignee will remain liable to the landlord on the covenants in the lease even if he should further assign the lease and thus cease to be in privity of estate with the landlord.

24. Covenants which touch and concern the land. The best way to understand what constitutes a covenant which touches and concerns the land is to consider some examples.

The following are covenants which touch and concern the land:

    (*a*) by the landlord:

        (*i*) for quiet enjoyment (*Spencer's Case* (1583));

        (*ii*) to repair (*ibid.*);

        (*iii*) to renew the lease (*Muller* v. *Trafford* (1901));

    (*b*) by the tenant:

        (*i*) to pay rent (*Parker* v. *Webb* (1693));

        (*ii*) to repair (*Martyn* v. *Clue* (1852));

        (*iii*) not to assign without consent (*Goldstein* v. *Sanders* (1915));

        (*iv*) to insure (*Vernon* v. *Smith* (1821));

        (*v*) to use the premises for a specific purpose (*Wilkinson* v. *Rogers* (1863)).

The following are covenants which do not touch and concern the land:

    (*a*) by the landlord:

        (*i*) a covenant that the tenant shall have an option to buy land other than the demised premises (*Collinson* v. *Lettsom* (1815));

        (*ii*) to keep in repair other land (*Dewar* v. *Goodman* (1908));

        (*iii*) permitting the tenant to display advertisements on other land (*Re No. 1 Albermarle Street* (1959));

    (*b*) by the tenant:

        (*i*) to pay rates in respect of other land (*Gower* v. *Postmaster-General* (1887));

        (*ii*) not to employ men from other parishes (*Congleton Corporation* v. *Pattison* (1808));

25. The enforceability of covenants by and against an assignee of the reversion. The question here is, if the landlord assigns his reversion, can the new landlord enforce the tenant's covenants against the tenant? Similarly, can the tenant enforce the landlord's covenant against the new landlord? The rule is that an assignee of the reversion can sue or be sued upon the covenants in the lease which have "reference to the subject-matter of the lease." This rule is contained in the Law of Property Act 1925, ss. 141 (benefit of tenant's covenants) and 142 (burden of landlord's covenants). The words "reference to . . . ." have the same meaning as the words "touch and concern." Accordingly, the cases in **24** above can be used to illustrate what this rule applies to. The rules which govern the situation described in this paragraph are entirely statutory and derive originally from the Grantees of Reversions Act 1540.

26. The position after an assignment of the reversion. Where the reversion is assigned, the Law of Property Act 1925, s. 141 provides that the assignee acquires all "the benefit" of the tenant's covenants. The courts have held that the effect of this is that after an assignment the assignee alone is entitled to sue the tenant for breaches of a covenant in the lease, whether the breaches occurred before or after the assignment.

Re King (1963). In 1895 T let to B a factory for 80 years at £100 per year. B covenanted to keep the premises in repair. In 1908 the lease vested in K. In the 1950's the freehold interest of T was compulsorily acquired by the LCC and the sale was completed in 1960. After completion the question arose who was entitled to sue K for breaches of covenant occurring before the assignment, i.e. was it T or the LCC? HELD by the Court of Appeal: Under s. 141, the rights of the assignor to sue the lessee for breaches occurring before the assignment passed on the assignment to the assignee as part of "the benefit" of every covenant under s. 141. This meant that the LCC had the right to sue for breaches of the repairing covenants.

Arlesford Trading Co. Ltd. v. *Servansingh* (1971). L let land to T who failed to pay rent. T assigned the lease to A. Later, L assigned the reversion to R. Accordingly there was never any privity of either contract or estate between R and T. R sued T for the rent which he had failed to pay. HELD: R could sue T for the rent by virtue of the Law of Property Act 1925, s. 141, even though there had never been privity between them. The right to sue for this rent was one of the "benefits" which passed to R under s. 141. T was liable as original tenant (*see* **21**).

27. Liability between tenant and assignee. When the lease is assigned to an assignee, he becomes responsible for the performance of the covenants and for the payment of the rent. It has already been seen that the original tenant continues to be liable contractually for the performance of the covenants and the payment of the rent. As between the tenant and the assignee, it is the assignee who is primarily liable. In order to protect the original tenant, there is implied by statute in every conveyance after 1925 of the interest created by a lease, a covenant by the assignee that he will pay all the rent and perform the covenants in the lease and indemnify the assignor against any proceedings costs and claims arising from any omission to pay the rent or any breach of the covenants: Law of Property Act 1925, s. 77. Frequently the deed of assignment contains an express covenant of indemnity.

The original tenant is also entitled, at common law, to an indemnity from the assignee responsible for any breach. This indemnity arises from general principles of the law of restitution or quasi-contract. Thus in most cases where an assignee defaults to observe a covenant and the original tenant is sued by the landlord, he can recover from the assignee what he has been compelled to pay (*a*) on any express covenant, or (*b*) on the statutorily implied covenant, or (*c*) under the rules of quasi-contract.

28. The enforceability of covenants against and by an underlessee. Until now this chapter has been concerned with the enforcement of covenants by or against assignees of the lease or the reversion. It is now necessary to consider this question in relation to an underlessee. The position is more straight forward. Suppose L grants a lease to T who grants a sub-lease to S. The position is as follows:

(*a*) between L and T there is privity of contract and of estate;

(*b*) between T and S there is privity of contract and of estate;

(*c*) between L and S there is neither relationship.

This means that the covenants in S's sub-lease are enforceable only between T and S. If therefore S should commit a breach of covenant, only T can sue S; L cannot sue S. L could in many cases sue T since S's breach of covenant would probably be a breach of the terms of T's lease.

29. Exceptions. There are only two exceptions to the above rule. First, where there is an express contract between the sub-tenant (S) and the head landlord (L), L can sue S. This may arise where L only allows the sub-letting on condition that S enters into a direct contract with him. The second exception is where the head lease contains a covenant restricting user. The covenant may then be enforceable against the sub-tenant by virtue of the general principles of restrictive covenants: *see Tulk* v. *Moxhay* (1848).

30. Example. The foregoing paragraphs deal with a number of difficult principles. The following example is intended to illustrate all the principles.

EXAMPLE: L lets land to T who assigns to A who then assigns to B who sub-lets to S. S commits a breach of covenant. The position is as follows:

(*a*) S is liable to B by privity of estate and of contract (*see* **28**);

(*b*) S is not liable to L unless there is a direct contract between

them or the breach relates to a restrictive covenant and S is
liable under the general principles of restrictive covenants;

(c) B is liable to L by privity of estate or by a direct contract
if there is one;

(d) A is not liable to L unless there is a direct contract between
them (see 23);

(e) T is liable to L by privity of contract (see 21);

(f) T is entitled to an indemnity from A by reason of the
Law of Property Act 1925, s. 77 (see 27);

(g) T is entitled to an indemnity from B at common law (see
27);

(h) A is entitled to an indemnity from B by reason of the Law
of Property Act 1925, s. 77 (see 27).

DEVOLUTION OF LEASES

31. Introduction. It is now necessary to consider a matter associated
with the question of assignment. It concerns the way in which a
lease passes or "devolves" upon the happening of the following
events:

(a) the death of the tenant (see 32);

(b) the bankruptcy of the tenant (see 33).

32. Devolution on death of tenant. Where a tenant dies, the lease
vests in his personal representatives: Administration of Estates Act
1925, s. 1. In the case of a tenant who dies leaving a will, the vesting
takes place at the time of the testator's death by operation of law.
In the case of a tenant who dies intestate, the administrator derives
title only from the moment that the court grants letters of administration; until then the lease vests in the probate judge: Administration of Estates Act 1925, s. 9. The personal representatives
then hold the lease and will be responsible for the payment of rent
and the performance of the covenants. Their liability is limited,
however, to the extent of their estate.

33. Bankruptcy of the tenant. On the bankruptcy of the tenant the
lease vests in his trustee in bankruptcy: Bankruptcy Act 1914,
s. 53. The trustee becomes liable for the rent and for the performance of the covenants. The trustee may assign the lease or
avoid liability altogether by disclaiming the lease: s. 54(1). In certain cases disclaimer must be with the leave of the courts: s. 54(3).
If the bankrupt acquires any lease after his bankruptcy but before
his discharge, that automatically vests in his trustee.

PROGRESS TEST 6

1. How do you distinguish between an assignment and a sub-letting? **(4)**

2. L lets property to T for seven years from 1st January 1980. T purports to sub-let the property to S for five years from 1st January 1984. What is the effect of the transaction? **(4)**

3. What formalities are required on the making of an assignment? **(3)**

4. What is the effect of a covenant by the tenant against: (a) sub-letting and assigning; (b) assigning; (c) parting with possession? **(12, 13)**

5. What is the difference between a qualified and an absolute covenant against alienation? **(10)**

6. What is the effect on a qualified covenant of
   (a) s. 144 of the Law of Property Act 1925, and
   (b) s. 19(1) of the Landlord and Tenant Act 1927? **(7)**

7. L grants to T a lease of premises on terms that T should not assign or sub-let without the consent of L. T assigns the lease to A without seeking L's consent. Advise L. **(7)**

8. Give examples of the grounds on which a landlord may (a) reasonably, and (b) unreasonably, withhold his consent to an assignment. **(14, 15)**

9. L grants to T Ltd. a lease of Rent-Act protected property for seven years. The lease prohibits assigning or sub-letting without consent. At the end of the term T Ltd. wishes to assign the lease to A who is a director of T Ltd. Advise L. **(16)**

10. Explain the difference between "privity of estate" and "privity of contract." **(20)**

11. "An original tenant is always liable on the covenants in a lease." What are the exceptions to this rule? **(22)**

12. L lets land to T who assigns the lease to A. Advise L which of the following covenants he can enforce against A: (a) repairing; (b) insurance; (c) option to buy other land. **(24)**

13. What is the effect of the Law of Property Act 1925, s. 141 on the assignment of the reversion of a lease? **(25)**

14. L lets land to T who assigns the lease to A. At the end of the lease, the property is in disrepair and L sues T for damages. Advise T. **(27)**

15. L lets land to T who sub-lets a part to S. What remedies does L have against S if he is in breach of covenant? **(28, 29)**

16. What happens to a lease on (a) the death, and (b) the bankruptcy of a tenant? **(31–33)**

CHAPTER VII

Termination of Tenancies

INTRODUCTION

1. The different methods of termination. The main ways in which a tenancy may be ended are as follows:

(*a*) effluxion of time (*see* **2**);

(*b*) under a power (*see* **3**);

(*c*) operation of a condition subsequent (*see* **4**);

(*d*) merger (*see* **5–7**);

(*e*) surrender (*see* **8–11**);

(*f*) notice to quit (*see* **12–20**);

(*g*) disclaimer (*see* **21–22**);

(*h*) forfeiture (*see* **23**);

(*i*) frustration (*see* **24**).

EFFLUXION OF TIME

2. Generally. This only applies to a tenancy for a fixed term. At common law the tenancy will end on the expiry of the term and the landlord will then be entitled to possession. In practice the landlord's right to possession has been restricted by the modern legislation which operates to continue certain types of tenancy beyond the expiry of the term. For example, in the case of a tenancy of business premises the term is continued by statute until it is determined in accordance with any of the specified methods of termination (*see* the Landlord and Tenant Act 1954, Part II).

UNDER A POWER

3. Generally. A tenancy may contain a term enabling either party to end the tenancy at a particular time or on the happening of a particular event. This is often called a "break clause" and is normally found in tenancies for a fixed term.

EXAMPLES: (1) L lets land to T for a term of 14 years with a term enabling T to end the tenancy by notice at the end of the seventh year.

(2) L lets land to T for a term of 14 years with a term enabling L to end the tenancy by six months' notice given at any time in the event of his intending to demolish the buildings on the land and to rebuild.

In order to exercise a break clause a party must comply strictly with the conditions attached to it. So, in the first example, the tenant can only end the tenancy at the end of the seventh year—no earlier and no later. In the second example, L must show that he actually intends to demolish and to rebuild. It is usual to provide that notice of determination should be given within a certain period. In such a case time will be of the essence. Of course, a power of determination may be vested in a tenant as well as a landlord.

CONDITION SUBSEQUENT

4. Operation. The duration of a tenancy may be limited by a condition, in which case the tenancy will continue until the condition is satisfied. The following is a common example:

An employer provides his employee with accommodation subject to the condition that the employee's tenancy shall determine on the termination of his employment. When the employment ends the condition is fulfilled and the tenancy will determine.

MERGER

5. Definition. When a tenancy and the reversion immediately expectant on it are held by the same person in the same capacity, the term is said to merge with the reversion. The effect of merger is that the term and the reversion become one. It is essential that the same person holds the two interests in the same capacity. If, for example, he held one as a trustee and the other in his own right, the two interests could not merge.

6. Effect of merger on sub-tenancies. At common law the merger of a term of years and the reversion destroyed the covenants in any sub-tenancy. It is now provided by the Law of Property Act 1925, s. 139, that where a reversion expectant on a lease is merged, the reversioner becomes the immediate reversioner on any sub-tenancies and is entitled to the benefit of (and must bear the burden of) the sub-tenant's covenants.

EXAMPLE: L grants a lease of land to T who sub-lets to S. X, a third party, buys the interests of both L and T. At common law the sub-lease to S would be of no effect because of the merger of L's and T's interests which amounts to the termination of T's lease. The effect of s. 139 is that X would become S's landlord and would be entitled to enforce S's covenants against S. Similarly S would be entitled to enforce T's covenants against X.

7. Retention of reversion. Where a merger occurs it is sometimes convenient to keep the reversion and the lease in being notwithstanding that they are vested in the same person in the same capacity. It is possible to achieve this in two ways. One is by including a declaration against merger in the appropriate instrument, e.g. in the example in the last paragraph the transfer to X might contain an express statement that no merger was intended. The other method is by the operation of the doctrine of equity that merger will not be taken to have occurred where it would be against the interests of the parties involved for there to be a merger.

At common law, merger was automatic; the equitable doctrine set out above now prevails by express statutory provision: Law of Property Act 1925, s. 185.

SURRENDER

8. Generally. Surrender takes place where the tenant gives up his interest to his landlord and is therefore akin to merger. A surrender may be either:

(a) an express surrender; or
(b) a surrender by operation of law.

9. Express surrender. An express surrender takes place where the parties expressly agree to the making of a surrender. The following formalities must be complied with:

(a) if the lease is for a period not exceeding three years and is at the best rent which can reasonably be obtained without taking a fine, the surrender may be made in writing signed by the surrenderor: Law of Property Act 1925, ss. 53(1), 54(2);

(b) if the lease is for a period exceeding three years, the surrender must be by deed: Law of Property Act 1925, s. 52.

A formal deed of surrender is usual.

10. Surrender by operation of law. In certain cases the conduct of the parties is such that the law implies a surrender. This is called a surrender by operation of law, and is also sometimes called an implied surrender. It occurs where the conduct of the parties is inconsistent with the continued existence of the old lease. The following cases illustrate this form of surrender.

Lyon v. *Reed* (1844). L granted to T a new lease that was to begin before T's old lease expired. The old lease was therefore impliedly surrendered. T was bound by the terms of the new lease.

Wallis v. *Hands* (1893). L granted a lease to T. Later, during the currency of T's lease, L granted a new lease to X. T consented to this and gave up possession to X. T's old lease was impliedly surrendered.

Cannan v. *Hartley* (1850). L granted to T a lease. During the currency of the lease T gave up possession to L who unequivocally accepted it. T's lease was impliedly surrendered.

The last case illustrates one of the more common forms of surrender by operation of law. It may sometimes be a difficult question whether the tenant has actually given up possession to the landlord. There is a sufficient giving up if the tenant gives up the keys and the landlord accepts them with the intention of ending the tenancy. In contrast, if the landlord simply enters the premises to carry out essential repairs, or the tenant simply abandons the premises, there will be no surrender by operation of law until the landlord does some act whereby he treats the tenancy as at an end.

The essential components of a surrender by operation of law are

(*a*) the actual giving up of possession to the landlord; and

(*b*) an intention on the part of both parties that the tenancy shall be brought to an end.

Sometimes the parties prefer to end the lease by an implied surrender rather than by an express surrender, e.g. to save stamp duties.

11. The effect of surrender on sub-tenancies. The surrender of a tenancy does not affect any sub-tenancies created out of that tenancy. On surrender, by virtue of the Law of Property Act 1925, s. 139, the head-landlord becomes the reversioner to any sub-tenant as in the example in **6** above.

NOTICE TO QUIT

12. Introduction. A periodic tenancy can be determined by the service of a notice to quit. The notice may be served by either the landlord or the tenant. In the absence of an express term in the lease, the period of notice required is determined by the rules at common law. If the parties make an express agreement as to the manner of giving notice, the notice is governed by that agreement. It is not, however, open to either party to deprive himself permanently of his right to serve a notice to quit.

Centaploy v. *Matlodge Ltd.* (1973). L granted to T a weekly tenancy which was "to continue until determined by T." The question arose whether this provision deprived L of the right to determine the tenancy. HELD: The tenancy could be determined by L serving notice to quit notwithstanding the words of the agreement because to hold that L had no such right was repugnant to the nature of the tenancy granted. Per Whitford J.: "It must be basic to a tenancy that at some stage the person granting the tenancy shall have the right to determine it and a tenancy in which the landlord is never going to have the right to determine at all . . . . . . is a complete contradiction in terms."

It is, however, open to either party to limit his right to serve a notice to quit provided he does not permanently deprive himself of the right.

Re Midland Railway Company's Agreement (1971). A half-yearly tenancy was made determinable by three months' notice, subject to a proviso that the landlords could only serve notice if they required the land for the purpose of their undertaking. The question arose whether this proviso was void as being repugnant to the nature of a periodic tenancy. The Court of Appeal HELD: The proviso was not repugnant to the nature of a periodic tenancy and was a valid restriction.

13. Period of notice. If the parties have not made any express agreement, the periods of notice required to determine a periodic tenancy are as follows:

    (*a*) a yearly or greater tenancy—six months' notice;
    (*b*) a quarterly tenancy—one quarter's notice;
    (*c*) a monthly tenancy—one month's notice;
    (*d*) a weekly tenancy—one week's notice.

It can be seen that, except in the case of yearly tenancies, the period of notice must equal the period of the tenancy.

14. Residential tenancies. The rule described above has been modified in the case of residential tenancies. The Protection from Eviction Act 1977, s. 5 (re-enacting part of the Rent Act 1957) requires a minimum of four weeks' notice to determine a periodic residential tenancy. This means that **13** (*d*) above is modified in the case of residential tenancies.

15. Agricultural holdings. The rules described above have also been modified in the case of tenancies of agricultural holdings. In summary, a year's notice expiring at the end of the current year of the tenancy is required to determine a tenancy of an agricultural holding: *see* XXIV.

16. Business tenancies. A notice determining a tenancy of business premises must be at least six months in duration: *see* XI.

17. Expiration of notice to quit. The notice to quit must not only satisfy the requirements relating to the period of the notice, but it must also expire at the end of a period of the tenancy. If this requirement is not satisfied the notice will be bad. If, for example, a yearly tenancy began on 1st January, its period ends each year on 31st December. Strictly speaking therefore, the notice to quit must take effect on 31st December. The courts have construed the end of the period of the tenancy to include the anniversary of the commencement of the tenancy: *see Sidebotham* v. *Holland* (1895). The result is that, in the example above, a notice to quit would be effective if it took effect on either 1st January or 31st December.

It is often difficult to ascertain when a tenancy began, and accordingly it is often difficult to know when the notice to quit should take effect. To avoid the danger of an error like this invalidating the notice to quit, it is the practice in drafting such a notice:

(*a*) to specify as the date on which the notice will expire the date on which it is believed the tenancy expires; and

(*b*) to add general words of the following sort "or at the end of the (year or other period) of the tenancy which will expire next after the end of (one half-year or other period required to determine the tenancy) from the date of the service of this notice."

By doing this an error as to the specific date given under (*a*) should not invalidate the notice because the general words should provide a date which will be the anniversary of the tenancy: *Addis* v. *Burrows* (1948).

18. Form of the notice to quit. A notice to quit must satisfy the following requirements:

(*a*) it must be clear and unambiguous;

(*b*) it need not be in any specific form unless this is required by the terms of the tenancy or the provisions of a statute. In theory, a notice may be given orally, although this would be inadvisable because of the evidential problems it would cause;

(*c*) it must relate to the whole of the land let under the tenancy; notice to quit part only of the land is void unless there is a provision to that effect in the agreement.

NOTE: There is now one statutory requirement of form in relation to common law notices to quit. The Protection from Eviction Act 1977, s. 5, requires that a notice to quit in respect of any premises let as a dwelling must be in writing and contain certain prescribed information. This information is designed to tell the tenant what his rights are under the Rent Act.

19. Service of notice to quit. The following points must be noted with regard to service:

(*a*) The notice to quit must be given by the landlord to his immediate tenant or by the tenant to his immediate landlord.

(*b*) The notice may be given in any of the following ways:

    (*i*) by ordinary post;

    (*ii*) by registered or recorded delivery post;

    (*iii*) by or on an authorised agent;

    (*iv*) by personal service; or

    (*v*) by any other means prescribed by the lease.

20. Conduct subsequent to the notice to quit. It is often the case that something done (notably the acceptance of rent by the landlord) after the service of notice to quit amounts to the grant of a new tenancy. This gives rise to difficult questions and the following points should be noted.

(*a*) Whether a new tenancy has been granted will depend on whether there was an intention to create a new tenancy.

(*b*) The payment and acceptance of rent will only create a new tenancy if it is shown that there was a common intention to create a new tenancy: *dee Doe d. Cheney* v. *Batten* (1775); *Clarke* v. *Grant* (1949). So if the landlord accepts rent "without prejudice" to his rights under a notice to quit there can be no intention to create a new tenancy.

(*c*) The court will not imply an intention to create a new tenancy simply because a tenant protected in his occupation by statute continues to occupy the demised premises and makes payment for his occupation; such a tenant's occupation is attributable to his statutory right and not to the creation of a new tenancy: *Marcroft Wagons Ltd.* v. *Smith* (1951) (*see* III, **13**).

The process just described is sometimes called "waiver" of the notice to quit. This term is inaccurate since the notice to quit has full effect to end the tenancy; the acceptance of rent creates a new tenancy by implication.

DISCLAIMER

21. Introduction. In certain cases a lease may be disclaimed by the person in whom it is vested:

(*a*) where a lease is vested in a bankrupt, his trustee in bankruptcy may disclaim it under the Bankruptcy Act 1914, s. 54; the disclaimer must be in writing and be made within 12 months of the appointment of the trustee;

(*b*) where a lease is vested in a company which is being wound up, the liquidator may disclaim it under the Companies Act 1948, s. 323.

The trustee or liquidator will generally wish to disclaim the lease if he cannot assign it for value or put it to some beneficial use.

22. The effect of disclaimer. In order to consider the effect of disclaimer it is necessary to distinguish between two situations:

(*a*) where the disclaimed lease is still vested in the original tenant; and

(*b*) where the disclaimed lease is vested in an assignee and not in the original tenant.

In the first situation, the disclaimer operates to terminate the lease which ceases to exist: *see Stacey* v. *Hill* (1901). The rights and liabilities of the bankrupt or the company cease to exist. In the second situation, the disclaimer terminates only the rights and liabilities of the assignee, but the original lessee remains liable on the covenants in the lease.

Warnford Investments Ltd. v. *Duckworth* (1978). W granted a lease of business premises to D. With W's consent, D later assigned the lease to L Ltd., a company, which went into voluntary liquidation. The liquidator of L disclaimed the lease. W sued D for rent falling due after the date of the disclaimer. HELD: Where a lease has been assigned to a company which goes into liquidation and the liquidator disclaims the lease, leaving the lease without an owner until a vesting order is made in respect of the lease, the disclaimer does not destroy the lease. D remained directly and primarily liable to W for the rent throughout the remainder of the term.

23. Forfeiture. This is dealt with in chapter VIII.

FRUSTRATION

24. Introduction. The doctrine of frustration is a part of the general law of contract. Under the doctrine a contract will be discharged and both parties released from further contractual obligations where the circumstances surrounding the contract are radically altered by unforeseen events so that the whole basis of the contract changes, e.g. destruction of the subject-matter of the contract by war, fire, earthquake.

At one time, it was not clear whether the doctrine of frustration applied to leases because a lease created an estate in land which, it was said, endured irrespective of changes in the nature of land. Until 1981 the law was stated in the following case.

Cricklewood Property and Investment Trust Ltd. v. Leightons Investment Trust Ltd. (1945). The question here was whether a building lease for 99 years was frustrated by war-time building restrictions. The House of Lords HELD: On these facts the lease was not frustrated for the restrictions were of a temporary nature. Lords Russell and Goddard took the view that the doctrine of frustration could not apply to a lease of land. Lords Simon and Wright, however, considered that the doctrine might apply if the alleged frustrating event was more permanent than on these facts and affected the land for the whole term. The fifth law lord expressed no view.

It has now, however, been held by the House of Lords that the doctrine of frustration does, in principle, apply to leases, though the cases in which it can properly be applied are limited.

National Carriers Ltd. v. Panalpina (Northern) Ltd. (1981). A warehouse was let to the tenants for ten years from January 1974. The only vehicular access to the warehouse was by a road which the local authority closed in May 1979 because of the dangerous condition of a nearby derelict building. The period of closure was likely to be 20 months. The landlord sued for arrears of rent and the tenant argued that the lease was frustrated. The House of Lords HELD: The doctrine of frustration was in principle applicable to a lease but on the facts here it did not apply.

PROGRESS TEST 7

1. What are the various ways in which a lease may come to an end? **(1)**

2. Does the doctrine of frustration apply to leases? **(24)**

3. What is a "break clause"? How does it operate? **(3)**

4. Why is no notice to quit necessary at the end of a tenancy for a fixed term? **(2)**

5. What is the effect of a lease subject to a condition? **(4)**

6. How does the merger of a lease and the reversion expectant on the same affect a sub-tenancy created out of the term? **(6)**

7. What are the two kinds of surrender? What is the difference between them? **(8)**

8. What formalities are necessary for a surrender? **(9)**

9. How does a surrender affect sub-tenants? **(11)**

10. What period of notice is required to end (a) a weekly tenancy; (b) a yearly tenancy; (c) a tenancy for a fixed term? **(13)**

11. Can a landlord deprive himself of the right to serve notice to quit? **(12)**

12. What special requirements apply to notices to quit: (a) residential property; (b) business property; (c) agricultural land? **(14–16)**

13. L grants to T a yearly tenancy running from 1st January 1978. In September 1980 L decides that he wishes to end the tenancy. When is the earliest date on which he can do this? Would your answer be different if the tenancy was (a) a weekly tenancy; (b) a monthly tenancy; or (c) a quarterly tenancy? **(17)**

14. Can notice to quit be given orally? **(18)**

15. What is "waiver of a notice to quit"? **(20)**

16. What is the effect of a disclaimer of a lease? Who may disclaim a lease? **(21)**

17. L lets property to T on a weekly tenancy. L wishes to end the tenancy. Consider the validity of a notice to quit by L served on: (a) T; (b) T's wife; (c) T's solicitor; and (d) T's next door neighbour. **(19)**

18. What is the effect of *Warnford* v. *Duckworth*? **(22)**

CHAPTER VIII

Forfeiture

INTRODUCTION

1. Generally. A lease will normally contain a clause which enables the landlord, in certain specified circumstances, to terminate the lease and to re-enter the demised premises. This is called a forfeiture clause or a proviso for re-entry. The specified circumstances will normally be where the tenant is in breach of any of his obligations under his tenancy. The clause may, however, be drafted so as to cover other matters, e.g. the bankruptcy of the tenant. If there is no express proviso for re-entry in a lease, the law will *not* imply one. Even if there is no express proviso the landlord may still be able to re-enter if the tenant is in breach of a condition of his tenancy. The law has developed various rules relating to forfeiture and this is therefore a complicated subject. In this chapter the subject is dealt with in the following sequence:

  (*a*) breach of a condition (*see* **2**);
  (*b*) construction of forfeiture clauses (*see* **3**);
  (*c*) their operation (*see* **4**);
  (*d*) re-entry (*see* **5–7**);
  (*e*) the effect of forfeiture (*see* **8–9**);
  (*f*) waiver (*see* **11–14**);
  (*g*) restrictions on forfeiture (*see* **15** *et seq.*)

2. Breach of a condition. If a term of the tenancy is framed as a condition rather than as an ordinary covenant, the landlord is entitled to re–enter the premises if the tenant is in breach of that condition. Whether a clause is a condition is a question of construction of the words used. The distinction between a covenant and a condition is not always clear; the use, however, of words such as "provided always" or "upon condition that" will generally, though not always, give rise to a condition.

Doe d. Henniker v. *Watt* (1828). L let land to T. By the lease it was "stipulated and conditioned" that T should not assign, transfer or underlet any part of the land other than to his immediate family. HELD: By this clause a condition was created, for the breach of which L might re-enter the land.

OPERATION OF FORFEITURE CLAUSES

3. Construction of forfeiture clauses. There is a general rule of construction that contractual terms are construed against the party for whose benefit they have been inserted (the *contra proferentem* rule). Applying this rule, the courts construe forfeiture clauses against the landlord and in favour of the tenant. The following cases illustrate this.

Doe d. Spencer v. *Godwin* (1815). A forfeiture clause referred to the covenants "thereinafter" contained. In fact the covenants were all contained *before* the forfeiture clause. HELD: The forfeiture clause was of no effect.

Doe d. Abdy v. *Stevens* (1832). A forfeiture clause referred to the tenant doing "any act matter or thing contrary to and in breach of the covenants" in the lease. HELD: This wording did not extend to a breach of a repairing covenant which was an omission and not an act.

4. Operation of a forfeiture clause. A typical clause may be in the following form:

"provided that if the rent hereby reserved or any part thereof is at any time in arrear and unpaid for 21 days after it is due, whether legally demanded or not, or if there shall be any breach of any of the covenants on the part of the tenant contained herein then it shall be lawful for the landlord at any time thereafter to re-enter the demised premises and thereupon the term shall absolutely cease and determine."

Such a clause operates in the following way. If the tenant commits an act of forfeiture (i.e. if the rent is unpaid and in arrear and unpaid for 21 days or if he is in breach of another covenant), the landlord may elect to do one of two things. He may treat the lease as continuing or he may forfeit it. The tenant's conduct does not therefore end the lease but makes it determinable by the landlord at his option. It is therefore only the landlord who can end the lease on forfeiture; the tenant cannot end it in this way.

5. The landlord's right to forfeit. If the landlord decides to forfeit the lease (rather than allowing the lease to continue) he may enforce his right either by:

(a) actually re-entering on the land (*see* **6**); or

(b) bringing proceedings for possession (*see* **7**).

6. Actual re-entry on the land. This will normally take the form of a re-occupation of the premises or a re-letting of them to another person. There are certain statutory restrictions on this method of enforcing a right of re-entry. As a result this method of re-entry is not often relied on by landlords. The restrictions are:

(a) the Criminal Law Act 1977 (*see* IX, **4**);

(b) the Protection from Eviction Act 1977. Section 2 of this Act provides that where premises are let as a dwelling on a lease containing a right of re-entry it is not lawful to enforce the right otherwise than by proceedings in court while any person is lawfully residing in the premises or any part of them.

7. Bringing proceedings for possession. Currently, the normal method of enforcing a right of re-entry is by issuing proceedings claiming possession of the premises. The writ must contain an unequivocal demand for possession in order to operate as an effective re-entry.

8. When the forfeiture takes effect. It used to be thought that it was the issue of the writ which operated as the landlord's final election to determine the lease. In fact it is the service of the writ upon the tenant which operates as the final election: *Canas Property Co. Ltd.* v. *K.L. Television Services Ltd.* (1970). This means that from the date of service of the writ the lease is at an end.

9. The effect of forfeiture. When a landlord actually forfeits his tenant's lease by taking either of the steps above, it has the following effect:

(a) the lease comes to an end;

(b) any underlease derived from the lease also ends;

(c) the landlord can only claim rent falling due before the forfeiture took place; thereafter his claim is for mesne profits;

(d) the right of re-entry is no longer capable of being waived (*see* **11**).

NOTE: Although the lease is at an end, the tenant may enforce the landlord's covenants if he is pursuing an application for relief from forfeiture: *Peninsular Maritime Ltd.* v. *Padseal Ltd.* (1982).

WAIVER OF FORFEITURE

10. Introduction. If, before he has exercised his right of re-entry, the landlord with knowledge of the breach does some act which acknowledges the continuance of the tenancy, he will be taken to have elected not to forfeit the lease. The landlord is said to have waived the forfeiture.

11. Elements of waiver. The elements of waiver are:

(*a*) the landlord's knowledge of the breach;

(*b*) an act by the landlord which recognises the continuation of the tenancy prior to the exercise by the landlord of his right to re-enter.

12. Knowledge of the breach. It is a prequisite for waiver that the landlord knows of the breach. The expression "knowledge" in this context has a wide meaning as is illustrated by the following cases.

Central Estates (Belgravia) Ltd. v. *Woolgar* (1972). T commited a breach of covenant. L employed managing agents who instructed their staff to refuse rent from T. The instructions did not reach one of the clerks who sent out a demand for rent to T; he paid the rent and was then sent a receipt by the agents. HELD: There was a waiver of the forfeiture because L, through the agents, knew of the breach and still accepted rent.

David Blackstone Ltd. v. *Burnetts (West End) Ltd.* (1973). A lease contained a covenant against sub-letting without L's consent. L gave his consent to a proposed sub-letting by T to A and B. In fact T sub-let to a company owned by A and B, i.e. a different person in law to the proposed sub-lessee. T told L's solicitors of this change. Later, while the solicitors were still considering if this change amounted to a breach of covenant, an employee in an associated company of L sent out a rent demand. HELD: L had knowledge of the breach because he knew of it through his solicitors.

13. Examples. The following are examples of acts which, with the appropriate knowledge, amount to waiver:

(*a*) demanding or accepting rent due after the breach (*David Blackstone Ltd.* v. *Burnetts (West End) Ltd.* (1973));

(*b*) distraining for rent (*Green's Case* (1582));

(*c*) express consent to the breach;

(d) acceptance of rent "without prejudice" (*Segal Securities Ltd.* v. *Thoseby* (1963)).

The following are examples of acts not amounting to waiver:

(a) accepting rent due before the breach (*Green's Case* (1582));
(b) standing by and seeing a breach incurred;
(c) assigning the reversion "subject to the lease" (*London & County (A. & D.) Ltd.* v. *Wilfred Sportsman Ltd.* (1971))

14. Waiver and different types of breach. A breach may be either a "continuing" breach or a "once and for all" breach. A breach of a repairing covenant is an example of a continuing breach for it continues to exist until it is remedied by the execution of the necessary repairs. A breach of the covenant against sub-letting is a once and for all breach because it consists of a single, non-recurring act, i.e. the grant of the sub-lease. If there is a waiver of a once and for all breach, the right to forfeit for that breach is lost forever. In contrast, if there is a waiver of a continuing breach, a fresh right of forfeiture will arise on the day after the waiver because the breach continues from day to day.

RESTRICTIONS ON FORFEITURE

15. Introduction. It is now necessary to consider certain rules which restrict the operation of forfeiture clauses. It is said that the law leans against forfeitures: this means simply that the law restricts the landlord's rights under the clause. This is apparent from the way in which the courts construe forfeiture clauses (*see* 3) and the rules relating to waiver (*see* 11). It also appears from the restrictions which, in summary, require

(a) that the landlord satisfy certain pre-conditions;
(b) that the tenant be granted relief from forfeiture in certain cases.

There are different rules relating to forfeiture for non-payment of rent and forfeiture for other breaches of covenant and these matters are therefore considered separately in the following paragraphs.

FORFEITURE FOR NON-PAYMENT OF RENT

16. Forfeiture for non-payment of rent. At common law a landlord could only forfeit a lease for non-payment of rent if he had made a formal demand for the rent due. A formal demand must be:

(a) made by the landlord or his authorised agent;

(b) for the exact sum due;

(c) made on the day it falls due; and

(d) made at the demised premises.

If a landlord failed to make a formal demand then he could not forfeit the lease. There therefore grew up a practice of providing in a forfeiture clause a term that the lease could be forfeited for non-payment of rent in arrear for a certain number of days "whether formally demanded or not." The effect is that a formal demand is no longer necessary.

Even if a lease contains no words dispensing with the necessity for a formal demand, it may be unnecessary if the Common Law Procedure Act 1852, s. 210, is satisfied. The statute provides that a formal demand is unnecessary where at least six months' rent is in arrears and no sufficient distress is to be found on the demised premises.

17. Relief against forfeiture for non-payment of rent. Originally equity granted relief against forfeiture for non-payment of rent to a tenant who paid all the arrears and any costs. In the main, the position is now governed by statute but the position is somewhat different according to whether the proceedings are in the High Court or the county court.

18. Relief in the High Court. If the landlord brings an action in the High Court for forfeiture on the ground of non-payment of rent, the tenant has the following rights.

(a) In cases where there are at least six months' arrears of rent, the tenant is entitled to an automatic stay of the proceedings if he pays all the arrears of rent and any costs into court or to the landlord before judgement is given: Common Law Procedure Act 1852, s. 212.

(b) If judgement is given in a case to which (a) applies, under s. 212 the tenant has the right to apply to the court for relief within six months of the landlord's actual entry under the court order.

(c) In cases to which s. 212 does not apply (i.e. where there is less than six months' rent in arrear or where the landlord re-enters peaceably without proceedings) relief is available under the Judicature Act 1925 s. 46. Relief is available in the same way as it was originally granted by the old courts of equity. This means that relief will normally be granted prior to re-entry by the landlord if the tenant pays all the rent and costs. After re-entry relief will only be granted if that would be just.

19. Relief in the county court. Here the position is governed by the County Courts Act 1984, s. 138, which provides that:

(a) if not less than five clear days before the date fixed for trial the tenant pays into court the arrears and the costs of the action the action will cease;

(b) if the action does not cease under (a), at the trial the court, if satisfied that the landlord is entitled to enforce the right of re-entry, will make an order in the following terms. The form is that the landlord "shall have possession unless the tenant pays into court all arrears and costs within (a specified time)." The specified time cannot be less than four weeks from the date of the order. If the tenant then pays the arrears and costs within the specified time he will continue to hold the premises under the lease. Also at any time before the landlord recovers possession, the tenant may apply to court for the period to be extended;

(c) if the order is enforced and the landlord recovers possession neither the county court nor the High Court has jurisdiction to grant relief because s. 138 (7) provides that "the lessee shall be barred from all relief": *Di Palma* v. *Victoria Square Pty Co. Ltd.* (1984). However, the opposite view was reached by a different judge in *Jones* v. *Barnett* (1984) and a decision of the Court of Appeal is now awaited to reconcile the two decisions;

(d) when the landlord forfeits the lease by actually re-entering, the tenant may apply to the county court for such relief as the High Court could have given provided he applies within six months of re-entry.

FORFEITURE FOR BREACHES OTHER THAN NON-PAYMENT OF RENT

20. Introduction. Where a tenant commits a breach of covenant other than the non-payment of rent, the landlord's right to forfeit is subject to two restrictions contained in the Law of Property Act 1925, s. 146. They are:

(a) in order to enforce a right to forfeit, the landlord must first serve on the tenant a special form of notice (called a s. 146 notice);

(b) the tenant has the right to apply for relief from forfeiture.

21. Service of a s. 146 notice. The Law of Property Act 1925, s. 146, provides that:

"A right of re-entry or forfeiture under any proviso or stipulation in a lease shall not be enforceable by action or otherwise unless and until the lessor serves on the lessee a notice:

(a) specifying the particular breach complained of; and

(b) if the breach is capable of remedy, requiring the lessee to remedy the breach; and

(c) in any case requiring the lessee to make compensation in money for the breach;

and the lessee fails within a reasonable time thereafter to remedy the breach if it is capable of remedy, and to make reasonable compensation in money to the satisfaction of the lessor for the breach."

22. Requirements of a valid s. 146 notice. Section 146(1) specifies three requirements. Requirement (a) is essential and cannot be omitted. It must make clear to the tenant what it is that the landlord is complaining of so that he will have an opportunity to remedy the breach before any proceedings are started: *Jolly* v. *Brown* (1914). Failure to comply with this requirement will invalidate the notice. Requirement (b) need not be included if the breach is incapable of rememdy (*see* **24**). Requirement (c) need not be included if the landlord does not want compensation in money: *Lock* v. *Pearce* (1893).

23. Effect of service of s. 146 notice. When a valid s. 146 notice has been served the landlord may then start proceedings for forfeiture of the lease; If the tenant is required to remedy the breach then it is normal to require him to do so within a reasonable period, the duration of which will depend upon the circumstances of the case. It is only at the expiration of that period that the proceedings can be started if the tenant has failed to remedy the breach.

24. Breaches incapable of remedy. The following are examples of breaches incapable of remedy:

(a) once and for all breaches (*see* **14**) such as a breach of the covenant against sub-letting: *Scala House & District Property Co. Ltd.* v. *Forbes* (1974);

(b) where the breach is of such a nature that it must cast a stigma on the premises, e.g. use for gambling or use as a brothel or for other immoral purposes: *see Rugby School Governors* v. *Tannahill* (1935).

It may not always be clear if a breach is capable of remedy. In cases of doubt it is therefore safest for a landlord to serve a notice requiring his tenant to remedy the breach adding such words as "if capable of remedy."

25. Method of service. A s. 146 notice must be served on the tenant or his duly authorised agent. If there are joint tenants the notice must be served on all of them.

26. Relief against forfeiture for breaches of covenant other than non-payment of rent. The Law of Property Act 1925, s. 146(2) makes provision for relief in cases such as this in the following terms:

"Where a lessor is proceeding, by action or otherwise, to enforce such a right of re-entry or forfeiture, the lessee may in the lessor's action, if any, or in any action brought by himself, apply to the court for relief; and the court may grant or refuse relief, as the court, having regard to the proceedings and conduct of the parties under the foregoing provisions of this section, and to all the other circumstances, thinks fit; and in case of relief may grant it on such terms if any, as to costs, expenses, damages, compensation, penalty, or otherwise, including the granting of an injunction to restrain any like breach in the future, as the court, in the circumstances of each case, thinks fit."

27. The granting of relief. In granting relief the court considers various factors, including:

(*a*) the nature of the breach;

(*b*) whether the breach was serious or deliberate;

(*c*) whether the tenant is able and willing to remedy the breach.

These factors are not exhaustive. In *Hyman* v. *Rose* (1912), the House of Lords said that strict rules should not be laid down to guide the court in exercising its discretion because it was a matter for the court to consider in each case.

In appropriate circumstances the court may grant relief in respect of part only of the demised premises: *GMS Syndicate Ltd.* v. *Gary Elliott Ltd.* (1981).

28. The position of sub-tenants. Where a landlord forfeits a lease, the rule at common law is that any sub-tenancies end with the forfeited lease. This could be very unfair because the sub-tenant may not be at fault at all. The harshness of the rule has been mitigated by allowing a sub-tenant to apply for relief as against the person who has forfeited the lease. The relevant provisions are now contained in s. 146(4) of the 1925 Act which provides:

"Where a lessor is proceeding by action or otherwise to enforce a right of re-entry or forfeiture under any covenant, proviso or stipulation in a lease, or for non-payment of rent, the court may, on application by any person claiming as underlessee any estate or interest in the property comprised in the lease or any part thereof, either in the lessor's action (if any) or in any action brought by such person for that purpose, make an order vesting for the whole term of the lease or any less term the property comprised in the lease or any part thereof in any person entitled as underlessee to any estate in such property upon such conditions as to the execution of any deed or other document, payment of rent, costs, expenses damages, compensation, giving security, or otherwise, as the court in the circumstances of each case may think fit, but in no case shall any such underlessee be entitled to require a lease to be granted to him for any longer term than he had under his original sub-lease."

NOTE: This provision applies both to forfeiture for non-payment of rent and to forfeiture for other breaches of covenant.

29. Illustration. The following example is intended to illustrate the way in which the Law of Property Act 1925, s. 146(4) works.

EXAMPLE: L lets land to T who sub-lets half to S. T falls behind with his rent and L starts proceedings against T for forfeiture on this ground. T is unable to pay the arrears and L gets judgement against T for possession of the land and the arrears of rent. After judgement is entered against T, S applies to court for relief under s. 146(4). The court will normally grant him relief by ordering that he hold the term of his old sub-lease direct from L and that he enter into a deed with L for this purpose. S may also be ordered, as a condition of relief, to pay a proportion of the arrears due from T to L.

This is the normal practice in cases such as in the example: *see Chatham Empire Theatre Ltd.* v. *Ultrans Ltd.* (1961), where a sub-tenant was granted relief on terms that he pay a proportion of the arrears due from the intermediate tenant.

30. Sexual Offences Act 1965. Section 35(2) of this Act gives to a landlord a statutory right to determine a lease where the tenant is convicted of knowingly permitting the premises to be used as a brothel. The statutory right only arises if, first, the landlord requests the tenant to assign the lease to some person approved by the landlord and, second, the tenant fails to assign it within three months. If the tenant fails to assign the lease within that period, the landlord can get a summary order from the court for the delivery of possession.

PROGRESS TEST 8

1. What is the effect of the *contra proferentem* rule on forfeiture clauses? **(3)**

2. How may a landlord enforce his right to forfeit the lease? **(5)**

3. What is the effect of the Criminal Law Act 1977 and the Protection from Eviction Act 1977 on forfeiture clauses? **(6)**

4. When does a forfeiture take effect? **(8)**

5. What is the effect of a forfeiture on sub-tenancies? **(9, 28)**

6. How may a breach of covenant be waived? **(11)**

7. What is a Law of Property Act 1925, s. 146 notice? In what circumstances must it be served? **(20)**

8. How may a tenant apply for relief from forfeiture? **(18, 19, 26)**

9. How do the rules relating to relief from forfeiture for non-payment of rent differ from those relating to forfeiture for other breaches of covenant? **(26)**

10. L lets land to T at a rent of £2000 p.a. There is a forfeiture clause in the lease. T falls into arrears and L brings proceedings in the county court for forfeiture. Advise T. What would the position be if the proceedings were brought in the High Court? **(18, 19)**

11. What must a valid s. 146 notice contain? **(21)**

12. How does the court decide whether or not to grant relief from forfeiture for breaches other than non-payment of rent? **(27)**

CHAPTER IX

The Parties' Rights on Termination

COMMON LAW RIGHTS

1. Generally. This chapter is concerned with the parties' rights at common law at the end of a tenancy. The position has, of course, been changed considerably by statute and these changes are considered later. In summary the landlord's main right is to possession while the tenant's is to remove certain items.

LANDLORD'S RIGHTS

2. The landlord's rights. At common law at the end of the tenancy a tenant is bound to give up possession of the demised premises to his landlord. A lease will normally contain an express covenant to that effect; in the absence of such a covenant the law implies a term to that effect. If the tenant failed to give up possession, at common law a landlord could sue for damages. He would be entitled to recover

(*a*) a sum for use and occupation of the land for the period the tenant withholds possession, and

(*b*) subject to any question of remoteness of damage, any damages and costs the landlord incurs as a result of the tenant's failure to give possession; e.g. if the landlord had agreed to relet the premises and the new tenant was unable to take possession and suffered loss which he claimed from the landlord.

RECOVERY OF POSSESSION

3. Introduction. A landlord may enforce his right to possession by either,

(*a*) actually re-entering the premises provided he can do so without infringing the Criminal Law Act 1977; or

(*b*) bringing proceedings for possession.

4. Actual re-entry. A landlord can only enforce his right to possession by re-entering if he does so peaceably. Until 1977 this rule was contained in old statutes—the Statutes of Forcible Entry 1381 to 1623—which made it a criminal offence for a landlord to take forcible possession of premises. They have now been replaced by the Criminal Law Act 1977. Section 6 provides that any person who, without lawful authority, uses or threatens violence for the purpose of securing entry into any premises for himself or any other person is guilty of an offence if,

(a) there is someone on the premises who is opposed to the entry; and

(b) the person using the violence knows that is the case.

It is specifically provided by s. 6(2) that the fact that a person has any interest or right to possession of the premises (such as a landlord at the end of a tenancy) does not constitute lawful authority for the purpose of securing entry.

The effect of this provision is that a person seeking to recover possession of premises must use his civil remedies to recover possession rather than try to use or threaten violence. Section 6(4) provides that it is immaterial whether the violence is directed against person or property.

There is only one exception to the above rule. It is provided for in s. 6(3), which states that it is a defence to any proceedings to prove that the accused was a "displaced residential occupier" of the premises in question. Such a person is defined by s. 12 as a person who was occupying the premises as a residence immediately before being excluded from occupation by anyone who entered the premises as a trespasser. This is intended to assist a person who lives in premises, goes away for a time and returns to find that trespassers have entered the premises. Such a person has a defence to any proceedings brought if he should use or threaten violence to secure entry to the premises.

5. Recovery of possession by action. A landlord will normally enforce his right to possession by bringing an action for possession. He may combine this with any other claims that arise out of the tenant's occupation of the land e.g. a claim for arrears of rent or mesne profits (*see* 7) or a claim for damages for breach of covenant. The claim may be brought in the county court or the High Court. The county court only has jurisdiction where the net annual value of the premises for rating is less than £1000 (County Courts Act 1984, s. 21), unless the parties agree to an extended jurisdiction (*ibid.*, s. 18). In Rent Act cases, the county court has a very wide jurisdiction irrespective of rateable value. Proceedings in the county court are normally quicker and cheaper than in the High Court.

OTHER REMEDIES

6. Introduction. By statute there are two special and ancient remedies available to a landlord against a tenant holding over. In practice they are rarely used. They are:

(*a*) *An action for double value* under the Landlord and Tenant Act 1730, s.1 which provides that a landlord may sue for double the yearly value of the land where he gives notice under the Act (before the expiry of the tenancy) requiring the tenant to give up possession but the tenant then wilfully holds over. This action is not available where the tenant holds over by reason of statutory protection; nor is it available against weekly, monthly, or quarterly, tenants.

(*b*) *An action for double rent* under the Distress for Rent Act 1737, s. 18; this is available where a tenant gives a valid notice to quit and holds over after its expiry. Double rent can be recovered regardless of whether there is statutory protection.

7. Action for mesne profits. If the tenant remains in possession of the demised premises at the end of his tenancy (other than in right of some statutory protection) the landlord is entitled to recover from him "mesne profits" for the time that he so occupies the premises. Mesne profits are, in effect, a form of damages for the loss of the use of the land which the landlord has suffered by reason of the tenant's failure to give up possession. The way in which they are normally calculated is to consider what is the market rental of the land, since this is the benefit of which the landlord has been deprived.

NOTE: Mesne profits can only be claimed from the date when the tenant ceases to hold the premises as a tenant and holds them as a trespasser. Until that time the appropriate claim would be for rent.

8. Time-limits. A landlord must re-enter the land or bring his proceedings for possession within 12 years from the time when the right to re-enter or to bring proceedings accrued: Limitation Act 1980, s. 15(1). When the land is let under a written lease the landlord's right to possession accrues when the lease ends. When the land is let under an oral periodic tenancy the landlord's right to possession is deemed to have accrued at the end of the first year, or other period, of the tenancy or at the last time rent was received, whichever is the later. Accordingly if the landlord fails to bring proceedings for possession within the 12 years and there is no acknowledgement of the landlord's title by the tenant, the landlord's right of action will be barred and he will be unable to recover possession.

EXAMPLES: (1) L lets land to T on an oral yearly tenancy from 1st January 1960. The last receipt of rent by L is on 1st January 1962. In 1978 L tries to recover possession from T. L would not succeed because the limitation period for his claim expired on 1st January 1974, i.e. 12 years after the last receipt of rent.

(2) L lets land to T for a term of seven years from 1st January 1960. There is no renewal of the term and T remains in possession without paying any rent. In 1978 L tries to recover possession from T. L should succeed because the limitation period would not expire until 1st January 1979 i.e. 12 years after the expiry of the term.

TENANT'S RIGHTS

9. The tenant's rights on termination. At the end of a tenancy the main question which concerns a vacating tenant is whether he can remove articles which he has fixed to the demised premises.

10. Fixtures, generally. The general rule is that any article fixed to the land becomes part of the land and belongs to the owner of the land. This rule is expressed in the maxim *quicquid plantatur solo, solo cedit*—whatever is attached to the land becomes part of it. Consequently a tenant who attaches things to the demised premises may make them into a part of the land itself and they may thereby become the property of the landlord.

Terminology. Two expressions often used are "landlord's fixtures" and "tenant's fixtures". The former means fixtures which have been attached by the landlord and fixtures which have been added by the tenant but which he is not entitled to remove; the latter means fixtures which have been attached by the tenant and which he is entitled to remove in accordance with the following rules.

11. The difference between fixtures and chattels. A fixture is any article which is so attached to the land as to form in law a part of the land. If an article is not so attached to the land as to form in law a part of the land, then it remains a chattel. In many cases it will be clear whether or not an article is a fixture e.g. a fireplace. There are, however, many cases where it is difficult to decide if an article is a fixture or a chattel. There are two tests to decide this question:

(a) the degree of annexation; and

(b) the purpose of annexation.

12. The degree of annexation. This test must be considered first. If the article has some actual connection to the land, prima facie it is a fixture; e.g. a fireplace or panelling. If the article has no such connection, prima facie it is not a fixture, e.g. a free standing greenhouse, machinery resting on its own weight. The degree of annexation is not by itself decisive of the question whether any item is a fixture or chattel. It is necessary also to look at the object or purpose of the annexation.

13. The purpose of annexation. This test involves deciding whether the article has been affixed for its more convenient use as a chattel, in which case it remains a chattel, or for the more convenient use of the land to which it is attached. The leading case illustrates this.

> *Leigh* v. *Taylor* (1902). T owned some valuable tapestries. He fixed them to the wall of a house. He nailed strips of wood to the wall, he then stretched canvas over the strips, and the tapestry was fastened by tacks to the strips. Finally the tapestry was surrounded by a moulding. On T's death the question arose whether the tapestries were fixtures and passed with the house. HELD: The tapestries had not become fixtures. Per Vaughan Williams L.J.: "In my judgement it is obvious that everything which was done here can be accounted for as being absolutely necessary for the enjoyment of the tapestry."

14. The right to remove fixtures. If an article is a chattel the tenant can remove it; if it is a fixture it cannot be removed from the land and must be left for the owner of the land. There are exceptions to this last rule in so far as it affects landlord and tenant. Originally the rule was that all fixtures were landlord's fixtures and had to be left for the landlord. The law has mitigated this rule and there are now three exceptions. The following are tenant's fixtures:

(a) *Trade fixtures*. These are fixtures attached by the tenant for the purpose of his business or trade. They can be removed at any time during the term but not after the term has ended (*Poole's Case* (1703)).

(*b*) *Ornamental and domestic fixtures.* This covers things like mirrors, blinds, stoves. It is a pre–requisite that the removal will not cause substantial injury to the building (*Spyer* v. *Phillipson* (1931)).

(*c*) *Agricultural fixtures.* These do not fall within (*a*). By virtue of the Agricultural Holdings Act 1948, s. 13, a tenant of an agricultural holding who has attached fixtures to the land can take them away before the end of the term, or within two months after the end. The following conditions must be satisfied:

(*i*) the tenant must have performed or satisfied all his obligations to the landlord;

(*ii*) the tenant must have given the landlord written notice of his intention to remove the fixtures;

(*iii*) the landlord must not have served a counter–notice electing to purchase the fixtures;

(*iv*) the removal must not cause avoidable damage to the premises.

15. Removal of fixtures. The rule is that the tenant must remove the fixtures during the tenancy. If he fails to do so they will become the property of the landlord absolutely at the end of the tenancy. If a tenant surrenders his tenancy and is granted a new one of the same premises he loses his right to remove the fixtures unless there is an express provision to the contrary : *Leschallas* v. *Woolf* (1908).

In *New Zealand Government Property Corporation* v. *H.M. & S. Ltd.* (1981), however, it was held that, where there was a surrender of a tenancy by operation of law followed by the start of a new tenancy to the same tenant, there was a clear inference that it was not the intention of the parties that the tenant should be taken to give up his right to remove the fixtures on the determination of his old tenancy.

STATUTORY RIGHTS

16. Generally. So far this book has been primarily concerned with the position at common law between landlord and tenant. At law the relationship is governed by the combination of contract and land law. The parties are free to agree whatever terms they wish for the letting of land. At the end of the lease the landlord is entitled to possession and can evict the tenant or renegotiate the terms of the tenancy. This means that the landlord will generally be in a superior position. During the nineteenth century, this difference in bargaining power became more apparent with the increase in population and the need for more housing. As a result legislation was passed to try to redress the balance by improving the tenant's position. Such legislation has multiplied and today there are several different schemes affording protection to different types of tenants. The nature of these schemes has varied from time to time but, in essence, they do two things: first, they regulate the rent payable under a tenancy; secondly, they give security of tenure.

17. The nature of the protection. The extent of the protection enjoyed by a tenant will depend on the nature of the use to which he puts the premises and the type of tenancy he has. There are distinct codes of protection in respect of:

(*a*) business tenancies;

(*b*) residential tenancies other than long leases;

(*c*) residential tenancies which are long leases;

(*d*) agricultural holdings.

These different codes are considered in the following chapters.

18. Summary of the relevant statutes. The following is a chronological list of the main statutes with which students should be familiar.

(*a*) *Landlord and Tenant Act 1927, Part I:* this deals with a business tenant's entitlement, on leaving the demised premises, to compensation for improvements made to the demised premises.

(*b*) *Agricultural Holdings Acts 1948 and 1984:* these give tenants of agricultural holdings protection.

(*c*) *Landlord and Tenant Act 1954, Part I:* this gives security of tenure to tenants of residential premises who hold under long leases at low rents.

(*d*) *Landlord and Tenant Act 1954, Part II:* this gives security of tenure to the tenants of business premises.

(*e*) *Leasehold Reform Acts 1967 and 1979 :* These give tenants of houses under long leases at low rents the right to acquire the freehold of their house.

(*f*) *Rent (Agriculture) Act 1976:* this gives security of tenure to the occupiers of tied agricultural accomodation.

(*g*) *Rent Act 1977:* this gives security of tenure to tenants of residential property and controls the amount of rent recoverable from the tenant.

(*h*) *Housing Act 1980:* this gives security of tenure to local authority tenants.

The above is only an outline of the protection conferred by each statute. Whether protection is available and its extent in any case will depend upon the exact facts and the satisfaction of various, often complicated, conditions.

PROGRESS TEST 9

1. What were the Statutes of Forcible Entry?   (**4**)

2. If a tenant fails to give up possession of premises at the end of his tenancy what remedies does the landlord have? How has statute affected these remedies?   (**3, 4**)

3. How can a landlord enforce his right to possession at the end of a tenancy? What restrictions are placed on this right by the Criminal Law Act 1977?   (**4**)

4. What is a "displaced residential occupier"? What defence is available to such an occupier?   (**4**)

5. What is the difference between (*a*) an action for double value, and (*b*) an action for double rent?   (**6**)

6. How are fixtures and chattels distinguished? What tests are applied to distinguish them?   (**11**)

7. By when must fixtures be removed by a tenant?   (**15**)

8. What are the exceptions to the common law rules regarding fixtures?   (**14**)

9. What are mesne profits?   (**7**)

10. How does the Limitation Act 1980 affect a landlord's right to possession at the end of a tenancy?   (**8**)

11. When did the statutory regulation of landlord and tenant commence?   (**16**)

12. What are the main aims of statutory control?   (**16**)

13. What classes of lettings are now protected by statute?   (**17**)

PART TWO
BUSINESS TENANCIES

CHAPTER X
Business Tenancies

INTRODUCTION

1. Generally. In the absence of statutory protection a business tenant would be at a disadvantage at the end of his tenancy. He may have built up goodwill which attaches to the premises and which he will lose if he must move. Also, he may have altered the premises and improved them at his own expense for the particular purposes of his own business. At the end of the tenancy the landlord would be in a strong bargaining position to get a rent better than the market rent because the tenant would have a particular need to stay in the premises. For these reasons Parliament has intervened to give business tenants protection.

2. History. Business tenancies were first given protection by Part I of the Landlord and Tenant Act 1927 ("the 1927 Act"). This gave a tenant the right to a new tenancy if he could show that goodwill would be lost. It was replaced by Part II of the Landlord and Tenant Act 1954 ("the 1954 Act") which now forms the main code of protection. Various amendments were made to Part II of the 1954 Act by Part I of the Law of Property Act 1969 ("the 1969 Act").

PROTECTION OF TENANCIES

3. What tenancies are protected by Part II of the 1954 Act? Section 23(1) provides that Part II of the 1954 Act applies to "any tenancy where the property comprised in the tenancy is or includes premises which are occupied by the tenant and are so occupied for the purposes of a business carried on by him or for those and other purposes."

In order to satisfy s. 23(1), the following conditions must be satisfied:

(*a*) there must be a tenancy,

(*b*) the property comprised in the tenancy must be or include premises occupied by the tenant,

(*c*) the tenant must occupy those premises for the purposes of a business carried on by himself.

These requirements are considered in **4—6**.

4. There must be a tenancy. The word tenancy is given a wide definition in s. 59(1) of the 1954 Act. It means a tenancy created either immediately or derivatively out of the freehold, whether by an agreement for a lease or by a tenancy agreement or by statute. Certain transactions, however, do not fall within this definition and are therefore not protected. They are:

(*a*) *a licence*: *Shell-Mex and B.P. Ltd.* v. *Manchester Garages* (1971);

(*b*) *a tenancy at will* arising by implication of law: *Wheeler* v. *Mercer* (1957);

(*c*) *a tenancy at will* created by an express agreement: *Manfield & Sons Ltd.* v. *Botchin* (1970); *Hagee* v. *Erikson* (1975).

NOTES: (1) It has been held that an unlawful sub-tenancy (i.e. one created in breach of a covenant in the head-lease against sub-letting) is a tenancy protected by the 1954 Act; Part II: *D'Silva* v. *Lister House Development Ltd.* (1970)

(2) A tenancy at no rent or at a low rent would be protected by the 1954 Act, Part II.

5. Occupation. The property must be or include premises occupied by the tenant. It is enough for the purposes of s. 23(1) if the tenant only occupies a part of the demised premises. Accordingly a tenant can sub-let part of the demised premises and, provided he occupies the remainder, still retain the protection of Part II of the 1954 Act. If the tenant has sub-let the whole of the premises, generally it cannot be said that he occupies any part of the premises and he will not be protected. To this principle, however, there is an exception where the tenant's actual business is that of sub-letting (*see* **12**).

6. Character of occupation. There are several points regarding occupation by the tenant which should be noted:

(*a*) it must be genuine and not a sham;

(*b*) it need not be personal, i.e. a tenant can occupy through his servants or agents;

(*c*) it need not be wholly continuous, e.g. if the premises were being repaired and the tenant left in order that the repairs could be carried out, then he would still occupy;

(*d*) it may be sufficient if it is only for a part of the year if the business is seasonal and there is a link between the periods of occupation in each successive year; e.g. use of premises which are in a summer resort and which are unused in the winter months, may be sufficient occupation.

7. Example. The operation of the principle outlined in **6**(*c*) above was illustrated in *Morrison Holdings* v. *Manders Property* (*Wolverhampton*) *Ltd.* (1976). In that case, the tenants occupied premises for the purposes of their business. A devastating fire rendered the premises unfit for physical occupation. The tenants vacated the premises, but kept the keys and wrote to the landlord saying that they "wanted to get back into business as soon as possible." They subsequently acted in a way consistent with an intention to carry on business at the premises. The tenants applied for a new tenancy and there was a preliminary question for the court to decide as to whether the tenants "occupied" the premises. It was HELD by the Court of Appeal that the tenant was occupying. Scarman L.J. summarised the relevant principle in the following way: ".... in order to apply for a new tenancy under the 1954 Act a tenant must show either that he is continuing in occupation of the premises for the purposes of a business carried on by him, or, if events over which he has no control have led him to absent himself from the premises, that he continues to exert and claim his right to occupancy."

On the facts it was decided that there had been no abandonment of occupation by the tenants because they had at all times expressed their intention to go back to the premises.

8. Special cases of occupation. There are two special provisions where a tenancy is vested in a person other than the occupier. They are:

(*a*) where a tenancy is held on trust: Landlord and Tenant Act 1954, s. 41(*see* **9**);

(*b*) where a tenancy is held by a member of a group of companies: s. 42(*see* **10**).

9. Trust. Where a tenancy is held on trust, occupation by all or any of the beneficiaries is treated as occupation by the tenant: Landlord and Tenant Act 1954, s. 41(1).

EXAMPLE: L lets land to T who holds it on trust for B who occupies the land. The effect of s. 41 is that B's occupation is treated as occupation by T. This means that T will be protected by Pt. II notwithstanding that he himself does not occupy the premises.

10. Groups of companies. Two companies are members of a group of companies if,

(a) one is a subsidiary of the other; or

(b) both are subsidiaries of a third: Landlord and Tenant Act 1954, s. 42(1).

Where a tenancy is held by a member of a group of companies, occupation by another member of the group is treated as occupation by the member holding the tenancy: s. 42(2).

NOTE: The word "subsidiary" here means a subsidiary as defined by the Companies Act 1948: a company is a subsidiary of another if that other is a member of it and controls the composition of its board of directors, or if the holding company holds more than half of its equity share capital.

11. Occupation for business purposes. Two points must be considered here:

(a) The tenant is not actually required to carry on the business at the premises, but simply to occupy the premises for the purposes of a business. So, for example, a shopkeeper may rent separate premises for storing his goods and those premises would probably be protected by Part II of the Act although he does not carry on his business there.

(b) A tenant may use premises for two purposes, one being a business user and the other a non-business user, and still be protected; e.g. there may be a shop on the ground floor and a flat upstairs.

In regard to (b) the business activity must be a significant purpose of the occupation of the premises. Where the business activity was merely incidental to the residential occupation of premises and did not amount to a significant use of them, it was held that the premises were not occupied for the purposes of a business: *Cheryl Investments Ltd.* v. *Saldanha* (1979). In that case a medical practitioner had his consulting rooms near to a flat which he rented. He took the flat so that he could be near his consulting room and occasionally he saw patients at the flat. The main use was as a residence. The question arose whether the flat was subject to the Rent Act or to Part II of the 1954 Act. It was HELD that any use of the flat for professional purposes was not a significant use but was merely incidental to the residential occupation. Accordingly, the flat was not occupied for the purposes of a business and was not protected by Part II of the 1954 Act.

12. Sub-letting and occupation for the purposes of a business. There are several cases dealing with the situation where the tenant sub-lets the premises. Whilst this may often constitute a business, e.g. sub-letting furnished apartments, it may be difficult to decide if the tenant actually himself occupies the premises for the purposes of that business. Whether he does so will depend upon the extent of the control the tenant exercises over the premises.

Bagettes v. *G. P. Estates Co. Ltd.* (1956). T held a lease of premises comprising 13 flats let out, a caretaker's rooms, boiler rooms, storerooms, fuel stores and the common parts. T held the lease with a view to sub-letting for profit. T claimed a new tenancy of the whole premises under Part II at the end of the tenancy. The Court of Appeal HELD: T was not entitled to a new tenancy because although the entire premises were used by T for the purposes of a business carried on by him (i.e. sub-letting) he was not in occupation of the flats sub-let and the rest of the premises considered alone could not be said to be used for the purposes of any business carried on by him.

Lee-Verhulst (Investments) Ltd. v. *Harwood Trust* (1973). The tenant had a tenancy of a number of furnished apartments which were sub-let separately to individual occupiers. The tenant provided various services and had the right of access to all parts of the building in order to provide services. The Court of Appeal HELD: Having regard to the degree of control and the services provided, the tenant occupied the entire premises for the purposes of its business.

William Boyer & Sons Ltd. v. *Adams* (1975). The tenant had a tenancy of premises comprising various buildings. He sub-let parts of the demised premises for use for light industry and he occupied part of the premises as his residence. He also provided various services such as heating, electricity, cleaning and checking security to the sub-tenants. HELD: In view of the degree of control exercised by the tenant, he did occupy the premises for the purposes of a business.

13. Business. This is defined by the Landlord and Tenant Act 1954, s. 23(2) as including "a trade, profession or employment and includes any activity carried on by a body of persons whether corporate or unincorporate." The following cases illustrate the width of this definition.

Hills (Patents) Ltd. v. *University College Hospital Board of Governors* (1956). The activities of the governors in running the hospital were HELD to be a business.

Addiscombe Garden Estates, Ltd. v. *Crabbe* (1958). The organising of a members' tennis club was HELD to be a business.

Abernethie v. *A. M. & J. Kleiman Ltd.* (1969). The activity of running a Sunday school one hour every week was HELD *not* to be a business.

Town Investments Ltd. v. *Department of the Environment* (1977). The business of government carried on by the Crown was HELD by the House of Lords to fall within the definition of "business tenancy" in the counter-inflation legislation.

14. The holding. Section 23(3) provides that the expression "the holding" in relation to a business tenancy means that part of the demised premises which the tenant himself actually occupies. If, for example, the tenant has sub-let part of the premises but occupies the remainder, the holding will comprise only the retained part. The importance of the holding is in regard to the provisions concerning the tenant's entitlement to a new tenancy (*see* XIII, **3**). The tenant is entitled to a new tenancy of the holding only.

15. Business use in breach of covenant. The Landlord and Tenant Act 1954, s. 23(4) deals with the question whether a business use by a tenant which is in breach of covenant is within the scope of Part II of the Act. The effect of the sub-section is as follows:

(*a*) if the user covenant is in general terms, e.g. a covenant against any business, trade, profession or employment, use in breach will exclude the tenancy from the protection of the Act;

(*b*) if the covenant is against use for a specific business, e.g. not to use as a shop, use in breach will not exclude the tenancy from the Act;

(*c*) if the covenant is against use for any business except a specific business, use in breach will not exclude the tenancy from the Act;

(*d*) if the landlord has acquiesced in the breach, or the landlord's predecessor has consented to the breach, the tenancy is not excluded from the Act.

16. Exclusions from protection. By the Landlord and Tenant Act 1954, s. 43(1), the following tenancies are excluded from protection under Part II:

(*a*) tenancies of agricultural holdings;

(*b*) mining leases;

(*c*) tenancies of public houses and other on-licensed premises other than hotels, restaurants and places where the holding of the licence is ancillary to some other use;

(*d*) tenancies granted by reason of, and ceasing with the termination of, some office, appointment or employment, provided the tenancy is in writing and expresses the purpose for which it was granted;

(*e*) tenancies granted for a term certain not exceeding six months unless containing a provision for renewal beyond six months or unless the tenant has been in occupation for a period exceeding twelve months.

17. Other exclusions. The following are also excluded from protection under Part II.

(*a*) On the joint application of the parties, the court may authorise the grant of a tenancy for a term of years certain which will be outside the provisions of the Act concerning security of tenure: Act of 1954, s. 38(4)(b).

(*b*) Where the landlord of premises is a public authority (e.g. a local authority, statutory undertaker, government department) the relevant minister may issue a certificate that the landlord needs the premises. The effect of this is to deprive the tenant of his right to apply for a new tenancy: *ibid*. s. 57.

(*c*) Where the landlord of premises is a government department, the relevant minister may issue a certificate that the premises are needed for reasons of national security; the effect of the certificate is to deprive the tenant of his right to apply for a new tenancy: *ibid*. s. 58.

NOTE: In cases (*b*) and (*c*) the tenant has a right to compensation for disturbance.

18. Contracting out. The 1954 Act contains provisions to prevent the parties contracting out. Section 38(1) provides that any agreement will be void in so far as it purports to preclude a tenant from making an application for a new tenancy or it provides for the termination of his tenancy or penalises him if he should make such an application. Section 38(4) was added by the Law of Property Act 1969 in order to enable parties to contract out with the leave of the court (*see* **17**(*a*)). Section 38(4)(a) provides that on the joint application of the parties, the court may authorise the grant of a tenancy which will not be subject to the provisions of the Act regarding security of tenure. Further, s. 38(4)(b) provides that on the joint application of the parties, the court may authorise an agreement to surrender the tenancy at any time. The effect of an order under s. 38(4)(a) is that on the contractual termination of the tenancy, the tenancy will not be continued and the tenant's right to occupy will end. An agreement to surrender a business tenancy is void under s. 38(1) unless it is sanctioned by the court under s. 38(4)(b): *Joseph* v. *Joseph* (1967). Where a term of the lease requires the tenant to offer a surrender before he is entitled to licence to assign, the resulting agreement to surrender is unenforceable: *Allnatt London Pties Ltd.* v. *Newton* (1984).

19. Interaction of Part II with the Rent Act 1977. Where there is a tenancy with a mixed use, i.e. part business use and part residential, difficult questions may arise about whether the tenancy is protected by the Rent Act 1977 or by Part II of the 1954 Act (*see* XV, **35**). In essence, the rule is that a tenancy of premises put to such a mixed use will normally be protected by Part II of the 1954 Act unless the business use is insignificant.

20. The landlord. Another important preliminary matter is to consider who will be the landlord for the purposes of proceedings under Part II of the 1954 Act. This is a matter which is best considered when the different methods of termination have been considered as it is linked to that subject (*see* XI, **17**).

PROGRESS TEST 10

1. What is "the holding"? **(14)**
2. Which of the following interests is protected by Part II of the Landlord and Tenant Act 1954: (*a*) a tenancy at will; (*b*) a tenancy at no rent; (*c*) a licence? **(4)**

3. Which of the following are businesses for the purposes of Part II of the 1954 Act: (*a*) a bank; (*b*) a doctor's surgery; (*c*) a Sunday school; (*d*) a hospital? **(13)**

4. What are the requirements of protection under Part II of the 1954 Act? **(3)**

5. In what circumstances, if any, is a business use in breach of covenant protected by Part II? **(16)**

6. How can parties contract out of the provisions of Part II? **(18)**

7. Which of the following leases is protected by Part II: (*a*) a mining lease; (*b*) a lease of an hotel; (*c*) a lease of a block of flats which is sub-let in parts; (*d*) a lease of a suite of offices for three months? **(12, 16)**

8. L lets a shop with a flat over to T who uses the shop for his business and lives with his family in the flat. Is the tenancy protected by Part II? **(5)**

9. What special rules apply to (*a*) tenancies held by a member of a group of companies; (*b*) a tenancy held by a trustee on behalf of beneficiaries? **(8)**

10. T owns a factory. L lets to T a nearby piece of land which T uses as a staff car park. Is the tenancy protected by Part II? Would your answer be different if T used the land to store the goods made by the factory? **(6, 13)**

Security of Tenure

INTRODUCTION

1. Generally. The preceding chapter was concerned with the scope of Part II of the Landlord and Tenant Act 1954; it is now necessary to consider how Part II works. Broadly, it protects the tenant in the following ways:

(*a*) it limits the ways in which a tenancy may come to an end;

(*b*) unless the tenancy is ended in one of the specified ways it will continue automatically;

(*c*) it gives to the business tenant the right to apply for a new tenancy at the end of his current tenancy (*see* XII);

(*d*) if the landlord wishes to oppose the grant of a new tenancy to the tenant, he can only do so if he establishes one, or more, of certain specified grounds (*see* XII, **6** *et seq*);

(*e*) a tenant who has to leave may be entitled to compensation (*see* **20**).

2. Automatic continuance. This is central to the operation of Part II of the 1954 Act. Section 24(1) provides that a tenancy to which Part II of the 1954 Act applies will not come to an end unless terminated in accordance with the provisions of the Act. The effect is that a tenancy will automatically continue on the same terms unless it is properly determined by one of the methods specified in the Act. The methods specified by the Act are, in summary:

(*a*) some of the common law methods of termination; and

(*b*) service of one of the special kinds of statutory notice.

3. The common law methods of termination. The Landlord and Tenant Act 1954, s. 24(2) provides that, notwithstanding the various statutory methods of termination, a tenancy protected by Part II of the 1954 Act may still be ended by the following common law methods:

(*a*) notice to quit given by the tenant;

(*b*) surrender (while an actual surrender is effective an agreement to surrender may be void by s. 38(1): *see* **X, 18**);

(*c*) forfeiture;

(*d*) forfeiture of a superior tenancy.

In cases (*a*) and (*b*) the notice or surrender will be ineffective if given or made before the tenant has been in occupation of the premises in right of the tenancy for at least one month: s. 24(2)(a), (b). This provision is designed to prevent evasion of the Act by a landlord granting a tenancy on condition that the tenant executes a surrender of it or gives notice to quit *before*, or soon after, he takes the tenancy.

METHODS OF TERMINATION

4. Statutory methods. The statutory methods of termination laid down by Part II are:

(*a*) by a landlord's notice under s. 25;

(*b*) by a tenant's request for a new tenancy under s. 26;

(*c*) by a tenant's notice under s. 27.

5. Landlord's notice under s. 25. A landlord may terminate a tenancy to which Part II of the 1954 Act applies by the service of a notice complying with the requirements of s. 25. The requirements of a valid "s. 25 notice" (as it is commonly known) are as follows:

(*a*) it must be in the form prescribed by regulations made under the 1954 Act or in a form substantially to the like effect;

(*b*) it must be given not more than twelve nor less than six months before the termination date specified in the notice;

(*c*) it must specify the date at which the tenancy is to come to an end ("the date of termination");

(*d*) it must require the tenant within two months after the giving of the notice to notify the landlord in writing whether he will be willing to give up possession at the date of termination;

(*e*) it must state whether the landlord would oppose an application to the court for a new tenancy and, if so, on which of the statutory grounds in s. 30.

6. The date of termination. There are special rules for ascertaining the date of termination and they are contained in the Landlord and Tenant Act 1954, s. 25. The rules are that the date must not be earlier than:

(*a*) in the case of a tenancy determinable by notice to quit, the earliest date on which the tenancy could have been brought to an end by notice to quit given by the landlord on the date of giving the s. 25 notice. The date of termination, however, need not be the actual date on which a common law notice would have had effect —it simply must not be earlier than that date;

(b) in the case of a tenancy for a fixed term, the date on which it would have expired by effluxion of time.

EXAMPLES: (1) L grants to T a yearly tenancy running from 1st January. At common law such a tenancy had to be determined by six months' notice to quit given to expire on 31st December or 1st January (see VI, **17**). So if L wished to serve a s. 25 notice in March 1979, the earliest date on which the tenancy could be ended at common law would be 31st December 1979. Therefore the s. 25 notice served in March 1979 must specify a date of termination not earlier than 31st December 1979. If the notice specifies an earlier date it will be of no effect. The notice could, however, specify a later date, e.g. 1st February 1980, provided it is not more than 12 months ahead.

(2) If in the example above, L decided in August 1979 that he wished to serve a s. 25 notice, the earliest date on which the tenancy could be determined at law would be 31st December 1980. Therefore the s. 25 notice must specify a date not earlier than 31st December 1980. This means that L will be unable to serve the notice until 31st December 1979 because the notice must be given not more than twelve nor less than six months before the date of termination specified in the notice (see **5**(b)).

(3) L grants to T a tenancy for a term of ten years from 1st January 1969. The term will expire at midnight on 31st December 1979. A s. 25 notice specifying a date of termination earlier than 31st December 1979 will be invalid as it specifies a date earlier than the date on which the term expires. A notice specifying 31st December 1979, however, would be valid because that is the date on which the tenancy comes to an end by effluxion of time: *Re Crowhurst Park* (1974).

7. Break clauses and s. 25 notices. A lease for a fixed term may contain a break clause entitling the landlord to determine the term at a specific point of time. The rule is that a single notice will be sufficient to operate such a clause and also to satisfy s. 25, provided it satisfies the requirements of s. 25 and the contract: *Scholl Manufacturing Ltd.* v. *Clifton (Slim Line) Ltd.* (1967). If the landlord gives a notice which complies with the contractual requirements but not with the statutory requirements the effect will be to determine the contractual tenancy but the tenancy will be continued by s. 24. If the landlord then wishes to end the tenancy, he will have to serve a separate s. 25 notice.

EXAMPLE: L grants to T a lease for a term of 15 years with a break clause at the end of the fifth and tenth years. At the end of the fifth year L exercises his powers under the break clause. Unless the notice exercising the break clause complies with s. 25, the tenancy will be continued by s. 24 until it is terminated by a s. 25 notice or one of the other methods of termination permitted by the Act. A landlord may use this to his advantage. Suppose in this example L knows that he will want to re-develop the premises in the eighth year but there is no break clause in that year, L can end the tenancy in that year by exercising his right under the break clause in the fifth year; the tenancy will then continue under s. 24 and in the seventh or eighth year, he can serve a s. 25 notice to end the continued tenancy.

8. Continuation tenancy. As is apparent from the last example when a tenancy is continued under the Landlord and Tenant Act 1954, s. 24 it must still be terminated by one of the methods prescribed by the Act. In such a case the landlord may select any date of termination for the s. 25 notice subject only to the rule that it must be not more than twelve months nor less than six months from the date of service of the notice.

EXAMPLE: A tenancy is granted for five years expiring 1st May 1975. It continues under s. 24 of the Act. The landlord serves a s. 25 notice on 1st July 1979. It may specify as the date of termination any date between 1st January 1980 and 30th June 1980.

9. The effect of a s. 25 notice. When a tenant receives a s. 25 notice he must decide whether he wishes to apply for a new tenancy. If he does,

(a) within two months of the giving of the s. 25 notice he must give to the landlord written notice that he is unwilling to give up possession; and

(b) between two and four months after the giving of the s. 25 notice he must apply to the court for a new tenancy.

If the tenant fails to do either of these things, he will lose the right to apply to the court for a new tenancy and the current tenancy will determine on the date specified in the s. 25 notice.

10. Tenant's request for new tenancy under s. 26. This is the second of the statutory methods of termination. In practice a tenant will generally wish his tenancy to continue because he will then continue paying the existing rent which, because of inflation, is likely to be lower than the current market rent. Accordingly this procedure is not very common. This alternative method may, however, be used where the tenant wishes to regularise his position by having a new tenancy of a definite duration rather than a continued tenancy liable to be determined at six months' notice.

11. Requirements of tenant's request for new tenancy. A tenant can only make a request for a new tenancy under the Landlord and Tenant Act 1954, s. 26 if his current tenancy is for a term of years certain exceeding one year or for a term of years certain and thereafter from year to year. This means that yearly tenancies, lesser periodic tenancies and tenancies for terms of less than one year are outside s. 26. The actual request must, by s. 26:

(*a*) be in the prescribed form or a form substantially to the like effect;

(*b*) set out the tenant's proposals for the terms of the new tenancy;

(*c*) be for a tenancy commencing not more than twelve and not less than six months after the making of the request,

(*d*) specify as the date of commencement a date not earlier than the date on which the current tenancy would have ended by effluxion of time, or the earliest date on which the current tenancy could be brought to an end by a tenant's notice to quit.

NOTES: (1) A request cannot be made after the service of a s. 25 notice.

(2) Once a tenant has made a valid request for a new tenancy, he cannot withdraw it and serve a fresh request at a later date: *Polyviou* v. *Seeley* (1979).

12. The effect of a tenant's request. When a tenant has made a request, the effect is as follows:

(*a*) the landlord has two months within which to give notice whether he will oppose the grant of a new tenancy and, if so, the grounds on which he will oppose it;

(*b*) the tenant must apply to the court for the grant of a new tenancy within not less than two nor more than four months after the making of the request;

(*c*) subject to the provisions of the Act regarding interim continuation (*see* **15**), the tenancy will terminate on the date specified in the request for the commencement of the new tenancy.

NOTE: If the landlord fails to comply with (*a*) or the tenant with (*b*), they will respectively lose the right to oppose the grant of a new tenancy and the right to a new tenancy. It is therefore essential for the parties to comply with the time limits.

13. Termination by a tenant's notice under s. 27. The Landlord and Tenant Act 1954, s. 27 provides two methods whereby a tenant under a fixed term may end his tenancy. They are:

(*a*) where the tenancy has not yet come to an end, provided it has at least three months to run, the tenant may give written notice to his immediate landlord that he does not desire the tenancy to be continued. The effect of this is that s. 24 will not apply to the tenancy and, when the tenancy expires by effluxion of time, it will not be continued;

(*b*) where the tenancy has reached its contractual expiry date and is being continued by s. 24, the tenant may end it by giving to the immediate landlord not less than three months' written notice ending on any quarter day: s. 27(2).

It is important to note that these provisions only apply to tenancies for a fixed term. In the case of a periodic tenancy the tenant's right to serve ordinary notice to quit is preserved by s. 24(2) (*see* **3**). The service by the tenant of an ordinary notice to quit or a s. 27 notice does not give him any right to apply to the court for a new tenancy.

14. Effect of Part II ceasing to apply to a tenancy. There is another important aspect of termination which remains to be considered, i.e. the effect of the Act ceasing to apply to a tenancy. An example of the way in which the Act may cease to apply arises if the premises cease to be used for business purposes. Section 24(3) of the Act contains special provisions dealing with this. In summary their effect is as follows:

(*a*) In the case of a tenancy for a term of years certain, if Part II ceases to apply to it before its expiry there will be no continuation under s. 24 because the tenancy is not one to which Part II applies;

(*b*) In the case of a tenancy for a term of years certain, if Part II ceases to apply to it after the expiry of the term but while it is being continued by s. 24, the tenancy will not end simply because Part II has ceased to apply; but the landlord can terminate the continued tenancy by giving to the tenant not less than three nor more than six months' written notice: s. 24(3)(a). The tenant has no right to apply to the court for a new tenancy.

(c) In the case of a periodic tenancy, if Part II ceases to apply to it, the landlord can serve an ordinary common law notice to quit which will determine the tenancy. The tenant has no right to apply to the court for a new tenancy.

(d) Once a notice has been served by a landlord under (b) or (c) above, the tenant cannot avoid the effect of that notice by changes which would otherwise bring the tenancy back into the Act because s. 24(3)(b) provides that the operation of such a notice will not be affected by reason that the tenancy becomes one to which Part II applies after the giving of the notice.

EXAMPLES: (1) L lets business premises to T for a term of three years. At the end of the term T no longer occupies the premises for the purposes of his business. Part II will therefore not apply and the tenancy will not be continued under s. 24: *see* (a) above.

(2) L lets business premises to T for a term of three years. At the end of the term, T still occupies the premises for the purposes of his business. The tenancy will therefore be continued by s. 24(1). At the end of the fourth year, T closes down his business and ceases to occupy the premises for the purposes of his business. In order to determine the continued tenancy, L must serve a notice under s. 24(3)(a): *see* (b) above.

(3) In example (2) L serves a valid notice under s. 24(3)(a). Two months after service of the notice T starts up his business again at the premises. T is not protected because s. 24(3)(b) operates to prevent T defeating L's notice in this way: *see* (d) above.

15. Interim continuation of tenancies. An important provision of the Landlord and Tenant Act 1954, Part II is contained in s. 64, which operates in the following way. Where a landlord serves a s. 25 notice or a tenant makes a request under s. 26, both have the effect of ending the old tenancy on the date specified in the notice or the request. Section 64(1), however, provides that where a notice or request has been given or made and it has been followed by an application to the court, the old tenancy will not end until three months after the date on which the tenant's application has been finally disposed of. The reference to the date on which an application is finally disposed of means the earliest date on which the proceedings on the application have been determined and any time for appealing has expired. Appeals will be from the High Court or the county court to the Court of Appeal, and the normal time for appealing is four weeks.

EXAMPLE: L serves on T a s. 25 notice specifying as the date of termination 25th December 1979. T duly applies to the county court. The parties agree some of the terms but are unable to agree the rent. This issue goes to the county court for determination. The county court gives its decision on 1st June 1980. Neither party appeals. The application is therefore finally disposed of on 29th June (i.e. four weeks after the determination of the application). By s. 64(1) the old tenancy is continued until three months after that date.

In most cases, therefore, interim continuation will be for a period of approximately four months. If the tenant withdraws his application to the court, the period of three months will run from the date of the withdrawal.

16. The nature of a continued tenancy. A tenancy which is continued by Part II of the 1954 Act is much the same creature as the preceding contractual tenancy. It will continue on the same terms as in the contractual tenancy. It is not like a statutory tenancy under the Rent Act (which is a purely personal right); it can be assigned and transmitted in the same way as an ordinary contractual tenancy, subject to any restrictions in the terms of the old contractual tenancy. The only way in which the continued tenancy is changed is in regard to the ways in which it can be determined.

MEANING OF "THE LANDLORD"

17. The landlord. It is now possible to consider who is the landlord for the purposes of the machinery of Part II. Proceedings under Part II are conducted between the business tenant in possession and the "competent landlord." This means either

(a) the owner for the time being of the fee simple; or

(b) the owner of a tenancy which will not come to an end within 14 months and, if it satisfies this requirement, in respect of which no notice has been given by virtue of which it will come to an end within 14 months or any period of interim continuance pending a determination of the court.

In a case where there is a chain of interests more than one of which satisfies these conditions, the competent landlord will be the owner of the interest lowest down the chain which satisfies the requirements.

This is a complicated provision and it may be conveniently summarised by saying that the competent landlord is the first landlord up the chain of tenancies above the business tenant who has an interest which will not come to an end within 14 months by effluxion of time, provided no notice has been given to him to bring his interest to an end within 14 months.

The significance of establishing who is the competent landlord is to determine who should serve a s. 25 notice on a business tenant and who should be served with a s. 26 request by a business tenant. Each of the following examples is intended to show who is the competent landlord in relation to the person at the bottom of the chain of leasehold interests.

EXAMPLES: (1) L lets premises to T who sub-lets it all to S who occupies it for the purposes of his business. At the relevant time T's contractual tenancy has 12 months to run. The competent landlord of S is therefore L because T's tenancy will end within 14 months by effluxion of time.

(2) L lets land to T who sub-lets it all to S who occupies it for the purposes of his business. At the relevant time T's contractual tenancy has two years to run. The competent landlord of S is therefore T.

(3) L lets land to T who sub-lets a part to S. T occupies the remainder for the purposes of his business. At the relevant time T's contractual tenancy has one month still to run. T will be the competent landlord of S, because his tenancy will not come to an end within 14 months but will continue under s. 24.

(4) As in the preceding example but at the relevant time L has served a s. 25 notice which will end the tenancy at the end of two months. L will be the competent landlord of S because a notice has been given whereby the tenancy of T will come to an end within 14 months.

(5) L lets land to T who sub-lets it all to S who further sub-underlets it all to R who occupies it for the purposes of his business. At the relevant time S's tenancy has six months to run and T's tenancy has two years to run. T will be the competent landlord of R because his tenancy will not come to an end within 14 months whereas S's tenancy will come to an end within that period.

It is essential to ascertain who is the competent landlord since if a notice under s. 25 or a request under s. 26 is served by or on the wrong landlord it will be of no effect.

18. Provision of information. The Landlord and Tenant Act 1954, s. 40, imposes on landlord and tenant of business premises a duty to give information to each other. In particular, a tenant of premises used for business purposes may be required, by his immediate landlord giving him notice in the prescribed form, to state whether he occupies the premises for the purposes of a business carried on by him and whether he has sub-let and, if so, to give particulars of the sub-letting. Similarly, if his tenancy is for more than a year, a tenant may require his immediate landlord or any superior landlord to state whether he is the owner of the freehold and, if he is not, to give particulars of his interest. Information cannot, however, be required under these provisions more than two years before the date when apart from 1954 Act the term would expire: s. 40(4). This provision will help the parties to know on whom and by whom notice should be served by helping them to determine who is the competent landlord.

PROGRESS TEST 11

1. What is a s. 25 notice? **(5)**

2. In which of the following ways may a business tenancy be lawfully terminated: (*a*) notice to quit served by the landlord; (*b*) an agreement to surrender; (*c*) effluxion of time; (*d*) forfeiture? **(3)**

3. What are the statutory methods of ending a business tenancy? **(4)**

4. What are the requirements of a valid s. 25 notice? **(5)**

5. L grants a yearly tenancy of business premises to T. The tenancy runs from 1st March 1975. In April 1978 L decides that he wishes to end the tenancy. What is the earliest date on which L can end the tenancy and why? What would your answer be if it was in February 1978 that he decided? **(6)**

6. L lets premises to T on a tenancy which is protected by Part II of the 1954 Act. L serves T with a s. 25 notice. Advise T what he must do to retain possession of the premises. **(9)**

7. What is a tenant's request for a new tenancy? What are the requirements of a valid one? **(11)**

8. L lets premises to T on a tenancy protected by Part II of the 1954 Act. At the end of the tenancy T serves on L a request for a new tenancy. Advise L how he can oppose this. **(12)**

9. L lets premises to T for a term of seven years from 1st January 1971; the tenancy is protected by Part II. At the end of the lease T wishes to leave. What formalities, if any, must he comply with? Would your answer be different if T had not decided to leave until after the contractual tenancy had ended and been continued by Part II? **(14)**

10. How is a business tenancy protected? **(1)**

11. What are the terms of a continued tenancy? **(16)**

12. What are the interim continuation provisions of s. 64? **(15)**

13. Can a tenant assign his continued tenancy? **(8)**

14. Who is the competent landlord for the purposes of proceedings under Part II of the 1954 Act? **(17)**

CHAPTER XII

The Tenant's Application to the Court for a New Tenancy

INTRODUCTION

1. Generally. The effect of the notice procedure described in the preceding chapter is that the parties can see where they stand in relation to each other. The landlord may be willing to grant a new tenancy of the premises to the tenant in which case he will say so in his notice under the Landlord and Tenant Act 1954, s. 25, or in his notice in reply to the tenant's request for a new tenancy. If the landlord opposes the grant of a new tenancy, he must say so in one of those notices and also state the grounds upon which he opposes the grant. If the tenant wants a new tenancy, he must put forward the terms he proposes and the landlord can then consider if they are agreeable to him. Often the parties will be able to agree the terms of the new tenancy and it will be unnecessary to resort to the courts and to litigation. The tenant must always apply to the court within the prescribed period no matter how near to agreement the parties are, for if he fails to do so he will lose his right to a new tenancy.

THE APPLICATION

2. The tenant's application to the court. As appears from the preceding chapter a tenant's right to apply to the court for the grant of a new tenancy depends on:

(*a*) the landlord having served a s. 25 notice or the tenant having served a s. 26 request;

(*b*) if the application follows a s. 25 notice, the tenant having notified the landlord within two months after the giving of the notice that he was unwilling to give up possession;

(*c*) the tenant having applied to the court not less than two months and not more than four months after the giving of the s. 25 notice or the s. 26 request.

It is important that the tenant should have complied strictly with all the time limits; any failure to comply will deprive the tenant of his right to the grant of a new tenancy. The only exception is that the landlord can expressly or impliedly waive the time limits: *Kammins Ballrooms* v. *Zenith Investments* (1971).

In calculating the period of months that elapses after service of a notice, the general rule is that the period ends on the corresponding date in the appropriate subsequent month, irrespective of whether that month is longer than others; so, if a 25 notice is given on 30th September 1984 application to the court must be made by 30th January and not 31st January 1985: *Dodds* v. *Walker* (1981).

3. Form of the application. Where the rateable value of the holding is less than £5,000 the application is made to the county court; where it exceeds £5,000 the application is to the High Court: Landlord and Tenant Act 1954, s. 63. The parties are free, however, to agree that a case be transferred from the High Court to the county court and vice versa. The application to the court is by way of an originating application in the county court and by an originating summons in the High Court and there are detailed rules of procedure governing such applications in the County Court Rules 1981, Ord. 43 and the Rules of the Supreme Court 1965, Ord. 97.

4. Special cases: joint tenancies and partnerships. The application to the court must be made by the tenant. Where there are joint tenants the old rule was that all the tenants must apply whether or not they were still active in the business: *Jacobs* v. *Chaudhuri* (1968). This rule has now been altered in certain situations by the 1954 Act, s. 41A, which provides that where a tenancy is held by joint tenants and,

(*a*) at one time a business was carried on in partnership by all the joint tenants; and

(*b*) the tenancy was then partnership property; and

(*c*) the business is now being carried on by one or some only of the joint tenants ("the business tenants"); and

(*d*) the other joint tenants are occupying no part of the property comprised in the tenancy for the purposes of a business they carry on,

the business tenants alone may apply to the court for the grant of a new tenancy instead of all the joint tenants.

5. The procedure on a tenant's application. If the parties agree terms for the grant of a new tenancy, the normal procedure is for the tenant to withdraw his application to the court, or for the parties to consent to an order by the court for the grant of a new tenancy upon the terms agreed. If the parties are unable to agree terms, the matter will go to trial and the court will decide the terms that the parties have not agreed. Each party will put forward his evidence in support of the terms which he proposes and the judge will decide on that evidence what is appropriate.

Where the landlord opposes the grant of a new tenancy, the court will normally hear and consider the evidence relating to that as a preliminary issue: *Dutch Oven Ltd.* v. *Egham Estates & Investment Co. Ltd.* (1968). If the landlord succeeds, the cost of disputing the terms will have been saved; if he fails, the parties will try to agree the terms and in default of agreement the court will determine them.

OPPOSITION

6. The grounds of opposition. The grounds on which a landlord may oppose an application for a new tenancy are contained in the Landlord and Tenant Act 1954, s. 30(1). It must be remembered that a landlord can only rely upon the ground(s) that he has specified in his s. 25 notice or in his notice in opposition to the tenant's request for a new tenancy. Similarly, if a landlord sells his interest after having served a s. 25 notice, the purchaser landlord can only rely upon the ground(s) specified in the vendor landlord's notice.

The grounds are as follows:

(*a*) where under the current tenancy the tenant has any obligations as respects the repair and maintenance of the holding, that the tenant ought not to be granted a new tenancy in view of the state of repair of the holding, being a state resulting from the tenant's failure to comply with the said obligations;

(*b*) that the tenant ought not to be granted a new tenancy in view of his persistent delay in paying rent which has become due;

(*c*) that the tenant ought not to be granted a new tenancy in view of other substantial breaches by him of his obligations under the current tenancy, or for any other reason connected with the tenant's use or management of the holding;

(*d*) that the landlord has offered and is willing to provide or secure the provision of alternative accommodation for the tenant, that the terms on which the alternative accommodation is available are reasonable having regard to the terms of the current tenancy and to all other relevant circumstances, and that the accommodation and the time at which it will be available are suitable for the tenant's requirements (including the requirement to preserve goodwill) having regard to the nature and class of his business and to the situation and extent of, and facilities afforded by, the holding;

(e) where the current tenancy was created by the sub-letting of part only of the property comprised in a superior tenancy and the landlord is the owner of an interest in reversion expectant on the termination of that superior tenancy, that the aggregate of the rents reasonably obtainable on separate lettings of the holding and the remainder of that property would be substantially less than the rent reasonably obtainable on a letting of that property as a whole, that on the termination of the current tenancy the landlord requires possession of the holding for the purpose of letting or otherwise disposing of the said property as a whole, and that in view thereof the tenant ought not to be granted a new tenancy;

(f) that on the termination of the current tenancy the landlord intends to demolish or reconstruct the premises comprised in the holding or a substantial part of those premises or to carry out substantial work of construction on the holding or part thereof and that he could not reasonably do so without obtaining possession of the holding;

(g) that on the termination of the current tenancy the landlord intends to occupy the holding for the purposes, or partly for the purposes, of a business to be carried on by him therein, or as his residence.

It should be noted that grounds (a), (b), (c), and (e) are discretionary in that even if the facts are established the court has to consider whether in the circumstances, "the tenant ought not to be granted a new tenancy." In relation to the other grounds, if the facts are established the court must find for the landlord.

7. Ground (a); failure to repair. This is one of the cases where the court has a discretion. The landlord must show that the state of repair is such that a new tenancy ought not to be granted. The court will consider the seriousness of the disrepair and any attempts to remedy it. The relevant date at which the court must consider this is the date of the hearing.

8. Ground (b); persistent delay in paying rent. Again the landlord must show that a new tenancy ought not to be granted in view of the delay in paying rent.

9. Ground (c); substantial breaches of other obligations. This is another of the discretionary grounds. The court will have to consider the nature of the obligation and the extent of the breach. The user of the premises by the tenant may be such that, while no actual breach of covenant is involved, the court will refuse to order a new tenancy.

10. Ground (d); alternative accommodation. The alternative accommodation must be provided or secured by the landlord. The terms must be reasonable having regard to the terms of the current tenancy. The accommodation must be suitable to the tenant's requirements having regard to the nature and class of his business and to the situation and extent of the holding.

11. Ground (e); letting of property as a whole. This ground is rarely used in practice since it is very difficult for the requisite circumstances to arise and it is not therefore considered here.

12. Ground (f); the landlord requires possession to demolish or reconstruct. This is one of the most important grounds. It comprises the following elements which are considered in the subsequent paragraphs:

(a) the landlord intends (see **13**);

(b) to demolish or reconstruct the premises comprising the holding or a substantial part of the premises or to carry out substantial works of construction (see **14**);

(c) and that he could not reasonably do so without obtaining possession of the holding (see **15**).

13. The landlord intends. The following points should be noted.

(a) The intention must be established at the time the court hears the application: *Betty's Cafes Ltd.* v. *Philips Furnishing Stores Ltd.* (1959).

(b) A landlord can rely on a s. 25 notice served by himself or by his predecessor in title. If he relies on a notice served by a predecessor in title it does not matter that the notice was served by a predecessor who then had no intention himself: *Marks* v. *British Waterways Board* (1963).

(c) In order to establish "intention" it must be shown that there is a firm and settled intention to do something which there is a reasonable prospect of bringing about: *Reohorn* v. *Barry Corporation* (1956); *Cunliffe* v. *Goodman* (1950).

(d) If such matters as planning permission and consent under the building regulations are needed, it will assist the landlord's case if he has secured the grant of them by the time of the hearing; not having them by then will not necessarily be fatal provided there is a reasonable chance of getting them: *Gregson* v. *Cyril Lord* (1962).

14. To demolish or reconstruct the premises, etc. Whether this requirement is satisfied in any case will be a question of fact, and two examples may show how the courts treat such cases.

Joel v. *Swaddle* (1957). L intended to change a small shop with two storage rooms into part of a large hall to be used as an amusement arcade. HELD: There was an intention to reconstruct within the scope of case (*f*).

Atkinson v. *Bettison* (1955). The mere putting into premises of a new shop front was HELD not to be a reconstruction of a substantial part of the premises or the carrying out of substantial works.

15. He could not reasonably do so without obtaining possession. This requirement has to be considered in the light of the Landlord and Tenant Act 1954, s. 31A, which provides that under ground (*f*) the court must not hold that the landlord "could not reasonably do so without obtaining possession of the holding" if

(*a*) the tenant agrees to the inclusion in the new tenancy of terms giving to the landlord access and other facilities for carrying out the work intended and the landlord could thereby reasonably carry out the work without obtaining possession of the holding and without interfering substantially with the tenant's use of the holding; or

(*b*) the tenant is willing to accept an economically separable part of the holding and either

(*i*) condition (*a*) above is satisfied with respect to that part; or

(*ii*) possession of the remainder of the holding would be reasonably sufficient to enable the landlord to carry out the intended work.

The practical effect of this provision is that the landlord's right to possession under ground (*f*) is restricted if the tenant is prepared to agree to either (*a*) or (*b*) above.

Section 31A(2) provides that a part of a holding will be deemed to be an economically separable part if, and only if, the aggregate of the rents reasonably obtainable, after the completion of the intended works, for the part and the remainder would not be substantially less than the rent which would then reasonably be obtainable on a letting of the whole.

16. *Heath* v. *Drown*. A landlord will be unable to rely on ground (*f*) where he could in fact carry out the works under the terms of the existing lease. In *Heath* v. *Drown* (1972), T occupied premises for the purposes of her business under two leases each of which reserved to L the right to enter and carry out necessary repairs. L served notices on T under s. 25, relying on ground (*f*) to resist the grant of a new tenancy to T. It was conceded by L that he could carry out the works under the reservations in the current tenancies. The House of Lords HELD: It was not reasonably necessary for L to obtain possession of the holding as it was conceded that he could carry out the works under the reservations, and therefore L could not bring himself within the words of s. 30(1)(f).

17. Ground (*g*); the landlord intends to occupy the holding. The landlord must show a firm intention to occupy the premises for the purposes of his own business or as his residence. The matters discussed above (*see* **13**) will be relevant to a consideration of intention. Other points to note are:

(*a*) the landlord can rely on this ground even though he intends to use the premises in partnership with someone else: *Clift* v. *Taylor* (1948);

(*b*) the intention to occupy must be for a period which is more than minimal: *Willis* v. *Association of Universities of the British Commonwealth* (1965);

(*c*) the intended business must be the landlord's, except:

(*i*) where the landlord is a trustee and the business is that of a beneficiary: Act of 1954, s. 41;

(*ii*) where the landlord has a controlling interest in a company and the company will occupy the premises: s. 30(3);

(*iii*) where the landlord is a company in a group and another member of the group is to occupy the premises: s. 42;

(*d*) the ground applies where the holding is to be used partly for the purposes of the business; the use need not therefore relate to the entire holding;

(*e*) the ground also applies where the landlord intends to use the premises as his residence.

NOTE: This ground and ground (*f*) are the grounds which in practice are most often relied upon by a landlord opposing the grant of a new tenancy.

18. The exclusion of ground (*g*). A landlord cannot rely upon ground (*g*) if his interest was purchased or created within the period of five years prior to the termination of the current tenancy and at all times since the purchase or creation of that interest the holding has been comprised in a tenancy to which Part II of the 1954 Act applies: s. 30(2).

EFFECT OF OPPOSITION

19. Successful opposition by landlord. The rules here are as follows.

(*a*) If the landlord succeeds in his opposition the court cannot make an order for the grant of a new tenancy: Landlord and Tenant Act 1954, s. 31(1). The tenant will have four weeks within which to decide if he wishes to appeal to the Court of Appeal. If he appeals his tenancy will be continued by the interim continuation provisions in s. 64 until the outcome of the appeal. If he does not appeal, the tenancy will also be continued by s. 64 (*see* XI, **15**).

(*b*) If the landlord relies on any of the grounds (*d*), (*e*) and (*f*) and the court is not satisfied that the ground has been established, but would have been satisfied if the date specified in the s. 25 notice or the tenant's request had been a date up to a year later, it will make a declaration stating the date on which it would have been satisfied but will not order the grant of a new tenancy: s. 31(2). The tenant may then apply within 14 days for the declared date to be substituted in the landlord's notice or the tenant's request in which case the tenancy will continue until that date. If the tenant does not so apply, the position is as if the landlord had successfully opposed the application.

20. The tenant's right to compensation. Where the landlord successfully opposes an application for a new tenancy on grounds (*e*), (*f*) or (*g*), compensation will be payable to the tenant under s. 37. The compensation payable is an amount equal to the product of $2\frac{1}{4}$ and the rateable value of the holding as at the date of the s. 25 notice or the s. 26 request. The tenant can recover twice this amount if the premises have been occupied for business purposes for at least 14 years and the occupiers in that period have carried on the same business. In order to secure his compensation, the tenant need not pursue his application through the courts if the landlord specifies grounds (*e*), (*f*), or (*g*) and no other ground. The tenant can abandon his application if he sees that the landlord will make out his ground and this will not prejudice his claim for compensation: s. 37(1).

21. Unsuccessful opposition by the landlord. If the landlord fails in his opposition the position is as follows. If the landlord's ground of opposition was decided as a preliminary issue, the matter will be adjourned for the parties to agree terms or, in default of agreement, for the court to determine them. If the parties have agreed terms, the court will order the grant of a new tenancy upon those terms. The Landlord and Tenant Act 1954, s. 36 provides that the effect of the order is that the landlord is bound to grant and the tenant to take a tenancy on the terms agreed or, if the court has had to determine the terms, on those ordered by the court.

If the tenant has second thoughts at this stage and is unwilling to take a new tenancy on the terms ordered by the court, he may take advantage of the following provisions. Section 36(2) gives the tenant the right, within 14 days after the making of the order, to apply to the court for the revocation of the order. On such an application the court is bound to revoke the order. The court will also order the tenancy to continue for such a period as will afford to the landlord a reasonable opportunity to re-let the premises. Normally a person will wish to exercise this right only where for some reason the tenancy is no longer an attractive proposition to him. A common reason will be where the court determines the rent and it is more than the tenant can afford.

LANDLORD'S APPLICATION FOR AN INTERIM RENT

22. Background. While dealing in this chapter with the tenant's application to the court for a new tenancy, it will be convenient also to consider an application which the landlord can make and which he will be well-advised to make as soon as is practical: this is an application for an "interim rent." It has already been explained that where a landlord has served a s. 25 notice or the tenant has made a request under s. 26 and it is followed by an application to the court, the current tenancy is continued by the interim continuation provisions of s. 64 until three months after the time at which the tenant's application is finally disposed of (*see* XI, **15**).

As is apparent from this provision, a tenant who draws out the negotiations for the terms of his new tenancy, who takes every opportunity to have his application adjourned and who appeals against the court's decision may secure himself a considerable advantage. Throughout the period he will be paying the old rent which, in times of inflation, will often be considerably less than the market rent which he will have to pay under his new tenancy. It was to deal with this unsatisfactory situation that s. 24A of the 1954 Act was added by the 1969 Act.

23. Applications under s. 24A. It is provided by the Landlord and Tenant Act 1954, s. 24A, that where the landlord has given notice under s. 25 or the tenant has made a request under s. 26, the landlord may apply to the court to determine a rent which it would be reasonable for the tenant to pay while the tenancy is continuing by virtue of Part II of the Act. When the court determines such a rent, the new rate is payable from the date on which the proceedings for an interim rent were started or from the date specified in the landlord's notice or the tenant's request, whichever is the later: s. 24A(1). In determining the rent the court must have regard to the rent payable under the terms of the current tenancy, but otherwise determines the rent in accordance with s. 34(1),(2) (these are the provisions concerning the determination of the new rent under a new tenancy: *see* XIII, **6**) as if a new tenancy from year to year were to be granted to the tenant. The assumption of an annual tenancy means that the rent determined as the interim rent is generally less than that determined for the new tenancy ordered by the court. The reason is that in the open market a tenant will pay less for an annual tenancy than he will for a lease for a fixed period of, say, seven years. The values upon which the court reaches its decision are those prevailing at the time when the period of continuation starts: *see English Exporters Ltd.* v. *Eldonwall Ltd.* (1973). It was held in the same case that the court is not bound to determine an interim rent; in practice it is usually willing to do so.

NOTE: Unless the rents in the market are falling, it will normally be in the landlord's interest to apply to the court for an interim rent as soon as he can.

PROGRESS TEST 12

1. How may a landlord protect himself during the currency of proceedings under Part II of the Landlord and Tenant Act 1954? **(22)**

2. When may a tenant apply to the court for a new tenancy? **(2)**

3. Which is the appropriate court to hear applications under Pt. II of the 1954 Act?   **(3)**

4. How are proceedings under Part II conducted?   **(5)**

5. L lets property to A, B, C and D who are partners in a business. D dies and B leaves the business. Who should make application to the court for a new tenancy? **(4)**

6. Which are the discretionary grounds for possession? In what way are they discretionary? **(6)**

7. What are the elements of ground (g)? **(17)**

8. What is the effect of s. 31A on ground (f)? **(12)**

9. L lets premises to T on a tenancy protected by Part II. The tenancy is for 20 years from 1st January 1960. L sells his interest to X in 1978. X wishes to occupy the premises for his own purposes. Advise X. **(18)**

10. What is the effect of successful opposition by a landlord to a tenant's application for a new tenancy? What is the effect of unsuccessful opposition? **(19, 21)**

11. What compensation is a tenant entitled to if a landlord succeeds in his opposition to the grant of a new tenancy? **(20)**

12. What is ground (e)? **(6, 11)**

13. What is the effect of a tenant's failure to apply to the court for the grant of a new tenancy within the prescribed time? **(2)**

14. What is an interim rent? How is it assessed? **(22)**

CHAPTER XIII

Terms of New Tenancy Ordered to be Granted by the Court

1. Generally. The way in which Part II of the Landlord and Tenant Act 1954 works is that the court is only involved if the parties are unable to reach agreement. In practice the parties will often be able to agree. There are two main ways in which the court may become involved to determine the terms. First, if the landlord opposes the grant of a new tenancy, his ground of opposition will normally be tried as a preliminary issue. If the landlord fails in his opposition, the court will adjourn the matter for the parties to agree the terms or, if they cannot agree, for them to be determined by the court. Secondly, if the landlord does not oppose the grant, but the parties cannot agree terms, then the court will become involved in determining the terms.

2. The provisions concerning the terms are:

   (*a*) the property: s. 32 (*see* **3**);
   (*b*) the duration: s. 33 (*see* **4, 5**);
   (*c*) the rent: s. 34 (*see* **6**);
   (*d*) other terms: s. 35 (*see* **7**).

3. The property. Section 32(1) provides that the property to be comprised in the new tenancy will be the holding (*see* XI, **15**) as at the date of the court's order. There are two exceptions:

   (*a*) where the landlord opposes under ground (*f*) and the court grants a tenancy of part of the holding under s. 31A (*see* XII, **15**);

   (*b*) where the landlord exercises a power given to him by s. 32(2) to require the tenancy to comprise the entire premises comprised in the current tenancy not just the holding.

The effect of these provisions is that the tenant only has the right to a tenancy of the holding. Under s. 32(2), however, the landlord has the right to require the new tenancy to comprise the entire premises.

4. The duration of the new tenancy. Section 33 provides that where the court orders the grant of a new tenancy, the tenancy will be of such duration as the parties may agree, or in default of agreement, such as the court determines in all the circumstances to be reasonable. When the court determines the duration, there is an upper limit of 14 years on the term that may be ordered. Where a landlord cannot successfully rely on grounds (*f*) or (*g*) but satisfies the court that he is likely to be able to establish the ground in the near future, the court may order a short tenancy to be granted. The court is entitled to order a periodic tenancy to be granted.

It has been held that the court may insert in the new tenancy a break clause: *McCombie* v. *Grand Junction Co. Ltd.* (1962). The court may do this where it appears that at a future date the landlord is likely to require the premises for redevelopment.

5. The commencement of the new tenancy. The commencement date of the new tenancy is the date on which the current tenancy comes to an end. By reason of the interim continuation provisions in s. 64 (*see* XI, **15**), the new lease will generally start on the expiry of three months after the application is finally disposed of.

6. Rent. The Landlord and Tenant Act 1954, s. 34(1) provides that the rent determined by the court must be at such rent as, having regard to the terms of the tenancy, the holding might reasonably be expected to be let in the open market by a willing lessor. The court must disregard:

(*a*) any effect on rent attributable to occupation by the tenant or his predecessors in title;

(*b*) any goodwill attached to the holding by reason of the carrying on of the tenant's business;

(*c*) improvements carried out by the tenant other than in pursuance of an obligation to his landlord and either:

(*i*) carried out during the current tenancy, or

(*ii*) completed not more than 21 years before the application for a new tenancy was made where the preceding tenancies were all protected by Part II of the 1954 Act and the tenant did not quit at the end of each tenancy;

(*d*) where the holding comprises licensed premises, any addition in value due to the licence held by the tenant.

It should be noted that s. 34(3) gives the court power to include such a term for varying the rent as may be specified in its determination:

this gives the court power to insert a rent review clause into the tenancy. Unless premises have an uncommon use such as an hotel, a petrol filling station, a theatre or a racecourse, where profitability may be relevant to rent, the court will not normally order the discovery of trading records to determine the rent: *W.J. Barton Ltd.* v. *Long Acre Securities Ltd.* (1982).

7. Other terms. Section 35 of the 1954 Act provides that the other terms of the tenancy will be such as may be determined by the court in default of agreement. Regard must be had to the terms of the current tenancy and to all relevant circumstances. Normally the court will adhere to the terms of the old tenancy unless either party can produce good reasons for changing them. If a variation in the terms would prejudice the tenant's business, the court is unlikely to accept it.

Gold v. *Brighton Corporation* (1956). T applied for a new tenancy. Under the old tenancy he had traded in new and second-hand clothes. L sought to have included a term preventing T from carrying on the sale of second-hand clothes. The Court of Appeal HELD: It would be wrong to introduce this clause into the new tenancy as it would limit the business which the tenant had previously carried on.

O'May v. *City of London Real Property Co. Ltd.* (1982). In this case, L sought to transfer the risk and burden of services and repairs from himself to T by imposing a service charge with a reduced rent for the risk. The House of Lords HELD that the burden was on the party seeking to change the terms of the current lease to show that the change was fair and reasonable in all the circumstances. The landlord had failed to discharge this burden as the proposed variation required T to assume an unpredictable liability disproportionate to his interest.

Adams v. *Green* (1978). The court has power to insert a break clause for redevelopment.

Cairnplace Ltd v. *CBL (Property Investment) Co. Ltd.* (1984). The court has power to order a term that the tenant provide guarantors. However, it cannot order the tenant to pay the costs of preparing the lease.

PROGRESS TEST 13

1. In what circumstances must the court determine the terms of

a new tenancy under the Landlord and Tenant Act 1954, Part II?
(1)

2. What is the maximum term of a new tenancy ordered by the court? **(4)**

3. When will the court insert a break clause in a new tenancy?
(4)

4. From when does the new tenancy start? **(5)**

5. In what circumstances will a tenancy of property other than the holding be ordered? **(3)**

6. How does the court assess the new rent under the tenancy?
(6)

CHAPTER XIV

Business Tenancies: Compensation for Improvements

1. Generally. Part I of the Landlord and Tenant Act 1927 (ss. 1–17) and Part III of the Landlord and Tenant Act 1954 (ss. 47–50) make provision for the payment of compensation to the tenant of business premises, upon quitting the premises, for improvements made by him to the demised premises. The following points have to be considered:

  (a) the premises (*see* **2**);
  (b) the improvements (*see* **3**);
  (c) pre-conditions to a claim (*see* **4**);
  (d) the claim for compensation (*see* **5**);
  (e) the amount of compensation (*see* **6, 7**);
  (f) the rights of mesne landlords (*see* **8**).

2. The premises. Part I of the 1927 Act applies to any premises used wholly or partly for trade, professional or business purposes. The provisions do not apply to mining leases or to written leases where the tenant is expressed to be the holder of an office or employment under the landlord. The premises to which Part I of the 1927 Act apply and those to which Part II of the 1954 Act apply are not entirely the same. In particular, there are the following differences:

  (a) tenants of licensed premises may claim compensation under the 1927 Act, but are not generally protected by Part II of the 1954 Act (*see* X, **16**);
  (b) the business of sub-letting flats is expressly excluded from the operation of the 1927 Act but such a business tenancy may be protected by Part II of the 1954 Act (*see* X, **12**).

3. The improvements. By s. 1 of the 1927 Act a tenant can claim compensation for any improvement made by him or his predecessors in title which adds to the letting value of the holding at the end of the tenancy. The following points must be noted about this:

(*a*) improvements include the erection of any building but not any trade or other fixture which the tenant is by law entitled to remove: s. 1(1);

(*b*) the right to compensation does not apply to improvements made before 1927; s. 2(1)(a);

(*c*) the Act does not apply to improvements which the tenant was under an obligation to make in pursuance of a contract entered into for valuable consideration: s. 2(1)(b).

4. Pre-conditions to making a claim. Section 3 of the 1927 Act provides that in order to make a claim for compensation:

(*a*) the tenant must have served on the landlord notice of his intention to carry out the improvements together with a specification and plan showing the proposed improvement; and

(*b*) if the landlord gave notice of objection within three months, the tenant must have obtained a certificate from the court that the improvement was a proper one (such a certificate will not be granted if the landlord proves that he has offered to carry out the improvements himself in consideration of a reasonable increase in rent); and

(*c*) the tenant must have carried out the improvements within the time agreed with the landlord or fixed by the court.

5. The claim for compensation. The claim must be made by the tenant within the period prescribed by the Landlord and Tenant Act 1954, s. 47. That period varies with the manner in which the tenancy is ended.

(*a*) if the tenancy is ended by the giving of notice to quit or notice under Part II of the 1954 Act, a claim may be made at any time within three months beginning on the date on which the notice is given: s. 47(1);

(*b*) if the tenancy comes to an end by effluxion of time, a claim may be made at any time not more than six months and not less than three months before the coming to an end of the tenancy: s. 47(2);

(*c*) if the tenancy is terminated by forfeiture or re-entry, a claim may be made at any time within the period of three months from the effective date of the possession order by the court or the date of the re-entry: s. 47(3).

NOTE: The effective date of the possession order means the date on which the order is stated to take effect, or the date on which it ceases to be subject to appeal whichever is the later: s. 47(4).

6. The amount of compensation. By s. 1(1) of the 1927 Act the amount to be paid as compensation must not exceed the lesser of:

(*a*) the net addition to the value of the holding as a whole which is the direct result of the improvement; or

(*b*) the reasonable cost of carrying out the improvement at the end of the tenancy, subject to a deduction of an amount equal to the cost (if any) of putting the works constituting the improvements into a reasonable state of repair.

In practice this may be limited by s. 1(2) which provides that in determining item (*a*), regard must be had to the purposes for which it is intended to use the premises at the end of the tenancy. If it is shown that it is intended to demolish or alter the premises or change the use, regard must be had to the effect of these acts on the additional value due to the improvement and to the length of time likely to elapse between the end of the tenancy and the demolition, alteration or change of use.

NOTE: In practice, s. 1(2) of the 1927 Act will often operate to reduce the amount of compensation to which a tenant is entitled.

7. Determination of disputes. Section 1(3) of the 1927 Act provides that, in the absence of any agreement between the parties, questions as to the right to compensation or the amount must be determined by the court. The appropriate court will depend upon the rateable value of the holding: if the rateable value exceeds £5,000 it will be the High Court; otherwise it will be the county court.

8. Mesne landlords. There are special provisions dealing with the position where there is a chain of tenancies. By s. 8 of the 1927 Act, a mesne landlord who has paid or is liable to pay compensation under the 1927 Act is entitled, at the end of his own term, to compensation from his immediate landlord in like manner and on the same conditions as if he had himself made the improvements in question. This right is conditional on the mesne land landlord, at the prescribed time, having served on his immediate landlord copies of all documents sent to him and relating to proposed improvements and claims under the Act. Where a mesne landlord has served on a superior landlord copies of such documents, the superior landlord has the same rights of opposing a

proposed improvement or a claim for compensation as the mesne
landlord. By these provisions where there is a chain of tenancies
each landlord, who satisfies the relevant conditions may pass on his
liabilities under the 1927 Act.

PROGRESS TEST 14

1. What are the main differences between premises to which
Part II of the 1954 Act applies and those to which the 1927 Act
applies? **(2)**

2. What improvements are excluded from the compensation
provisions? **(3)**

3. How does a tenant make his claim for compensation under
the 1927 Act? **(4)**

4. What are the statutory limits on the amount of compensation? **(6)**

5. Which court determines disputes regarding compensation
under the 1927 Act? **(7)**

6. L lets property to T who sub-lets it to S who makes improvements to it. At the end of his tenancy S claims compensation
under the 1927 Act from T. Advise T of his rights against L and
S. **(8)**

PART THREE

THE RENT ACT 1977

CHAPTER XV

Residential Tenancies: The Rent Act 1977

HISTORY

1. Introduction. The relevant history starts in 1915. It is a long and complex history which originated with the housing shortage brought about by the First World War and which constantly reflects political change. It culminates in the Rent Act 1977 which is a consolidating Act. A clear understanding of the history is helpful in securing a clear understanding of the protection as there have been different types of protection with their origins in different Acts.

TERMINOLOGY

2. Historical table. The following are the main Acts since 1915 and summaries of some of their effects.

(*a*) *Increase of Rent and Mortgage Interest (War Restriction) Act 1915.* This Act introduced control for the first time. It restricted the rent chargeable and the landlord's right to possession. It applied only to houses in certain rental and rateable value brackets.

(*b*) *Increase of Rent and Mortgage Interest (Restriction) Act 1920.* This replaced the 1915 Act and the same system of protection.

(*c*) *Rent and Mortgage Interest Restrictions Act 1923*; *Rent and Mortgage Interest Restrictions Act (Amendment) Act 1933*; *Increase of Rent and Mortgage Interest (Restriction) Act 1938.* These three Acts provided for a certain measure of de-control.

(*d*) *Rent and Mortgage Interest Restriction Act 1939.* This ended the period of de-control and started what was called "new" control.

(*e*) *Rent Act 1957.* This provided for immediate de-control of dwellings over a certain rateable value and a gradual de-control thereafter as old tenancies ended and new tenancies were granted. It also provided a new method of calculating rents for dwellings still subject to control.

(*f*) *Rent Act 1965.* This brought back controls on dwellings decontrolled by the 1957 Act. It also provided for a new method of calculating rents. Tenancies deriving their protection from this Act, or its later re-enactments, are called regulated tenancies.

(*g*) *Rent Act 1968.* Prior to this Act the law was contained in a number of Acts running back to 1920. This Act consolidated the bulk of the earlier provisions.

(*h*) *Housing Finance Act 1972.* This provided for automatic conversion of controlled to regulated tenancies.

(*i*) *Rent Act 1974.* This brought furnished tenancies fully within the protection of the Rent Acts for the first time.

(*j*) *Rent Act 1977.* This consolidated the earlier Acts, and forms the basis of the present law.

(*k*) *Protection from Eviction Act 1977.* This brought together in one Act various provisions relating to notices to quit, restrictions on enforcing rights of re-entry in relation to residential property and other restrictions on the recovery of possession of residential property.

(*l*) *Housing Act 1980.* This gives security of tenure and the right to buy to tenants of local authorities and other bodies.

3. Terminology. Before considering the nature of the protection under the legislation it is important to be clear about the names given to different types of tenancies involved. There are two important distinctions:

(*a*) *between controlled and regulated tenancies.* This has already been touched upon in the history: essentially it distinguishes between tenancies enjoying the old style protection under the pre-1957 Acts and those enjoying the protection created by the Rent Act 1965. Its significance has been greatly reduced by the Housing Act 1980.

(*b*) *between protected and statutory tenancies.* A protected tenancy is a contractual tenancy which is within the Rent Act. Thus, for instance, a monthly tenancy or a tenancy for a fixed term, being a contractual tenancy, will be a protected tenancy (provided it satisfies various conditions). A statutory tenancy is a tenancy which arises, by virtue of the Rent Act at the end of a contractual (protected) tenancy and which continues as long as the tenant continues to reside in the dwelling-house.

EXAMPLES: (1) L lets a dwelling to T on a monthly tenancy. The letting is within the Rent Act. L serves notice to quit on T but T continues to reside in the house. Until the notice to quit takes effect T has a protected tenancy; from the date it takes effect T has a statutory tenancy.

(2) L lets a dwelling to T for a term of seven years from 1st January 1970. The tenancy is within the Rent Act and T continues to reside there at the end of the term. Until 31st December 1977 T has a protected tenancy and thereafter he has a statutory tenancy so long as he occupies the dwelling as his residence.

PROTECTED TENANCIES

4. Introduction. Section 1 of the 1977 Act provides that a tenancy under which a dwelling-house (which may be a house or part of a house) is let as a separate dwelling is a protected tenancy. In addition, the rateable value of the dwelling-house must come within certain limits and the tenancy must not fall within certain specified exceptions. There are therefore five matters to be considered:

(*a*) there must be a tenancy (*see* **5**);

(*b*) of a dwelling-house (*see* **6, 7**);

(*c*) which is let as a separate dwelling (*see* **8** *et seq.*);

(*d*) whose rateable value is within the limits (*see* **12** *et seq.*);

(*e*) and the tenancy does not fall within the exceptions (*see* **18** *et seq.*).

5. A tenancy. It is first necessary to ensure that there is in fact a tenancy. If there is not then there can be no question of the Rent Act applying. The distinction between tenancies and licences has already been considered in II, **12**. Recent decisions of the Court of Appeal have shown the importance of this requirement and how the protection of the Rent Act may be excluded by the landlord granting a licence, rather than a tenancy, to occupiers of his property. Reference has already been made to the case of *Marchant* v. *Charters* (1977) and also to *Somma* v. *Hazlehurst* (1978); students should refer to that section which shows how a properly drafted licence can exclude the operation of the Rent Act (*see* II, **12** *et seq.*). Provided there is a tenancy there can be Rent Act protection whatever the form of the tenancy. A tenancy granted for 99 years can in principle be a protected tenancy as much as can a weekly tenancy. Even a tenancy at will can be a protected tenancy for the purposes of the Rent Act: *Francis Jackson Developments Ltd.* v. *Stamp* (1945).

6. Of a dwelling-house. The Rent Act 1977, s. 1 provides that a dwelling-house may be a house or part of a house. There is no other definition of a dwelling-house in the Act. There have been various cases on the meaning of the words and they show that the court has considered whether the premises are the "home" of the tenant, i.e. the place where he carries on his ordinary domestic life. A flat is a dwelling-house for the purposes of the Rent Act. A single room may also be one.

7. Let as a dwelling. This is closely connected to the preceding requirement. If a dwelling-house is not let as a dwelling-house, it will not be protected. If there is a user covenant in the tenancy, it will determine how the dwelling is let. If the user covenant is for use other than as a residence, the premises will not be let as a dwelling and the tenancy will not be protected. If there is no user covenant, the court looks at the circumstances of the letting. The position was summarised by Denning L.J. in *Wolfe* v. *Hogan* (1949) in the following terms:

"In determining whether a house or part of a house is 'let as a dwelling' within the meaning of the Rent Acts, it is necessary to look at the purpose of the letting. If the lease contains an express provision as to the purpose of the letting, it is not necessary to look further, but, if there is no express provision, it is open to the court to look at the circumstances of the letting. If the house is constructed for use as a dwelling-house, it is reasonable to infer that the purpose was to let it as a dwelling, but if, on the other hand, it is constructed for use as a lock-up shop, the reasonable inference is that it was let for business purposes. If the position were neutral, it would be proper to look at the actual user. It is not a question of implied terms. It is a question of the purpose for which the premises were let."

8. Let as a separate dwelling. This paragraph is concerned with the use of the word "separate" in s. 1. The effect of this word is that the dwelling must be exclusive to the tenant and not involve any sharing with some other person. What is required was helpfully summarised by MacKinnon L.J. in *Cole* v. *Harris* (1945) in the following terms:

"It is, I think, difficult to formulate any principle of law which separates what I have called the contrasted conceptions of (1) a demise of part of a house as a separate dwelling, and (2) an agreement to share the use and occupation of a house. But I think Morton L.J. provides the best formula by saying that to create (1) there must be an agreement by which the occupier has the exclusive use of the essential *living* rooms of a separate dwelling-house. After all, a dwelling-house is that in which a person dwells or lives, and it seems reasonable that a separate dwelling should be one containing essential living rooms. A w.c. may be essential in modern days, but I do not think it is a living room, whereas a kitchen, I think, is."

The cases show that, in deciding whether a room is or is not an "essential living room" within the meaning of the words of Mac-Kinnon L.J., the courts have distinguished between rooms such as a bedroom, sitting room or kitchen where people spend a good deal of their time and rooms such as a lavatory, bathroom or garage which are not used such a great deal. So if a tenant has to share any of the rooms in the former category there will be no separate dwelling; but if he has to share any of the rooms in the latter category that sharing will not prevent there being a separate dwelling. If there is a separate dwelling the tenancy can (if it satisfies the other conditions) be a protected tenancy; if there is no separate dwelling there can be no protected tenancy.

9. Special cases. The rules described in the preceding paragraph have been altered by the Act in two special cases. They are where:

(*a*) the tenant has exclusive occupation of some accommodation and shares the other accommodation with his landlord (s. 21); and

(*b*) the tenant has exclusive occupation of some accommodation and shares other accommodation with persons other than his landlord (s. 22).

NOTE: The word "accommodation" here means the essential living rooms as defined in the preceding paragraph.

10. Tenant sharing with his landlord. Section 21 of the 1977 Rent Act provides that where under any contract:

(*a*) a tenant has the exclusive occupation of any accommodation, and

(*b*) the terms on which he holds it include the use of other accommodation in common with his landlord or in common with his landlord and other persons, and

(c) by reason of (b) the accommodation in (a) is not a dwelling-house let on a protected tenancy,

the contract has the status of a "restricted contract." This is a special form of protection which gives the tenant a limited or restricted form of security of tenure only and not the full Rent Act security. It is considered in XIX.

11. Tenant sharing with person other than landlord. Section 22 provides that where a tenant has the exclusive occupation of accommodation ("the separate accommodation") and

(a) the terms as between the tenant and his landlord on which he holds the separate accommodation include the use of other accommodation ("the shared accommodation") in common with another person or other persons, not being or including the landlord; and

(b) by reason of the circumstances in (a), the separate accommodation would not be a dwelling-house let on or subject to a protected or statutory tenancy,

the separate accommodation is deemed to be a dwelling-house let on a protected tenancy or, as the case may be, subject to a statutory tenancy. This means that in relation to the separate accommodation the tenant has full Rent Act protection. This protection is secured by two special provisions in s. 22. They are as follows:

(a) a possession order cannot be made in respect of the shared accommodation unless an order is also made in respect of the separate accommodation: s. 22(5);

(b) while the tenant is in possession of the separate accommodation, any term of the contract of tenancy modifying or providing for the modification of his right to the use of any of the shared accommodation will be ineffective: s. 22(3).

12. The rateable value. The policy of the Rent Acts has always been to exclude from protection dwelling-houses of a comparatively high rateable value. This is dealt with in s. 4(1) of the 1977 Act which provides that a tenancy is not a protected tenancy if the dwelling-house falls within one of the three classes in s. 4(2). These classes specify various rateable value limits on certain days. In order to decide into which class a house falls (and therefore whether the rateable value is within the limits) it is first necessary to consider what is the "appropriate day" in relation to the dwelling-house. When the appropriate day is determined, the house can be placed in one of the three classes and it can be seen whether the rateable value is within the limits.

13. The appropriate day. Section 25(3) defines the appropriate day in the following way:

(*a*) where the dwelling-house had a rateable value shown in the valuation list on 23rd March 1965, that is the appropriate day;

(*b*) in relation to any other dwelling, it means the date on which a rateable value was first shown in the valuation list, i.e. it will be a date after 23rd March 1965.

EXAMPLES: (1) A house is built in 1945 and is then entered in the valuation list. The appropriate day is 23rd March 1965.

(2) A house is built in 1969 and is entered in the valuation list on 1st January 1970. The appropriate day is 1st January 1970.

NOTE: The significance of 23rd March 1965 is that it was the date on which the Bill which became the Rent Act 1965 was introduced into the House of Commons. It was that Act which created the new form of protection given to regulated tenancies.

14. The rateable value limits. Having considered the meaning of the "appropriate day," it is now possible to consider the limits. A tenancy is not a protected tenancy if the dwelling-house falls within one of the classes set out below. Where alternative values are mentioned, the higher value applies if the dwelling-house is in Greater London and the lower value if it is elsewhere.

(*a*) *Class A*. The appropriate day in relation to the dwelling-house falls or fell on or after 1st April 1973 and the dwelling-house on the appropriate day has or had a rateable value exceeding £1,500 or £750.

(*b*) *Class B*. The appropriate day in relation to the dwelling-house fell on or after 22nd March 1973, but before 1st April 1973, and the dwelling-house

(*i*) on the appropriate day had a rateable value exceeding £600 or £300; and

(*ii*) on 1st April 1973 had a rateable value exceeding £1,500 or £750.

(*c*) *Class C*. The appropriate day in relation to the dwelling-house fell before 22nd March 1973 and the dwelling-house

(*i*) on the appropriate day had a rateable value exceeding £400 or £200; and

(*ii*) on 22nd March 1973 had a rateable value exceeding £600 or £300; and (*iii*) on 1st April 1973 had a rateable value exceeding £1,500 or £750.

15. Historical explanation of the limits. At first sight these limits are complicated; it will assist students to know the historical explanation for them:

(*a*) 23rd March 1965 is the date on which the Rent Bill 1965 was first introduced in the House of Commons.

(*b*) 22nd March 1973 was the date on which the Counter-Inflation Act 1973 was passed. This Act increased the limits so as to take account of the effect of inflation on the assessment of rateable values.

(*c*) 1st April 1973 was the date on which a new valuation list came into effect, following a generous re-assessment of premises for rating purposes.

16. Operation of the limits. With this historical explanation in mind, it is now necessary to consider how the limits operate. There are the following steps:

(*a*) determine the appropriate day; then

(*b*) determine, by reference to the appropriate day, which of the three classes the dwelling-house falls into; then

(*c*) consider whether the rateable value on each day specified in the class was exceeded.

If the rateable value on any of the days specified in the relevant class is not exceeded the dwelling-house comes within the limits.

17. Examples. The following examples illustrate the way in which the limits operate.

EXAMPLES: (1) A flat built in Mayfair in the nineteenth century. It has the following values on the following dates: 23rd March 1965: £450; 22nd March 1973: £650; 1st April 1973: £1,200. This flat would be within the limits. The appropriate day would be 23rd March 1965 (*see* **13** above). The class to consider is therefore class C. In that class conditions (*a*) and (*b*) are satisfied but condition (*c*) is not satisfied. Therefore the flat is within the rateable value limits. If the flat was in Bristol it would be outside the limits.

(2) A house in Manchester, built in 1972 and first appearing in the valuation list on 22nd March 1973. It has the following rateable values on the following dates: 22nd March 1973: £450; 1st April 1973: £800. The house is outside the rateable value

limits. The appropriate day is 22nd March 1973. The class to consider is class B. In that class both conditions (a) and (b) are satisfied in so far as the lower values are concerned. If the house was in London with the same rateable values, it would be within the limits since condition (b) would not be satisfied, the value being under £1,500.

(3) A house built in London in 1978 and first appearing in the list on 1st January 1979. The appropriate day is that date. If the rateable value is £1,500 or less, the house will be within the limits; if it is above £1,500, the house will be outside the limits. If the house was in Liverpool the relevant limit would be £750.

EXCEPTIONS TO PROTECTION

18. Introduction. If there is a tenancy of a separate dwelling whose rateable value is within the limits, the final question to consider is whether the tenancy falls within any of the exceptions. Those exceptions are as follows:

(a) tenancies at low rents: s. 5 (*see* **19–20**);

(b) dwelling-houses let with other land: s. 6 (*see* **21**);

(c) payments for board or attendance: s. 7 (*see* **22**);

(d) lettings to students: s. 8 (*see* **23**);

(e) holiday lettings: s. 9 (*see* **24**);

(f) agricultural holdings: s. 10 (*see* **25**);

(g) licensed premises: s. 11 (*see* **26**);

(h) resident landlords: s. 12 (*see* **27–28**);

(i) landlord's interest belonging to the Crown: s. 13 (*see* **29**);

(j) landlord's interest belonging to a local authority: s. 14 (*see* **30**);

(k) landlord's interest belonging to a housing association: s. 15 (*see* **31**);

(l) landlord's interest belonging to a housing co-operative: s. 16 (*see* **32**);

(m) an assured tenancy (*see* **XXIX**) is not a protected tenancy (*see* the Rent Act 1977, s. 16A (added by the Housing Act 1980, s. 56)).

19. Tenancies at a low rent. A tenancy is not a protected tenancy if under it either no rent is payable or the rent payable is less than two-thirds of the rateable value on the appropriate day: Rent Act 1977, s. 5(1). A tenancy falling within s. 5 is called a tenancy at a low rent, and such tenancies have always been outside the Rent

Acts. The reason for this is to exclude leases at a ground rent (i.e. leases where the rent only represents a payment for the use of the site and not the building on it).

EXAMPLES: (1) L lets a flat to T for no rent. The tenancy is within s. 5 and it is excluded from protection.

(2) L lets a house to T for £60 per year. On the appropriate day the rateable value was £100. The rent is therefore less than two-thirds of the rateable value and the tenancy is not protected.

In calculating whether a long tenancy (i.e. a tenancy granted for a term of more than 21 years) is a tenancy at a low rent, s. 5(4) requires that sums payable by the tenant in respect of rates, services, repairs, maintenance or insurance must be disregarded.

20. Qualifications to the operation of s. 5. There is an important limit on the working of s. 5, which applies where the appropriate day in relation to a dwelling-house fell before 22nd March 1973 and on the appropriate day the dwelling-house had a rateable value exceeding £400 in Greater London and £200 elsewhere: s. 5(2). The qualification is that in those circumstances s. 5(1) (*see* **19**) applies as if the reference to the appropriate day were a reference to 22nd March 1973.

The reason for the qualification is as follows. Prior to the changing of the rateable value limits under the Counter-Inflation Act 1973, a tenancy may have been outside the protection of the Rent Act by reason of its high rateable value. The 1973 Act may have brought that tenancy within the limits and the protection. In such a case, a concession is made to the landlord because, in determining if a tenancy is at a low rent, s. 5(2) requires that the comparison be between the rent and the rateable value on the 22nd March 1973. This means that if, as is probable, the rateable value increased between the appropriate day and 22nd March 1973, s. 5(2) may operate to exclude the tenancy from protection by making the tenancy one at a low rent.

21. Dwelling-houses let with other land. A tenancy is not a protected one if the dwelling-house which is subject to it is let together with land other than the site of the dwelling-house: Rent Act 1977, s. 6. This provision has to be read together with s. 26 which provides that any land or premises let together with a dwelling-house is, unless it is agricultural land of more than two acres, to be treated as part of the dwelling-house. The effect of the two provisions is that it is first necessary to consider if either, (*a*) the dwelling-house is let with other land, or

(*b*) other land is let with the dwelling-house.

The way in which to carry out this excercise is to consider the relative significance of the land and the house: *Pender* v. *Reid* (1948). If it is the land which is the more significant part of the letting, then the case falls within s. 6 and the letting is not protected by the Rent Act. If, on the other hand, it is the house which is the more significant part, the case falls within s. 26 and the land is treated as part of the house and the letting will be protected, provided all other necessary conditions are satisfied.

Feyereisel v. *Turnidge* (1952). A camping site was let together with a small bungalow. The Court of Appeal HELD: The bungalow was let as an adjunct to the camping site and therefore the letting was not protected.

Pender v. *Reid* (1948). A dwelling was let as a part of a coal yard used for a coal merchant's business. The house occupied less than one-third of the whole area. The tenant claimed the protection of the Rent Acts. HELD: The dwelling was merely an adjunct to the rest of the yard and was therefore let together with other land and was not protected by the Rent Acts.

22. Payments for board or attendance. A tenancy is not a protected one if the dwelling-house is bona fide let at a rent which includes payment in respect of board or attendance: Rent Act 1977, s. 7. "Board" means the provision of meals. It seems that there must be provided at least one main meal but not necessarily full board. "Attendance" means services personal to the tenant performed by an attendant provided by the landlord, e.g. delivering letters. It does not include the provision of the services normally provided in large blocks of flats: *see Property Holding Co. Ltd.* v. *Mischeff* (1948).

In the case of attendance s. 7(2) provides that a dwelling-house is not bona fide let at a rent which includes payments in respect of attendance unless the amount of rent which is fairly attributable to attendance forms a substantial part of the whole rent having regard to the value of the attendance to the tenant. The effect is that the court must consider what value the attendance is to the tenant in relation to the rent.

23. Lettings to students. A tenancy is not a protected one if it is granted to a person who is pursuing or intends to pursue a course of study provided by a specified educational institution and is so granted by that institution: Rent Act 1977, s. 8. "Specified" here means specified by the Secretary of State by regulations in a statutory instrument. Regulations have been made and the specified institutions include:

    (*a*) universities;
    (*b*) teacher training colleges;
    (*c*) polytechnics.

24. Holiday lettings. A tenancy is not a protected one if its purpose is to confer on the tenant the right to occupy the dwelling-house for a holiday: Rent Act 1977, s. 9. Where the parties to an agreement expressly say that it is a holiday letting, that is prima facie evidence that it is so, although it can be displaced by evidence that the expressed purpose was not the true one: *Buchmann* v. *May* (1976).

    Buchmann v. *May* (1976). B let to M a house on a series of short furnished tenancies. In late 1974 M sought a short renewal saying that she would be leaving England at its end. M signed an agreement for a new three month tenancy. It provided that "the letting hereby made is solely for the purpose of (M's) holiday." After the tenancy ended M remained in the house. B sued for possession claiming that the tenancy was outside the Rent Acts because it was a holiday letting. The judge took the view that the "purpose of the tenancy" had to be determined by the reality of the situation and held that the tenancy was not a holiday letting. B appealed to the Court of Appeal which HELD: Where a tenancy agreement expressly stated that the purpose for which it was made was for a holiday letting, that would be taken by the court as evidence of the purpose of the parties unless the tenant could show that the true purpose was different. In this case there was no such evidence by the tenant and it was therefore a holiday letting. B was entitled to possession.

25. Agricultural holdings. A tenancy is not a protected one if the dwelling-house is comprised in an agricultural holding within the meaning of the Agricultural Holdings Act 1948 and is occupied by the person responsible for the control (whether as tenant or as servant or agent of the tenant) of the farming of the holding: Rent Act 1977, s. 10.

26. Licensed premises. A tenancy of a dwelling-house which consists of or includes premises licensed for the sale of intoxicating liquors for consumption on the premises is not a protected one: Rent Act 1977, s. 11.

27. Resident landlords. Section 12 (as amended by the Housing Act 1980, s. 65) deals with the "resident landlord" exception. This was introduced by the 1974 Act which, it will be recalled (*see* **2**), gave furnished tenancies protection under the Rent Acts. At the same time, it introduced this new exception designed to assist landlords who "live in." The section provides that a tenancy is not a protected one if,

(*a*) it was granted on or after 14th August 1974; and

(*b*) the dwelling-house forms part only of a building and the building is not a purpose-built block of flats; and

(*c*) the tenancy was granted by a person who, at the time he granted it, occupied as his residence another dwelling-house which also formed part of the building;

(*d*) at all times since the tenancy was granted the interest of the landlord under the tenancy has belonged to a person who, at the time he owned that interest, occupied as his residence another dwelling-house which also formed part of that building.

A person is treated as occupying a dwelling-house as his residence if he fulfills the same conditions as have to be fulfilled by a statutory tenant (*see* **XVI**). Where there is a resident landlord, the tenant will not be a protected tenant but will be entitled to the more limited protection given to restricted contracts: *see* **XIX**.

Conditions (*a*)–(*d*) above apply to tenancies granted before 28th November 1980. The effect of the wording of the conditions, however, was considered to prevent the resident–landlord exception from applying to a person who owned a flat in a purpose-built block of flats and who let part of his flat but resided in the rest of it. The Housing Act 1980, s. 65(1), substituted for the last three conditions (above) the following conditions, and they will apply to lettings after 28th November 1980:

(*a*) the dwelling-house forms part of a building and, except in a case where the dwelling-house also forms part of a flat, the building is not a purpose-built block of flats; and

(*b*) the tenancy was granted by a person who, at the time when he granted it, occupied as his residence another dwelling-house which

(*i*) in the case mentioned in (*a*) above, also forms part of the flat; or (*ii*) in any other case, also forms part of the building; and

(*c*) at all times since the tenancy was granted, the interest of the landlord under the tenancy has belonged to a person who, at the time he owned that interest, occupied as his residence another dwelling-house which

(*i*) in the case mentioned in (*a*) above, also formed part of the flat; or

(*ii*) in any other case, also formed part of the building.

NOTE: The Rent Act 1977, Sch. 2, contains detailed provisions dealing with, primarily, the satisfaction of the residence condition where the interest of the landlord under the tenancy is transferred to a new landlord or is vested in personal representatives, trustees or the probate judge. The provisions of the Schedule were considered by the House of Lords in *Landau* v. *Sloan* (1981). It was as a result of the decision of the Court of Appeal in that case that the terms of Sch. 2 were amended. The provisions of that Schedule are complex and outside the scope of this book.

28. Exceptions to s. 12. This section does not apply to:

(*a*) tenancies granted before 14th August 1974; or

(*b*) a tenancy of a dwelling-house which forms part of a building if it is granted to someone who before it was granted, was a protected or statutory tenant of the same dwelling-house or another dwelling-house in the same building.

Exception (*a*) has already been examined (*see* 27(*a*)). Exception (*b*) prevents a landlord moving into a building, granting new tenancies to the existing tenants and then trying to rely on s. 12 to get them out.

29. Landlord's interest belonging to Crown. A tenancy is not a protected or statutory one at any time when the interest of the landlord belongs to Her Majesty in right of the Crown or to a government department or is held in trust for Her Majesty for the purposes of a government department: Rent Act 1977, s. 13(1) (as substituted by the Housing Act 1980, s. 73). The effect of this provision and of s. 13(2) is that tenants of the Crown who are tenants of (*a*) the Duchy of Lancaster, or (*b*) the Duchy of Cornwall, or (*c*) the Crown Estate Commissioners, can now be regulated tenants if they satisfy the other necessary conditions (*see* **4**).

30. Landlord's interest belonging to a local authority. The Rent Act

1977, s. 14 provides that a tenancy is not a protected one at any time when the interest of the landlord belongs to:

(a) a county council; or

(b) a district council; or

(c) the Greater London Council, the London Borough Councils or the City of London; or

(d) the Commission for New Towns; or

(e) a development corporation.

Such tenancies may, however, be secure tenancies (see XXVI).

31. Landlord's interest belonging to housing association. The Rent Act 1977, s. 15 provides that tenancies held from the following organisations are not protected:

(a) the Housing Corporation;

(b) a housing trust which is a charity;

(c) a housing association which is a registered association;

(d) a housing association which has applied for registration and the application has not been disposed of.

Such tenancies may, however, be secure tenancies (see XXVI).

32. Landlord's interest belonging to a housing co-operative. The Rent Act 1977, s. 16 provides that tenancies held of certain housing co-operatives are not protected.

REGULATED AND CONTROLLED TENANCIES

33. Generally. So far this chapter has been concerned with the general conditions which must be satisfied for a tenancy to be a protected tenancy. Until 28th November 1980 a protected tenancy could be either a regulated or a controlled tenancy. There were detailed provisions for determining which of the two categories a tenancy fell into. In summary, a controlled tenancy was one granted prior to 6th July 1957 in respect of a house erected before 24th August 1954 whose rateable value did not exceed £40 in London (£30 elsewhere) on 7th November 1956. If a tenancy was a controlled one there was a special basis for assessing the maximum rent lawfully recoverable.

Two attempts were made to convert controlled tenancies into regulated ones. First, there was provision in the Housing Finance Act 1972 for automatic conversion by reference to rateable value; the automatic conversion was, however, only partially implemented. Secondly, there was provision under Part VIII of the 1977

Rent Act for conversion where a dwelling was in good repair and provided with all the standard amenities.

34. Housing Act 1980, s. 64(1). This provision came into operation on the 28th November 1980 when "every controlled tenancy shall cease to be a controlled tenancy and become a regulated tenancy." Some controlled tenancies, however, were so classified notwithstanding that they had a business element in them. Section 64(2) of the 1980 Act provides that if the controlled tenancy is one to which Part II of the 1954 Act would apply, on ceasing to be a controlled tenancy (i.e. on 28th November 1980) it is treated as a tenancy continuing by virtue of s. 24 of the 1954 Act.

INTERACTION OF RENT ACT 1977 AND PART II OF THE 1954 ACT

35. Interaction of above Acts. The Rent Act protects the occupier of residential property; Part II of the Landlord and Tenant Act 1954 (*see* XI) protects the occupier of business property. Now, after the operation of the Housing Act 1980, s. 64 (*see* **34**), where a property has a mixed business and residential user the tenancy will normally be protected by Part II of the 1954 Act: *see* the Rent Act 1977, s. 24(3).

PROGRESS TEST 15

1. Outline the history of the Rent Acts. **(2)**
2. What is the difference between;

 (*a*) a controlled and a regulated tenancy;
 (*b*) a statutory tenancy and a protected tenancy;
 (*c*) a resident and a non-resident landlord? **(3, 27)**

3. What conditions must a tenant satisfy to be a protected tenant? **(4)**
4. Which of the following comprises a dwelling-house for the purposes of the Rent Act; (*a*) a cave; (*b*) Noah's Ark; (*c*) a cottage; (*d*) a flat; (*e*) a garden shed? **(6–8)**
5. Are the occupiers of the following premises protected by the Rent Act: (*a*) a YMCA room; (*b*) a shop with a flat over it; (*c*) a shop alone; (*d*) a flat; (*e*) a tied cottage? **(6–11)**
6. When are premises let as a dwelling? **(7)**
7. What is an essential living room? **(8)**

8. What protection does T have in the following cases:

(a) T shares a bathroom with L, his landlord, but he has the exclusive use of two other rooms;

(b) T shares accommodation with L's daughter but not with L;

(c) T lives in a flat in the same house as L.   **(9, 27)**

9. Explain how the rateable value limits operate. What is the difference between premises in and outside London?   **(12)**

10. What is the appropriate day in relation to (a) a house built in 1936; (b) a flat built in June 1973; (c) a shop built in 1978?   **(13)**

11. What is the significance of the following dates: (a) 23rd March 1965; (b) 22nd March 1973; (c) 1st April 1973; (d) 14th August 1974?   **(13, 15, 27)**

12. How does one determine whether a tenancy of mixed commercial and residential premises is protected by Part II of the 1954 Act or the Rent Act?   **(35)**

13. What is a tenancy at a low rent? What special rules apply to determining whether a long tenancy is at a low rent?   **(19)**

14. L lets to T a factory with a dwelling-house in its grounds. T lives in the dwelling and runs his business from the factory. Is T's occupation of the dwelling protected by the Rent Act?   **(21)**

15. What are (a) board, and (b) attendance?   **(22)**

16. What is the effect of a letting with (a) substantial board, and (b) substantial attendance?   **(22)**

17. The Oxbridge university lets one dwelling to S, a student at the university, and one to L, a lecturer there. At the end of the summer term L and S refuse to leave the dwellings. Advise the university. Would your answer be different if L had sub-let his entire dwelling to three students at the university?   **(23)**

18. What conditions must be satisfied if the resident-landlord exception is to apply?   **(27)**

19. What are the exceptions to the resident–landlord exception?   **(28)**

20. What is the effect of a letting by

(a) a landlord whose interest belongs to one of the following bodies; and

(b) a tenant whose landlord is one of the following bodies: (i) the Crown; (ii) a local authority, (iii) a housing association?   **(29, 30)**

CHAPTER XVI

Security of Tenure

STATUTORY TENANCIES

1. Introduction. The Rent Act gives security of tenure in two ways:

(*a*) a tenancy will be continued beyond its contractual date of termination so long as the tenant occupies the dwelling-house as his residence; this statutory continuation is called a "statutory tenancy";

(*b*) a landlord's right to recover possession can only be enforced by means of a court order, and this can only be granted in specific cases; in order to get such an order a landlord must establish one of the specified grounds for possession (*see* XVII).

2. Statutory tenancies and tenants. A statutory tenancy may arise in one of two ways:

(*a*) upon the determination of a previous protected tenancy; or

(*b*) by succession.

A statutory tenancy has been aptly described as a "status of irremovability."

3. Statutory tenancy by virtue of a previous protected tenancy. Section 2(1)(a) of the 1977 Rent Act provides that after the termination of a protected tenancy of a dwelling-house, the person who, immediately before that termination was the protected tenant of it, if and so long as he occupies it as his residence, will be the statutory tenant of it.

A statutory tenancy is therefore a form of protection which arises at the end of a protected tenancy and continues so long as the residential condition is satisfied. Section 2(1)(a) breaks down into the following requirements, all of which will have to be satisfied for a statutory tenancy to exist:

(*a*) there must be a protected (i.e. contractual) tenancy; and

(*b*) that tenancy must have ended; this may be by notice to quit, forfeiture or any of the other common law methods of termination; and (*c*) there must be a person who was a protected tenant before the termination; and

(*d*) that person must continue to occupy the dwelling-house as his residence.

Of these four elements the first three have already been considered in previous chapters. It is therefore only the last condition which has to be considered now. First it is necessary to deal with companies.

4. Companies. A company can be a protected tenant, but it cannot be a statutory tenant because it cannot satisfy the requirement that it occupy the dwelling-house as its residence: *Hiller* v. *United Dairies* (1934). Consequently, while a company may be a protected tenant, on the termination of its tenancy it will not become a statutory tenant and will therefore lose its Rent Act protection. Hence there is nowadays a practice for landlords to let dwelling-houses to companies only. The directors or other employees of the company are then allowed to occupy the premises as licensees.

5. Occupation as residence. This is the central requirement of a statutory tenancy. The rule is that a non-occupying tenant loses his status as a statutory tenant. It may, however, be difficult to decide if a tenant has ceased to occupy. The classic statement of the law was by the Court of Appeal in *Brown* v. *Brash* (1948); the judgment contains the following significant passage:

> "... absence of the [tenant] may be sufficiently prolonged or unintermittent to compel the inference, prima facie, of a cesser of possession or occupation. The question is one of fact and of degree ..... Notwithstanding an absence so protracted [i.e. five years or more] the authorities suggest that its effect may be averted if [the tenant has an intention to return and if] he couples and clothes his inward intention with some formal, outward and visible sign of it."

In summary therefore, when a tenant is not himself physically occupying the premises, his statutory tenancy will continue so long as,

(*a*) the tenant intends to return to the dwelling-house; and

(*b*) there is an outward physical sign of that intention.

6. Statutory tenancy by succession. A statutory tenancy may be transmitted to another person on the death of the statutory tenant by virtue of a previous protected tenancy ("the original tenant"). Schedule 1 to the Rent Act 1977 contains provisions which provide for two transmissions on death provided certain conditions are satisfied. The effect of the provisions is that:

(a) the surviving spouse (if any) of the original tenant, if residing in the dwelling-house immediately before the death of the original tenant, will after the death be the statutory tenant if and so long as he or she occupies the dwelling-house as his or her residence;

(b) where (a) does not apply, but a person who was a member of the original tenant's family was residing with him at the time of and for the period of six months immediately before his death, after the death, that person (or, if there is more than one such person, such one of them as may be decided by agreement, or in default of agreement, decided by the county court) will be the statutory tenant if and so long as he occupies the dwelling-house as his residence.

A person who becomes statutory tenant under these provisions is called the first successor. There may also be a second transmission under Sch. 1, para. 5. as follows:

(a) the surviving spouse (if any) of the first successor, if residing in the dwelling-house immediately before the death of the first successor, after the death will be the statutory tenant if and so long as he or she occupies the dwelling-house as his or her residence;

(b) if (a) does not apply, there are similar provisions to those in (b) above to determine who, if anyone, will be the statutory tenant. The provisions are the same, except that for the words "original tenant" there are substituted the words "first successor."

There can only be two transmissions on death of the statutory tenancy. When the successor to the first successor dies, the right to occupy the dwelling-house under a statutory tenancy ends and any members of that person's family will have to leave.

7. Meaning of "family." The word "family" as it is used in Sch. 1 is not defined in the Rent Act. The cases show that it includes:

(a) children, brothers and sisters of the deceased; and
(b) adopted children.

There have been several cases concerning mistresses. One of the more recent was the following.

Dyson Holdings v. *Fox* (1975). F, a spinster of 74, lived with W, a bachelor, for 40 years. They never married but lived together as man and wife in a rented house and used their joint income to pay the rent. W died in 1961 and F paid the rent in the name of Mrs W. In 1973, the landlords, D, discovered that F was not W's widow and they bought proceedings claiming possession from F on the ground that she was not protected by the Rent Acts. HELD by the Court of Appeal: The word "family" should not be construed in a technical sense but in the sense in which an ordinary man in the street would give to it. Here, having regard to the permanence and stability of the relationship, F would popularly have been said to be a member of W's family at the time of his death. Therefore F was entitled to the protection of the Rent Acts as a successor to W.

In fact there is an earlier decision of the Court of Appeal, *Gammans* v. *Ekins* (1950), which took a different approach, saying that a mistress will only be a member of the tenant's family if she bears his children. In *Dyson Holdings* the Court of Appeal distinguished *Gammans* on the ground that it was no longer in line with modern thinking, having regard to changes in social conditions. Until the House of Lords considers the matter there are now conflicting decisions of the Court of Appeal on the point. While the law on mistresses remains confused it is now established that two adults who live together in a platonic relationship can never establish a familial nexus for the purposes of Sch. 1.

Carega Properties v. *Sharratt* (1979). S, a young man, lived for 18 years with an elderly widow to whom he was not related. The relationship was platonic and filial and S looked after her in her last years. When she died S claimed to be entitled to remain in her rented flat as a statutory tenant by succession. The House of Lords HELD: The word "family" was to be given its ordinary natural meaning and did not here have the same meaning as the word "household." There was here no recognisable familial nexus, S was not therefore a member of the widow's family and was not entitled to become the statutory tenant by succession.

8. The nature of a statutory tenancy. A statutory tenancy is a purely personal right. It cannot be assigned or sold and it does not pass to the personal representatives of a deceased statutory tenant; nor will it pass to a trustee in bankruptcy. The reason is that it is dependent upon the occupation of the tenant himself and ceases to exist when he ceases to occupy the dwelling-house as his residence.

Similarly, a statutory tenant cannot sub-let the entire dwelling-house for his tenancy will then end.

9. The terms and conditions of a statutory tenancy. Section 3(1) of the Rent Act 1977 provides that so long as he retains possession, a statutory tenant must observe and will be entitled to the benefit of all the terms and conditions of the original contract of tenancy so far as they are consistent with the provisions of the Act. This means that the terms of the previous tenancy (e.g. as to repairs) will normally continue into the statutory tenancy. Some terms, however, will not so continue, since they are repugnant to the status of irremoveability that is conferred by a statutory tenancy (e.g. a provision allowing the landlord to determine the tenancy on the tenant ceasing to retain a certain employment).

Section 3(3) provides that a statutory tenant is entitled to give up possession of the dwelling-house if, and only if, he gives such notice as would have been required under the original contractual tenancy or, if no notice would have been so required, on giving not less than three months' notice.

10. Termination of a statutory tenancy. There are only two ways in which a statutory tenancy can come to an end:

(a) by the court making a possession order against the tenant; or

(b) by the tenant unequivocally giving up possession.

PROGRESS TEST 16

1. What is a statutory tenancy? **(3)**
2. What is the difference between:
   (a) a statutory tenancy by virtue of a previous tenancy; and
   (b) a statutory tenancy by succession? **(3, 6)**
3. What conditions must be satisfied for there to be a statutory tenancy? **(3)**
4. Why cannot a company be a statutory tenancy? **(4)**
5. Who may succeed to a statutory tenancy? What conditions must a person satisfy in order to qualify as a successor? **(6)**
6. How many successors can there be to a statutory tenancy? **(6)**
7. Which of the following, if any, can succeed to a statutory tenancy:

(*a*) a mistress; (*b*) a platonic friend; (*c*) a step-child; (*d*) a widower? **(7)**

8. In what ways may a statutory tenancy end? **(10)**

9. Under what terms does a statutory tenant hold? **(9)**

CHAPTER XVII

Recovery of Possession of
Dwelling-Houses Subject to the Rent Act

INTRODUCTION

1. Generally. One of the two main ways in which the Rent Act protects tenants is that it restricts the landlord's right to recover possession. This is done in two ways. The first is the statutory tenancy which (*see* XVI) gives to the tenant the right to stay in possession even though his tenancy has ended providing he continues to reside in the demised premises. The second way is that if the landlord does wish to recover possession, he must establish, to the satisfaction of the court, one of certain specified grounds or cases for possession. The Act prohibits the court from making a possession order except on those specified grounds.

2. Establishing a right to possession. It must always be borne in mind that the protection given by the Rent Act is in addition and not in substitution for the ordinary contractual rights of tenants. Consequently a landlord who seeks an order for possession has to pass two hurdles. First, he must show that as a matter of contract the tenancy is ended; secondly, he must establish one of the grounds for possession under the Rent Act 1977. For example, if the tenancy is a periodic one the landlord must determine it contractually by service of a notice to quit or other appropriate means before there can be any question of his entitlement to possession. Of course, once the tenancy has been determined as a matter of contract and has become a statutory one it is only the statutory grounds for possession which have any relevance.

GROUNDS FOR POSSESSION

3. Introduction. Section 98(1) of the Rent Act 1977 provides that a court must not make an order for possession of a dwelling-house which is let on a protected tenancy or is subject to a statutory tenancy unless the court considers it reasonable to make such an order and either:

(*a*) it is satisfied that suitable alternative accommodation is available for the tenant or will be available for him when the order takes effect; or

(*b*) the circumstances are as specified in any of the Cases in Part I of Sch. 15 to the Act.

The cases specified in Sch. 15, Part I are discretionary in that the court must consider if it is reasonable to make an order. There are in addition certain cases which are mandatory in that if the landlord makes them out the court must make an order: *see* s. 98(2). These cases are contained in Part II of Sch. 15.

4. Effect of s. 98. The following matters arise out of s. 98, and must be considered:

(*a*) suitable alternative accommodation (*see* **5, 6**);

(*b*) the discretionary cases in Part I of Sch. 15 (*see* **7** *et seq.*);

(*c*) the mandatory cases in Part II of Sch. 15 (*see* **20**);

(*d*) the powers of the court generally (*see* **32** *et seq.*).

SUITABLE ALTERNATIVE ACCOMMODATION

5. Introduction. The provisions relating to suitable alternative accommodation are contained in the Rent Act 1977, Sch. 15, Part IV. There are two ways in which the landlord may satisfy the requirements relating to suitable alternative accommodation:

(*a*) if the housing authority issues a certificate that it will provide suitable alternative accommodation for the tenant by a specified date; or

(*b*) if the court deems the accommodation to be suitable.

Only the second of these requires further consideration. The first is little used in practise since the local authority is understandably reluctant to issue certificates.

6. Deemed suitable by the court. The Rent Act 1977, Sch. 15, paras. 4, 5, provide that accommodation is to be deemed to be suitable when:

(*a*) the accommodation comprises premises to be let on a protected tenancy or with equivalent security of tenure; and

(*b*) it is similar as regards rental and extent to the accommodation offered by the housing authority in the area for persons whose needs are similar, or is reasonably suitable to the means and needs of the tenant; as regards extent and character; and

(c) it is reasonably suitable as regards proximity to place of work.

DISCRETIONARY CASES

7. The Cases in Schedule 15. Part I of this schedule contains ten cases where the court may order possession. The landlord must satisfy the court that:

(a) it is reasonable to make the order; and

(b) he has made out the case.

In the following paragraphs these cases are considered. In each paragraph the case is set out and, where appropriate, comments are made on it. In summary, it may be said that cases 5, 8 and 9 concern the landlord's needs while the remaining cases concern misbehaviour by the tenant. A landlord may rely on two or more cases. Sometimes the same facts may permit reliance on two cases, e.g. Cases 1 and 2.

8. Case 1. Where any rent lawfully due from the tenant has not been paid or any obligation of the protected or statutory tenancy has been broken or not performed.

This case is the one most commonly relied upon by a landlord. It covers a breach of any of the obligations of the tenancy except the covenant to give up possession of the premises at the end of the term.

9. Case 2. Where the tenant or any person residing or lodging with him or any sub-tenant of his has been guilty of conduct which is a nuisance or annoyance to adjoining occupiers, or has been convicted of using the dwelling-house or allowing the dwelling-house to be used for immoral or illegal purposes. Nuisance or annoyance here covers such things as noise, offensive activities, and using premises as a brothel.

10. Case 3. Where the condition of the dwelling-house has, in the opinion of the court, deteriorated owing to acts of waste by, or the neglect or default of, the tenant or any person residing or lodging with him or any sub-tenant of his and, in the case of any act of waste by, or the neglect or default of, a person lodging with the tenant or a sub-tenant of his, where the court is satisfied that the tenant has not, before the making of the order in question, taken such steps as he ought reasonably to have taken for the removal of the lodger or sub-tenant, as the case may be.

11. Case 4. Where the condition of any furniture provided for use under the tenancy has, in the opinion of the court, deteriorated owing to ill-treatment by the tenant or any person residing or lodging with him or any sub-tenant of his and, in the case of any ill-treatment by a person lodging with the tenant or a sub-tenant of his, where the court is satisfied that the tenant has not, before the making of the order in question, taken such steps as he ought reasonably to have taken for the removal of the lodger or sub-tenant, as the case may be.

12. Case 5. Where the tenant has given notice to quit and, in consequence of that notice, the landlord has contracted to sell or let the dwelling-house or has taken any other steps as the result of which he would, in the opinion of the court, be seriously prejudiced if he could not obtain possession.

Notice to quit here means the service of a proper notice; it does not mean informally agreeing to leave: *Standingford* v. *Bruce* (1926).

13. Case 6. Where, without the consent of the landlord, the tenant has at any time assigned or sub-let the whole of the dwelling-house or sub-let part of it, the remainder being already sub-let. This case can be relied upon against both the tenant and the sub-tenant: *Leith Properties Ltd.* v. *Springer* (1982).

14. Case 7. Where the tenancy is a controlled tenancy and the dwelling-house consists of or includes premises licensed for the sale of intoxicating liquor for consumption off the premises only, and either

(*a*) the tenant has committed an offence as holder of the licence; or

(*b*) the tenant has not conducted the business to the satisfaction of the licensing justices or the police authority, or

(*c*) the tenant has carried on the business in a manner detrimental to the public interest, or

(*d*) the renewal of the licence has for any reason been refused.

This case was repealed by the Housing Act 1980.

15. Case 8. Where the dwelling-house is reasonably required by the landlord for occupation as a residence for some person engaged in his whole-time employment, or in the whole-time employment of some tenant from him or with whom, conditional on housing being provided, a contract for such employment has been entered into, and the tenant was in the employment of the landlord or a former landlord, and the dwelling-house was let to him in consequence of that employment and he has ceased to be in that employment.

16. Case 9. Where the dwelling-house is reasonably required by the landlord for occupation as a residence for either:

(*a*) himself; or

(*b*) any son or daughter of his over 18 years of age; or

(*c*) his father or mother; or

(*d*) if the dwelling-house is let on or subject to a regulated tenancy, the father or mother of his wife or husband; and the landlord did not become landlord by purchasing the dwelling-house or any interest therein, after either:

(*i*) 7th November 1956, in the case of a tenancy which was then a controlled tenancy;

(*ii*) 8th March 1973, in the case of a tenancy which became a regulated tenancy by virtue of the Counter-Inflation Act 1973; s. 14;

(*iii*) 24th May 1974, in the case of a regulated furnished tenancy; or

(*iv*) 23rd March 1965, in the case of any other tenancy.

17. Case 9 explained. Case 9 is of some importance. It is often relied on by a landlord who is trying to recover possession of a dwelling-house for his own use or for the use of his immediate family. The following points should be noted:

(*a*) the dwelling-house must be reasonably required; this means that there must be a genuine need for the house;

(*b*) the landlord must not be a landlord by purchase, i.e. if a landlord grants a tenancy to a tenant and then sells his own interest to another person, that other person is a landlord by purchase and cannot rely on this case;

(*c*) the court has to consider the question of greater hardship when considering a claim under Case 9.

18. Case 9 and greater hardship. In considering a claim for possession under Case 9 the court must have regard to the question of greater hardship: Rent Act 1977, Sch. 15, Part III. In particular, a court must not make an order by reason of Case 9 if it is shown that, having regard to all the circumstances of the case, including the question whether other accommodation is available to the landlord or the tenant, greater hardship would be caused by granting the order than by refusing to grant it: Sch. 15, para. 1. The following points should be noted in regard to the question of greater hardship:

(*a*) the tenant must prove greater hardship;

(*b*) the mere fact that a tenant must move is not of itself evidence of greater hardship;

(*c*) the court considers all the factors as at the time of the hearing.

19. Case 10. Where the court is satisfied that the tenant has sub-let part of the dwelling at a rent in excess of the maximum rent recoverable under the Rent Act.

SCHEDULE 15, PART II

20. The mandatory cases in Part II. These are the cases in which the court must order possession where the dwelling-house is subject to a regulated tenancy. There is no discretion in the court and the question of reasonableness does not apply.

21. Case 11. Where a person who occupied the dwelling-house as his residence ("the owner-occupier") let it on a regulated tenancy and either:

(*a*) not later than the relevant date the landlord gave written notice to the tenant that possession might be recovered under this Case; and

(*b*) the dwelling-house has not, since

(*i*) 22nd March 1973, in the case of a tenancy which became a regulated tenancy by virtue of the Counter-Inflation Act 1973, s. 14;

(*ii*) 14th August 1974, in the case of a regulated furnished tenancy; or

(*iii*) 8th December 1965, in the case of any other tenancy; been let by the owner-occupier on a protected tenancy with respect to which the condition mentioned in paragraph (*a*) above was not satisfied; and

(*c*) the court is of the opinion that any of the conditions in the Rent Act 1977, Sch. 15, Part V, paras. (*a*), (*c*)—(*f*), is satisfied (for the conditions *see* **24**, below).

This case enables an owner-occupier who previously occupied a house as his residence and then let it, to recover possession where the court is satisfied that the house is required for one of the reasons specified in the Act (*see* **24** below). One of the joint owner-occupiers may rely on this case: *Tilling* v. *Whiteman* (1979).

22. Meaning of relevant date. As can be seen above notice must have been given to the tenant not later than the "relevant date" that possession might be recovered under this Case. The relevant date is defined by Sch. 15, Part III, para. 2 and is:

(*a*) in the case of a tenancy created before 8th December 1965, 7th June 1966;

(*b*) in the case of a tenancy becoming protected by virtue of the Counter-Inflation Act 1973, s. 14, and created before 22nd March 1973, 22nd September 1973;

(*c*) in the case of a regulated furnished tenancy created before 14th August 1979, 13th February 1975;

(*d*) in any other case, the date of commencement of the tenancy.

23. The court's discretion to dispense with notice. Where notice has not been served, if it considers it just and equitable to make an order for possession, the court may dispense with the requirement of notice under paragraphs (*a*) and (*b*) of Case 11.

24. Schedule 15, Part V. This was added to the Rent Act 1977 by s. 66 of the Housing Act 1980, and defines the Cases which an occupier may rely on to recover possession where he has served the appropriate notice. Paragraphs (*a*) and (*c*)—(*f*) apply to Case 11. Paragraphs (*b*)—(*e*) apply to Case 12. Paragraphs (*c*)—(*f*) apply to Case 20. The relevant provisions of Part V are as follows.

(*a*) The dwelling-house is required as a residence for the owner or any member of his family who resided with the owner when he last occupied the dwelling-house as a residence.

(*b*) The owner has retired from regular employment and requires the dwelling-house as a residence.

(*c*) The owner has died and the dwelling-house is required as a residence for a member of his family who was residing with him at the time of his death.

(*d*) The owner has died and the dwelling-house is required by a successor in title as his residence or for the purpose of disposing of it with vacant possession.

(*e*) The dwelling-house is subject to a mortgage, made by deed and granted before the tenancy, and the mortgagee

(*i*) is entitled to exercise a power of sale conferred on him by the mortgage or by the Law of Property Act 1925, s. 101; and

(*ii*) requires the dwelling-house for the purpose of disposing of it with vacant possession in exercise of that power.

(*f*) The dwelling-house is not reasonably suitable to the needs of the owner, having regard to his place of work, and he requires it for the purpose of disposing of it with vacant possession and of using the proceeds of that disposal in acquiring, as his residence, a dwelling-house which is more suitable to those needs.

25. Case 12. Where a person ("the owner") who acquired the dwelling-house or any interest therein with a view to occupying it as his residence at such time as he might retire from regular employment let it on a regulated tenancy before he has so retired and

(*a*) not later than the relevant date the landlord gave written notice to the tenant that possession might be recovered under this Case; and

(*b*) the dwelling-house has not, since 14th August 1974, been let by the owner on a protected tenancy with respect to which the condition mentioned in paragraph (*a*) above was not satisfied; and

(*c*) the court is of the opinion that any of the conditions in the Rent Act 1977, Sch. 15, Part V, paras (*b*)—(*e*) is satisfied (*see* **24**, above for the conditions).

This case concerns retirement homes bought and then let out pending retirement. Again, as in Case 11 the court has a discretion to dispense with the requirement of notice under (*a*) and (*b*).

26. Case 13. Where the dwelling-house is let under a tenancy for a term of years certain not exceeding eight months and

(*a*) not later than the relevant date the landlord gave written notice to the tenant that possession might be recovered under this Case; and

(*b*) the dwelling-house was, at some time within the period of 12 months ending on the relevant date, occupied under a right to occupy it for a holiday.

For the purposes of this Case a tenancy will be treated as being for a term of years certain notwithstanding that it is liable to determination by re-entry or on the happening of any event other than the giving of notice by the landlord to determine the term.

This Case concerns short lettings which follow holiday lettings and it operates as follows. If there is a holiday letting and within 12 months of it the landlord lets the property for a short term of less than eight months, he may serve notice at the start of that short term that he relies on this case. It is therefore intended to apply to those who own property which is normally let on holiday lettings but who let it out of season for short periods.

27. Case 14. Where the dwelling-house is let under a tenancy for a term of years certain not exceeding 12 months and

(*a*) not later than the relevant date the landlord gave written notice to the tenant that possession might be recovered under this Case; and

(*b*) at some time within the period of 12 months ending on the relevant date, the dwelling-house was subject to such a tenancy as is referred to in the Rent Act 1977, s. 8(1).

This case concerns short lettings which follow lettings to students within s. 8 of the Act (*see* XV, **23**), and is intended to enable those who let to students under s. 8 to let the property for short periods up to one year and then to recover possession.

28. Case 15. Where the dwelling-house is held for the purpose of being available for occupation by a minister of religion as a residence from which to perform the duties of his office and

(*a*) not later than the relevant date the tenant was given written notice that possession might be recovered under this Case; and

(*b*) the court is satisfied that the dwelling-house is required for occupation by a minister of religion as such a residence.

29. Cases 16–18. These cases all concern the recovery of dwelling-houses occupied by persons employed on, or responsible for, the control of agricultural units. They are particularly complicated even by the standards of the law of landlord and tenant and are outside the scope of this book.

30. Case 19. This case concerns protected shorthold tenancies (*see* XXVIII).

31. Case 20. This case was added to the Rent Act 1977 by the Housing Act 1980, s. 67, and deals with lettings by servicemen. Where the dwelling-house was let by a person ("the owner") at any time after 28th November 1980, and

(*a*) at the time when the owner acquired the dwelling-house he was a member of the regular armed forces of the Crown;

(*b*) at the relevant date the owner was a member of the regular armed forces of the Crown;

(*c*) not later than the relevant date the owner gave written notice to the tenant that possession might be recovered under this Case;

(*d*) the dwelling-house has not since 28th November 1980 been let by the owner on a protected tenancy with respect to which the condition mentioned in paragraph (c) above was not satisfied; and

(e) the court is of the opinion that either:

(i) the dwelling-house is required as a residence for the owner; or

(ii) that any of the conditions in the Rent Act 1977, Sch. 15, Part V, paras. (c)–(f) is satisfied (see **24**, above for the conditions).

If the court is of the opinion that, notwithstanding that the condition in paragraph (c) or (d) above is not complied with, it is just and equitable to make an order for possession of the dwelling-house, it may dispense with the requirements of either or both of these paragraphs, as the case may require.

32. The court's powers to make possession orders. Proceedings for possession are normally brought in the county court because it is quicker and cheaper. Proceedings may, however, be brought in the High Court. When the landlord relies on one of the discretionary cases in Part I on the making of an order for possession the court may

(a) stay or suspend the execution of the order; or

(b) postpone the date of possession;

for such period as it thinks fit: Rent Act 1977, s. 100 (3).

NOTES: (1) Under the Housing Act 1980, s. 75(2), where the court exercises its power in (a) or (b) above, it must impose conditions with regard to payment by the tenant of arrears of rent (if any) and current rent or mesne profits and may impose such other conditions as it thinks fit.

(2) Under the Housing Act 1980, s. 89, in dealing with the cases under Part II of Schedule 15 (the mandatory cases) the court must not postpone possession more than 14 days unless there is exceptional hardship, in which case the maximum is six weeks.

(3) There is a special speedy procedure in the county court for recovery of possession of a dwelling-house under:

(a) Cases 11, 12 or 20, provided

(i) the dwelling-house is required as a residence for the owner or for any member of the owner's family who resided with him at his death or, where the proceedings are brought under Case 11, for any member of the owner's family who resided with him when he last occupied the dwelling-house as a residence; and

(*ii*) the requisite notice was given; and
(*b*) Cases 13–19 (inclusive).

MISCELLANEOUS PROVISIONS CONCERNING SECURITY OF TENURE

33. Miscellaneous matters. The main provisions of the Rent Act concerning security of tenure have now been considered. There are however two miscellaneous matters which can be conveniently dealt with here. They are:

(*a*) unlawful eviction and harassment of residential occupiers (*see* **34–35**);
(*b*) sub-lettings (*see* **36–41**).

34. Unlawful eviction and harassment. Section 1(2) of the Protection from Eviction Act 1977 makes it an offence if any person unlawfully deprives a residential occupier of any premises of his occupation of the premises or any part of them, or if he attempts to do so, unless he proves that he believed, and had reasonable cause to believe that the residential occupier had ceased to reside in the premises. Section 1(3) makes it an offence if any person, with intent to cause the residential occupier of any premises

(*a*) to give up the occupation of the premises or any part of them, or
(*b*) to refrain from exercising any right or pursuing any remedy in respect of the premises or any part of them,

does acts calculated to interfere with the peace or comfort of the residential occupier or members of his household, or persistently withdraws or withholds services reasonably required for the occupation of the premises as a residence.

The reference to a "residential occupier" means a person occupying premises as a residence whether under a contract or by virtue of any enactment or rule of law giving him the right to remain in occupation or restricting the right of any other person to recover possession of the premises: Protection from Eviction Act 1977, s. 1(1). This is a wide definition and it covers not only protected tenants but also occupants under restricted contracts, residential licensees and service licensees. It is therefore intended to protect all lawful residential occupiers in their enjoyment of their occupation.

35. Unlawful eviction; civil proceedings. The preceding paragraph was concerned with criminal proceedings. Where a landlord harasses or evicts a residential occupier, that occupier will normally also have a civil remedy. He may seek an injunction to restrain the landlord from harassing him or may sue him for damages for the losses he has suffered. It has recently been held that where a landlord unlawfully evicts a protected tenant from his home, that tenant may recover what are called "exemplary damages".

Drane v. *Evangelou* (1978). D rented a flat from E. D applied to the rent officer for a review of his rent. The rent officer reduced the rent. Soon after this, while D was out of the premises E entered the flat, put D's belongings out in the yard and stopped him going back in. D applied to the court for an injunction putting him back in the flat. The court granted it and eventually E complied with it. D then went on and sued E for the loss he had suffered. The Court of Appeal HELD: This was a suitable case for an award of exemplary damages because it was a case where it was "necessary to teach a wrongdoer that tort does not pay." Damages totalling £1,000 were awarded.

36. Sub-lettings. A sub-tenancy which satisfies all the conditions of a protected tenancy will be a protected tenancy, notwithstanding the fact that it is a sub-tenancy. At common law, when the head tenancy ends the sub-tenancy ends with it. The Rent Acts have therefore always contained special provisions to protect sub-tenants who are protected or statutory tenants. The present provision is s. 137 of the 1977 Act. There are two situations which have to be considered:

(*a*) where the head tenancy is a protected or statutory tenancy (*see* **37**);

(*b*) where the head tenancy is not a protected or statutory tenancy (*see* **38**).

37. Sub-lettings where the head tenancy is a protected or statutory tenancy. In this situation there are two rules:

(*a*) If a court makes an order for possession of a dwelling-house from a protected or statutory tenant on one of the specified grounds in the Act, nothing in that order will affect the right of any sub-tenant to whom the dwelling-house or any part of it has been lawfully sub-let, nor will the order operate to give a right to possession against any sub-tenant: Rent Act 1977, s. 137(1).

(*b*) Where a protected or statutory tenancy is determined whether as a result of an order for possession or for any other reason, any sub-tenant to whom the dwelling-house or part of it has been lawfully sub-let will be deemed to become the tenant of the landlord on the same terms as if the tenant's statutory or protected tenancy had continued: *ibid.* s. 137(2).

EXAMPLES: (1) L lets a house to T who sub-lets part to S. When T fails to pay his rent he is taken to court by L who gets a possession order against him. The order does not operate against S: s. 137(1).

(2) L lets a house to T who sub-lets part to S. When T surrenders his interest to L, S is deemed to become L's tenant on the same terms as he held from T: s. 137(2).

NOTE: The sub-letting must be a lawful one. This means that if the sub-letting was created in breach of covenant and the landlord has not, by his conduct or expressly, accepted the subletting, the sub-tenant will not be protected by s. 137. The strict common law rules as to waiver of forfeiture (*see* VIII, **10**) do not apply to s. 137; in each case it is a question of fact whether the landlord's conduct amounts to an acknowledgment that the sub-tenancy is lawful: *Trustees of Henry Smith's Charity* v. *Willson* (1983).

38. Sub-lettings where the head tenancy is not a protected or statutory tenancy. Section 137(3) of the Rent Act 1977 deals with the situation where the head tenancy is not a protected or a statutory tenancy under that Act. It provides that where a dwelling-house both:

(*a*) forms part of premises which have been let as a whole on a superior tenancy but do not constitute a dwelling-house let on a protected or statutory tenancy; and

(*b*) is itself subject to a protected or statutory tenancy,

from the coming to an end of the superior tenancy, the Rent Act applies in relation to the dwelling-house as if, in lieu of the superior tenancy, there had been separate tenancies of the dwelling-house and of the remainder, for the like purposes as under the superior tenancy and at the rents equal to the just proportion of the rent under the superior tenancy. This provision will normally operate to protect a sub-tenant holding from a head tenant who is not protected by the Rent Act.

EXAMPLE: L lets to T business premises which include a flat. T sub-lets the flat to S and uses the rest for his business. T's lease will be subject to Part II of the 1954 Act and S's sublease to the Rent Act. At the end of T's tenancy he leaves the premises and his tenancy comes to an end but S stays on. The

effect of s. 137(3) is that instead of the head tenancy there are
deemed separate head lettings of the flat and of the rest. This
means that on the ending of the deemed head tenancy of the
flat, s. 137(2) (*see* **34**(*b*) above) will apply and S will become the
direct tenant of L.

**39. Sub-lettings where the head tenancy is a long lease at a low
rent.** In order to complete the protection given to sub-tenants,
the Rent Act 1977, s. 137(5) provides that where there is a superior
long tenancy of a dwelling-house which is at a low rent and which,
but for the fact that it was at a low rent, would have been a
protected tenancy, it is to be treated as a protected tenancy for the
purposes of s. 137(2). This means that where a sub-tenant who is
a protected tenant holds from an unprotected long leaseholder at a
low rent, the sub-tenant will have the same protection under
s. 137(2) (*see* **34**(*b*) above) as he would have had if the head
tenancy had been a protected tenancy.

**40. Effect on furnished sub-tenancy of the determination of a
superior unfurnished tenancy.** Section 138 of the Rent Act 1977 deals
with the curious situation where there is a superior tenancy which
was unfurnished and a sub-tenancy which was furnished and the
superior tenancy comes to an end. In such a situation the landlord under the superior tenancy has the right within six weeks from
the day on which the superior tenancy ends to serve notice on the
sub-tenant that he requires s. 138 to apply to the sub-tenancy. The
effect is that the terms on which the sub-tenant is (by virtue of
s. 137(2)) deemed to become the tenant of the landlord will not
include any terms as to the provision by the landlord of furniture or services: s. 138(1).

41. Obligation to notify sub-lettings. In conclusion on this section
on sub-tenancies, students should note that s. 139 provides that if the
tenant of a dwelling-house let on or subject to a protected or statutory tenancy sub-lets any part of the dwelling-house on a protected
tenancy, within 14 days after the sub-letting he must supply the landlord with a written statement giving particulars of the sub-letting.
Failure to do so or the supplying of a false statement is an offence.

PROGRESS TEST 17

1. What constitutes suitable alternative accommodation?   **(5)**
2. Why are the Cases in Part I of the Rent Act 1977, Sch. 15
discretionary? How does the court exercise its discretion?   **(7)**

3. Which Case is most commonly relied upon by a landlord seeking to recover possession? **(8)**

4. In what way can Cases 5, 8 and 9 be distinguished from the remaining cases in Part I? **(7)**

5. What are the elements of Case 9? **(16–18)**

6. How does the court consider the question of greater hardship? **(18)**

7. L lets premises to T on a protected tenancy. L sells his interest to X who wishes to have his daughter live in the premises. How, if at all, can X do this? **(16)**

8. Which Cases should a landlord rely upon in the following instance to recover possession from T, the tenant of a flat: (a) T uses the flat as a brothel; (b) T sub-lets the flat at an excessive rent; (c) T damages the furniture; (d) T damages the flat? **(2, 9, 11, 10)**

9. How may an owner-occupier let his house and be certain of recovering possession of it when he wishes to return to live there? **(21)**

10. What is the position of an owner-occupier who wishes to rely upon Case 11 but who has failed to give the necessary notice? **(22)**

11. Which are the mandatory Cases for possession? **(20)**

12. L lets flats to tourists in London on short holiday lettings. At the end of one of these, L lets a flat to T on a letting which is not a holiday letting and which is for six months. How can L recover possession from T? Would your answer be different if the letting to T was for nine months? **(26)**

13. Which court normally deals with possession proceedings? **(32)**

14. L lets a flat to T on a protected tenancy. L sells his interest to X Ltd., a property company, which cuts off T's electricity and water supplies, and bars his entrance to the flat. Advise X. **(34, 35)**

15. L lets a shop and flat to T who uses the shop as a business and sub-lets the flat to S. T surrenders his lease to L. Advise S. **(38)**

16. L lets a flat to X Ltd. which sub-lets it to S, one of its directors. X's tenancy comes to an end. Advise S. **(37)**

17. L lets a house to T on a lease for 99 years at a rent of £1 per year. T sub-lets the house to S at a full rent. T's lease comes to an end. Advise S. **(39)**

CHAPTER XVIII

Rent Control

RENTS UNDER REGULATED TENANCIES

1. Rents under regulated tenancies. There are two main situations to consider, and they are:

(*a*) where a rent is registered under the Rent Act 1977, Part IV; and

(*b*) where no rent is registered.

The actual process and mechanics of registration are dealt with later (*see* **13** *et seq.*). This section is concerned with the actual limits on the rent a landlord may recover under a regulated tenancy according to whether a rent is registered (*see* **2–4**) or not (*see* **5** *et seq.*).

2. The limit where a rent is registered. There are two cases to consider:

(*a*) when the tenancy is a contractual tenancy; i.e. the rent limit during contractual periods (*see* **3**); and

(*b*) when the tenancy is a statutory tenancy, i.e. the rent limit during statutory periods (*see* **4**).

3. Limit of rent during contractual periods. The Rent Act 1977, s. 44(1) provides that where a rent is registered the rent recoverable during any contractual period of a regulated tenancy is limited to the rent so registered. Section 44(2) provides that that where any rent payable under the tenancy exceeds the limit it is irrecoverable from the tenant.

Where the registered rent exceeds the contractual rent the landlord is unable to recover the excess so long as the contractual tenancy continues and the tenant will be bound only to pay the sum registered.

EXAMPLES: (1) L lets a flat to T at a contractual rent of £30 per week. A fair rent of £25 per week is registered. The rent limit is therefore £25 and the landlord cannot lawfully charge or recover more than that.

(2) L lets a flat to T at a contractual rent of £30 per week. The tenancy is for two years. A fair rent of £40 per week is registered. For the duration of the tenancy L cannot recover more than £30 because that is the maximum recoverable under the contract. L cannot increase the rent until the end of the two years unless the contract provides for an increase.

4. Limit of rent during statutory periods. During statutory periods the rent limit is the registered rent: Rent Act 1977, s. 45(2). The landlord cannot recover more than the registered rent: s. 45(2). During a statutory period, however, if the rent is less than the registered rent, the landlord can increase it up to the registered rent by means of a notice of increase. The amount by which it can be increased in any one year may be limited, for the Act provides that certain increases in rent must be "phased" i.e. increased in stages over a period of years.

5. Where no rent is registered. The relevant provisions are contained in the Rent Act 1977, ss. 51, 52, 54. Their effect can be summarised in the following way:

(*a*) where the tenant is a new tenant, there is no limit on rent payable under a contractual tenancy;

(*b*) where the tenant was tenant under a regulated tenancy and is granted a new tenancy of the same premises the rent limit is the amount payable at the end of the former tenancy;

(*c*) where the tenant is the tenant under a subsisting tenancy, the limit is the rent payable under that tenancy, i.e. the contractual rent under it;

(*d*) in the case of a statutory period, the limit is the rent payable during the last contractual period.

6. Lawful increases in the recoverable rent. The rent which the landlord can lawfully recover is subject to the above limits where no rent is registered. The Rent Act 1977, s. 51(1), however, gives the landlord a lawful means whereby he may increase the rent *provided* the tenant agrees and the agreement is in a specified form. The agreement is called a "rent agreement with a tenant having security of tenure," and means either:

(*a*) an agreement increasing the rent payable under a regulated tenancy; or

(*b*) the grant to the tenant under a regulated tenancy of another tenancy of the dwelling-house at a rent exceeding the rent under the previous tenancy: s. 51(1).

7. Form of the rent agreement. The Rent Act 1977, s. 51(3), (4) require the rent agreement to be in a specified form. Failure to comply with this requirement means that any increase in rent (other than an increase on account of rates payable by the landlord) is irrecoverable from the tenant: s. 54(1). The requirements are:

(*a*) the agreement must be in writing signed by the landlord and the tenant; and

(*b*) the document containing the agreement must contain a statement in characters not less conspicuous than those used in other parts of the agreement:

(*i*) that the tenant's security of tenure under the Act will not be affected if he refuses to enter into the agreement; and

(*ii*) that if the agreement were not made but instead a rent were registered under Part IV of the Act, part only of any increase over the rent previously recoverable by the landlord would be payable by the tenant during the first year (this is a new provision and was enacted by the Housing Act 1980, s. 68(1)); and

(*iii*) that entry into the agreement will not deprive the tenant or landlord of the right to apply to the rent officer for the registration of a fair rent, or words to that effect; and

(*c*) the statement in (*b*) must be set out at the head of the agreement.

8. Limit of rent during statutory periods. Section 45 provides that the rent payable for any statutory period is not to exceed the rent recoverable for the last preceding contractual period. Accordingly to determine the rent limit for any statutory period it is necessary to consider (*see* **3–7**) what was the rent limit under the contractual tenancy; that will be the limit in the statutory period. This limit may be increased or decreased by permitted adjustments. They are:

(*a*) adjustments with respect to rates: s. 46;

(*b*) adjustments with respect to the provision of services and furniture: s. 47.

The increase under s. 46 can only be made in pursuance of a notice of increase served by the landlord on the tenant (*see* **10**).

9. Miscellaneous matters. Before the system of registration is considered, there remain several miscellaneous matters to consider. They are:

(*a*) notices of increase (*see* **10**);

(b) phasing (see **11**); and
(c) the recovery of over payments (see **12**).

10. Notices of increase. Notices of increase are required in certain circumstances to increase the rent to a new limit. A notice of increase must be in the prescribed form: Rent Act 1977, s. 49(2). Where a notice of increase is served during a contractual period and the protected tenancy could have been ended by notice to quit given by the landlord at the same time, the notice of increase operates to convert the protected tenancy into a statutory tenancy: s. 49(4). Notices of increase are required:

(a) under s. 46: see **8** above;
(b) when a rent is registered and it is desired to increase the rent up to the registered rent.

11. Phasing. This is a process whereby certain rent increases are staged or phased over two or three years. There are complicated provisions for determining the actual amount of each phased increase. The most important case where there will be phasing is where a rent has been registered and the rent payable under the tenancy has to be increased up to that registered rent. By s. 55 it is provided that in that situation the increase must be phased.

12. Recovery of over-payment. Section 57 of the Rent Act 1977, enables a tenant who has paid rent in excess of the rent limit to recover it from the landlord or his personal representatives. Alternatively the tenant may set it off against future rent due to the landlord. It is only recoverable for up to two years after it was paid. In the case of a breach of s. 54(1) (see **7** above), the period is one year.

THE SYSTEM OF REGISTRATION OF FAIR RENTS

13. Registration of rents under regulated tenancies. This system was set up by the 1965 Act; the provisions are now contained in Part IV of the 1977 Act. There are separate registration areas each with its own rent officers and rent assessment committee. Applications are made first to the rent officer and can then be referred to the committee.

14. The register of rents. Section 66 of the Rent Act 1977 requires the rent officer for any area to prepare and keep up to date a register of rents available for inspection. It must contain:

(*a*) the rent payable;

(*b*) certain prescribed particulars;

(*c*) a specification of the dwelling-house.

15. Application for registration. An application for the registration of a fair rent may be made to the rent officer by:

(*a*) the landlord;

(*b*) the tenant;

(*c*) jointly by landlord and tenant; or

(*d*) the local authority.

The application must be made in the prescribed form and contain certain prescribed particulars. Where a rent is already registered prior to 28th November 1980, an application cannot be made within three years from the date on which the existing registration took effect. An application may be made in that three-year period on the ground that there has been a change, such as to make the registered rent no longer a fair rent, in

(*a*) the condition of the dwelling-house;

(*b*) the terms of the tenancy;

(*c*) the quantity, quality or condition of any furniture provided;

(*d*) any other circumstances considered when the rent was registered.

In the case of a rent registered after 28th November 1980, an application may be made after only two years: Housing Act 1980, s. 60. An application may be made in that two year period if there has been a change as set out above.

16. Procedure on application to rent officer. Schedule 11 to the Rent Act 1977 contains the detailed provisions for procedure on an application; in outline, it is as follows. The rent officer has power to, and may, require the giving of further information by the parties. Then he must give notice of the application to them and specify a period during which representations can be made to him. Thereafter he may, if necessary, consider in consultation with the parties (who may be represented) what rent ought to be registered. Then he must either determine a fair rent and register it or confirm the existing rent in the register and notify the parties of his decision. They can then object to it within 28 days. If they do object, the rent will automatically be referred to a rent assessment committee.

17. Determination by rent assessment committee. The committee consists of a chairman and one or two other members. The procedure before the committee is similar to that before the rent officer. The committee may first require the parties to give further information. Thereafter the landlord or the tenant may make representations in writing or request leave to make oral representations. Where a party requests leave to make oral representations the committee must give him an opportunity to be heard. Thereafter the committee will decide either to confirm the rent fixed by the rent officer or if it does not appear to it that it is a fair rent it will determine a fair rent. The landlord and tenant are then notified. The decision of the committee must be in writing, signed and contain the reasons for the decision. The decision may be challenged on a point of law in the High Court.

18. Certificate of fair rent. Section 69 of the Rent Act 1977 provides that a person intending either to provide a dwelling-house by the erection conversion or improvement of any premises, or to let on a regulated tenancy a dwelling-house which is not the subject of such a tenancy and for which no rent is registered or has been registered in the last two years, may apply to the rent officer for a certificate specifying the rent, which in the opinion of the rent officer, would be a fair rent. There are detailed provisions in Sch. 12 concerning certificates and applications for them. When a certificate has been issued, an application for registration in accordance with the certificate may be made within two years of the date of the certificate. In such a case the procedure on an application for registration is different and enquiry is directed to ensuring that:

(*a*) any works required by the certificate to be carried out have been carried out; or

(*b*) the condition of the house is the same as it was at the date of the issue of the certificate; or

(*c*) if furniture is provided it accords with the particulars given in the application for a certificate as being furniture to be provided when a letting takes place.

19. Determination of a fair rent. A "fair rent" is not defined. Section 70(1) provides that in determining a fair rent regard must be had to all the circumstances (other than personal circumstances) and in particular to

(*a*) the age, character, locality and state of repair of the dwelling-house; and (*b*) the quantity and quality and condition of any furniture which is provided.

No account is taken of scarcity of accommodation in assessing a fair rent: s. 70(2). By s. 70(3) there is also disregarded, in assessing a fair rent, the following:

(*a*) disrepair due to a failure by the tenant to carry out his obligations;

(*b*) improvements carried out by the tenant, other than those carried out in pursuance of an obligation;

(*c*) the provision in the locality after the material date, of any new amenity or the improvement of any existing amenity where the amenity is provided or improved at the cost of someone other than the landlord;

(*d*) any deterioration after the material date in the amenities of the locality;

(*e*) any improvement to the furniture by the tenant or any deterioration due to ill-treatment by the tenant.

The "material date" means where a rent is registered the date of registration, otherwise 8th March 1971.

20. Effect of registration of rent. The Rent Act 1977, s. 72 (as substituted by the Housing Act 1980, s. 61) provides that the registration of a rent takes effect as follows:

(*a*) if the rent is determined by the rent officer, from the date when it is registered;

(*b*) if the rent is determined by the rent assessment committee, from the date when the committee makes its decision;

(*c*) if the rent is confirmed by the rent officer, from the date when it is noted in the register;

(*d*) if confirmed by the rent assessment committee, from the date when the committee makes its decision.

PREMIUMS

21. Introduction. The provisions of the Rent Act concerning premiums are designed to prevent the evasion of the other provisions concerning rent restriction by the landlord or some other person demanding a capital sum for the grant of assignment of a protected tenancy. These provisions prohibit the taking of a premium in two situations:

(a) on the grant, renewal or continuance of a protected tenancy: Rent Act 1977, s. 119;

(b) on the assignment of a protected tenancy: s. 120.

22. Definition. A premium is defined as including

(a) any fine or other like sum;

(b) any other pecuniary consideration in addition to the rent; and

(c) any sum paid by way of a deposit, other than one which does not exceed one-sixth of the annual rent and is reasonable in relation to the potential liability in respect of which it is paid: Rent Act 1977, s. 128.

The usual form which a premium will take is that of a capital sum. By s. 123 of the Act, however, where the purchase of any furniture has been required as a condition of the grant, renewal, continuance or assignment of a protected tenancy, if the price exceeds the reasonable price for the furniture the excess is treated for the purposes of the Act as if it were a premium required to be paid as a condition of the grant, renewal, continuance or assignment of the interest.

23. Premiums on the grant, renewal or continuance of a protected tenancy. Section 119 provides that "any person" who, as a condition of the grant, renewal or continuance of a protected tenancy, requires in addition to the rent the payment of any premium or the making of any loan will be guilty of an offence. It extends also to any person who in connection with the grant, etc., receives any premium. The court by which the person is convicted may order the repayment of the premium to the person by whom it was paid.

24. Exceptions to s. 119. There are exceptions to the rule contained in s. 119. They are dealt with in s. 127 (as amended by the Housing Act 1980, s. 78). The exception concerns tenancies which are both a long tenancy and a protected tenancy. The detailed provisions are outside the scope of this book and reference should be made to other books on this point.

25. Premiums on the assignment of a protected tenancy. Section 120 of the Rent Act 1977 provides that "any person" who, as a condition of the assignment of a protected tenancy, requires the payment of any premium or the making of any loan will be guilty of an offence. It also extends to any person who in connection with the assignment of a protected tenancy receives any premium. There are, however, certain sums which, by virtue of s. 120(3), an assignor of a protected tenancy is entitled to require or receive from the assignee:

(*a*) outgoings paid by the assignor and referable to any period after the assignment takes effect;

(*b*) a sum not exceeding the amount of any expenditure reasonably incurred by the assignor in carrying out any structural alteration of the dwelling-house;

(*c*) where the assignor acquired the tenancy by an assignment, the amount of any sum he paid to his assignor under (*b*) above;

(*d*) if part of the premises are used for a business, payment for goodwill.

26. Exceptions to s. 120. There are three main exceptions to the rule (*see* **25**) in s. 120; they are:

(*a*) where a premium was lawfully required or received at the commencement of the tenancy: s. 120(5);

(*b*) where a premium was lawfully required on the grant, renewal or continuance of a regulated tenancy

   (*i*) which was granted before 8th March 1973; and

   (*ii*) which was brought into protection by the increasing of the rateable values by the Counter-Inflation Act 1973;

(*c*) on the assignment of a tenancy which satisfies the conditions in s. 127 (*see* **24** above).

As can be seen, the first two situations cover tenancies not originally subject to the restrictions on premiums (i.e. because the tenancy was not at the time of payment of the premium protected by the legislation) but which have subsequently become subject to the restrictions. In these circumstances it would obviously be unfair on the person who paid the lawful premium (at the time when the tenancy was not protected) to prevent him from receiving a payment for the tenancy. Sections 120(5), 121 therefore allow the tenant to require a premium calculated in accordance with the detailed provisions contained in Sch. 18. Broadly speaking this enables the tenant to require a premium which is a proportion of the lawful premium originally required. The proportion is, in effect, equal to the proportion which the residue of the term at the time of the assignment bears to the whole of the term.

27. The meaning of the words "any person". The words used in the Rent Act 1977, ss. 119, 120 are "any person who . . . . requires the payment of any premium". The meaning of these words has recently been considered by the House of Lords, in the following case:

> *Farrell* v. *Alexander* (1976). A had a protected tenancy of a flat which she wished to assign to F for £4,000 for "fixtures and fittings". The landlords were entitled under the terms of the tenancy to require a surrender of the tenancy but they were prepared to grant a new tenancy to F. An agreement was made between A and F that F would pay A £4,000 on the grant of the new lease. This duly took place. F then sued A to recover the amount by which the £4,000 exceeded the reasonable price of the furniture. The question arose whether A fell within the words "any person" or whether those words were confined to the landlord, in which case it would not affect this transaction. There were two earlier decisions of the Court of Appeal which supported the narrower construction. The House of Lords HELD: The words "any person" were not restricted to a landlord but included anyone who, as a condition of the grant of a tenancy, required the payment of a premium. It therefore extended to A who would have to pay back to F the difference between the £4,000 and the reasonable cost of the furniture.

28. The recovery of unlawful premiums. As can be seen (*see* **27**) from *Farrell* v. *Alexander*, it is possible to recover an unlawful premium by an action in the courts. This is the result of the Rent Act 1977, s. 125 which provides that where under any agreement any premium is paid and the whole or any part of it could not lawfully be required then the amount of it or, so much of it as could not lawfully be required, is recoverable by the person by whom it was paid. The normal way of recovering it will be by an action in the county court.

PROGRESS TEST 18

1. What details does the register of rents contain? **(14)**

2. Who may make an application for the registration of a fair rent? **(15)**

3. What is the procedure adopted on the determination of an application for the registration of a fair rent? **(16)**

4. What means is there of challenging a fair rent assessed by the rent officer? **(17)**

5. What criteria are adopted in determining a "fair rent"? **(19)**

6. What is a certificate of fair rent? **(18)**

7. For how long is a registered rent effective? **(15)**

8. What is the rent limit when a tenancy is a contractual tenancy? **(3)**

9. What is a rent agreement with a tenant having security of tenure? How does it limit the recoverable rent? What form must it take? **(7)**

10. What is the rent limit during statutory periods of a regulated tenancy? **(8)**

11. How may a landlord increase the rent payable by a regulated tenant up to the rent limit? **(8)**

12. How may a tenant recover rent which he has paid to his landlord over the rent limit? **(12)**

13. What is a premium? **(22)**

14. What restrictions apply to the taking of a premium on the grant or assignment of a protected tenancy? **(23, 25)**

15. In what circumstances may a landlord take a premium on the grant or assignment of a protected tenancy? **(24)**

16. What is the importance of the decision in *Farrell* v. *Alexander*? **(27)**

CHAPTER XIX

Restricted Contracts

INTRODUCTION

1. History. Until 1974 a tenancy could not be a protected one if the dwelling-house was let at a rent which included payments in respect of board, attendance or the use of furniture. A system was evolved to protect tenants under such tenancies, providing rent limits and a measure of security of tenure. Under the 1968 Act these contracts and other lettings where the tenant shared accommodation with his landlord were called "Part VI Contracts", Part VI being the Part of that Act in which they were dealt with.

In 1974 furnished tenancies were brought into line with unfurnished tenancies and given protection. At the same time the resident-landlord exception was created and tenancies falling within that exception were given the old Part VI protection. In the 1977 Act the contracts falling within the old Part VI have been given a new name—restricted contracts.

2. Definition. Section 19 of the Rent Act 1977 provides that a restricted contract is one whereby one person grants to another person, in consideration of a rent which includes payment for the use of furniture or for services, the right to occupy a dwelling as a residence (s. 19(1)). This is a wide definition and might appear to cover a large number of contracts including regulated tenancies. It is subject, however, to a number of exceptions and a contract is not a restricted contract if:

(*a*) it creates a regulated tenancy: s. 19(5)(a);

(*b*) the interest of the landlord belongs to the Crown or a Government Department but not the Duchy of Lancaster, the Duchy of Cornwall nor the Crown Estate Commissioners: s. 19(5) (b);

(*c*) the rent includes payment for board and the value of the board to the tenant is a substantial portion of the whole rent: s. 19(5)(c),

(*d*) it is a protected occupancy under the Rent (Agriculture) Act 1976: s. 19(5)(d);

(*e*) it is a housing association tenancy: s. 19(5)(e);

(*f*) it is a holiday letting: s. 19(7);

(*g*) the occupier does not have exclusive occupation of some part of the dwelling-house: s. 19(6);

(*h*) it is outside the rateable value limits (*see* **3**);

(*i*) the landlord's interest belongs to local authorities, the Commission for New Towns, a development corporation or the Development Board for Rural Wales.

3. The rateable value limits. A contract is not a restricted one if it falls within one of the classes in the Rent Act 1977, s. 19(4). These are as follows:

(*a*) *Class D.* The appropriate day in relation to the dwelling falls or fell on or after 1st April 1973 and the dwelling on the appropriate day has or had a rateable value exceeding £1,500 or £750.

(*b*) *Class E.* The appropriate day in relation to the dwelling fell before 1st April 1973 and the dwelling had a rateable value exceeding:

(*i*) on the appropriate day £400 or £200; and

(*ii*) on 1st April 1973, £1,500 or £750.

The meaning of "the appropriate day" has already been considered in relation to protected tenancies (*see* XV, **12**).

4. Where a restricted contract arises. The preceding two paragraphs contain what is, with its detailed exceptions, a complicated definition. It will most assist students simply to know what are the main situations where a restricted contract may arise. They are where:

(*a*) there is a resident landlord under the Rent Act 1977, s. 12 (*see* XV, **27**);

(*b*) the tenant shares accommodation with the landlord and comes within s. 21 (*see* XV, **10**);

(*c*) certain residential licences have been granted.

The resident-landlord exception and sharing under s. 21 have already been considered. It is therefore only necessary to consider which residential licences are restricted contracts. It should be noted that unlike the general protection given by the Rent Act, the protection given to restricted contracts applies to licences as well as to tenancies.

5. Residential licences. Section 19 requires that there be a contract whereby one person is granted the right to occupy a dwelling as a residence. This may apply to a lodger or other residential licensee.

Luganda v. *Service Hotels Ltd.* (1968). A student had a furnished room in an hotel. He had his own key to the room which was a bed-sittingroom with a gas-ring. The room was cleaned by the hotel owners. HELD: The student was a contractual licensee who came within the (old) Part VI protection.

R. v. *South Middlesex Rent Tribunal, ex p. Beswick* (1976). B lived in a single furnished room at a YWCA hostel. The room was her home and she was a permanent resident. She had the use of various communal facilities. HELD: She was a residential licensee and was entitled to the protection of Part VI of the 1968 Act.

6. The protection given to restricted contracts. The general scheme of protection is that:

(*a*) there is control of rents;

(*b*) there is a limited security of tenure.

The body responsible for assessing rents and deciding if a tenant should have security of tenure is the rent assessment committee which, when constituted to carry out these functions, is known as a rent tribunal (*see* the Housing Act 1980, s. 72).

RENT CONTROL

7. Rents under restricted contracts. A restricted contract may be referred to the rent tribunal for the appropriate district by the lessor, the lessee or the local authority: Rent Act 1977, s. 77. Where a restricted contract is referred to a rent tribunal and the reference is not, before the tribunal has entered upon consideration of it, withdrawn by the party or authority who made it, the tribunal must consider it: s. 78. After making appropriate enquiries and giving the parties an opportunity to be heard the tribunal may approve, reduce or increase the rent payable as they think is reasonable and must notify the parties of its decision. If a rent has already been registered under Part IV (i.e. registered rents under regulated tenancies) the rent tribunal cannot reduce the rent below that registered sum. It is the duty of the president of every rent assessment panel to keep an up-to-date register of rents under restricted contracts where the tribunal has considered the rent: s. 79. The register must contain details of the rent, the contract and the dwelling.

8. Reconsideration of registered rent. Where the rent payable for a dwelling has been entered in the register under the Rent Act 1977, s. 79 the lessor, lessee or local authority may refer the case to the tribunal for reconsideration of the rent entered. Where a rent has been entered within the last two years however, the tribunal cannot be required to hear a further reference in the two-year period unless either

(*a*) the application is made jointly by the lessor and lessee; or

(*b*) there has been a change in:

(*i*) the condition of the dwelling;

(*ii*) the furniture or services provided;

(*iii*) the terms of the contract; or

(*iv*) any other circumstances taken into consideration when the rent was last considered,

so as to make the registered rent no longer a reasonable rent: s. 80. In this context "lessor" and "lessee" indicate the owner and occupier of the property when the contract is a licence only.

9. Effect of registration of rent. Where the rent for any dwelling is entered in the register under the Rent Act 1977, s. 79, it is not lawful to require or receive on account of rent for that dwelling under a restricted contract payment of any sum in excess of the rent so registered: s. 81. Where any rent has been paid in contravention of s. 81, the amount of the excess is recoverable by the person by whom it was paid. It is also a criminal offence for any person to require or receive any payment in contravention of s. 81. Proceedings may only be commenced by the local authority.

10. Premiums. Section 122 of the Rent Act 1977 provides that where a rent is registered under s. 79, any person who as a condition of the grant, renewal, continuance or assignment of rights under a restricted contract requires the payment of any premium will be guilty of a criminal offence. This does not prevent a person from requiring the payment of:

(*a*) outgoings referable to any period after the grant or assignment takes place; or

(*b*) a reasonable amount in respect of the goodwill of a business trade or profession where the goodwill is transferred in connection with the grant or assignment.

SECURITY OF TENURE

11. Introduction. In relation to restricted contracts entered into before 28th November 1980, the statutory provisions operate in the following way. Where a notice to quit is served by the landlord, the operation of that notice may be deferred by the rent tribunal for one or more periods of up to six months depending upon the circumstances of the case. This means that the security of tenure provisions apply only to periodic tenancies, not to tenancies for a fixed term. There are two situations to be considered in relation to security of tenure. They are where notice to quit is served

(*a*) after a reference is made to the rent tribunal (*see* **12**); and

(*b*) before a reference is made but where reference is made before the notice to quit expires (*see* **13**).

12. Notice to quit served after reference to tribunal. Section 103 of the Rent Act 1977 provides that if after a reference by the lessee or the local authority the lessor gives notice to the lessee at any time before the decision of the tribunal is given or within the period of six months thereafter then the notice will not take effect before the end of that period. This is subject to two exceptions:

(*a*) notice to quit served by an owner-occupier; and

(*b*) where the period of notice is reduced under s. 106.

13. Notice to quit served by an owner-occupier. Section 105 of the Rent Act 1977 provides that s. 103 does not apply where a person who has occupied the dwelling as a residence ("the owner-occupier") has, by a restricted contract, granted the right to occupy the dwelling to another person, and

(*a*) at or before the time when the right was granted the owner-occupier had given written notice that he was the owner-occupier; and

(*b*) if the dwelling is part of a house, the owner-occupier does not occupy any other part of the house as his residence; and

(*c*) at the time the notice is to take effect, the dwelling is required as a residence for the owner-occupier or any member of his family who resided with him when he last occupied the dwelling as a residence.

14. Reduction of the period of notice on account of the lessee's default. Section 106(2) provides that where it appears to the tribunal on an application by the lessor for a direction that:

(a) the lessee has not complied with the terms of the contract; or

(b) the lessee of any person residing or lodging with him has been guilty of conduct which is a nuisance or annoyance to adjoining occupiers or has been convicted of using the dwelling or allowing the dwelling to be used for an immoral or illegal purpose; or

(c) the condition of the dwelling has deteriorated owing to any act of neglect of the lessee or any person residing or lodging with him; or

(d) the condition of any furniture provided for the use of the lessee has deteriorated owing to any ill-treatment by the lessee or any person residing or lodging with him;

the tribunal may reduce the period for the operation of the notice to quit.

15. Application to tribunal. In a case where

(a) notice to quit a dwelling subject to a restricted contract has been served; and

(b) the restricted contract has been referred to a rent tribunal; and

(c) the period of the notice to quit has not expired,

the lessee may apply to the tribunal for the extension of the period of the notice to quit: Rent Act 1977, s. 104(1). On an application by a lessee under s. 104, after making appropriate enquiries and giving the parties an opportunity of being heard, the tribunal may direct that the notice to quit have no effect until the end of such period as it may direct. The period cannot exceed six months from the date on which the notice to quit would have taken effect. At the end of the extended period a further application for a further extension can be made. Thus indefinite security of tenure can be given. If the tribunal refuses to make a direction the lessee cannot make a further application.

It should be noted that an application by a lessee under s. 104 is subject to s. 106 (see **14**) and so the landlord may apply for a direction reducing the period on the grounds specified in that section. If such a direction is made then no further application can be made by the lessee.

16. Recovery of possession. In order to recover possession of a dwelling which is subject to a restricted contract, the landlord must first serve notice to quit (assuming the tenancy is a periodic one). The tenant may then apply for security of tenure to the rent tribunal. If the tribunal directs that the notice is not to take effect for a specified period, the landlord must await the expiry of that period. At the end of that period (or any further extended period) he can recover possession. To recover possession, however, he will normally have to bring proceedings in the courts. This is the effect of the Protection from Eviction Act 1977, s. 3, which provides that it is not lawful for an owner to enforce his right to possession otherwise than by proceedings in the court.

17. Security of tenure under contract entered into after 28th November 1980. In relation to these contracts, the rent tribunal will have no jurisdiction to defer the operation of a notice to quit. Instead, in proceedings for possession, the court is given power to postpone the date for possession for up to three months: Rent Act 1977, s. 106a (added by the Housing Act 1980, s. 69(2)).

PROGRESS TEST 19

1. What were Part VI contracts? What effect did the Rent Act 1977 have upon them? **(1)**

2. What are the rateable value limits in relation to restricted contracts? **(3)**

3. In what main situations do restricted contracts arise? **(4)**

4. Is a holiday letting capable of being a restricted contract? **(2)**

5. In what ways does the protection given to an occupier under a restricted contract differ from that given to a tenant under a protected tenancy? **(15–17)**

6. What is a rent assessment committee? What is a rent tribunal, how is it constituted and what are its functions? What is the difference between these bodies? **(6)**

7. May a resident landlord charge a premium on the grant of a tenancy of a dwelling-house in the same building as that in which he lives? **(10)**

8. L lets a flat to T on a weekly tenancy. L is a resident landlord and serves notice to quit on T. Advise L what rights T has. What would be the position if T had a tenancy for a fixed term which had expired? **(15–17)**

9. How may a landlord recover possession of a dwelling subject to a restricted contract? **(16)**

PART FOUR

LONG LEASES

CHAPTER XX

Long Residential Leases

LANDLORD AND TENANT ACT 1954, PART I

1. Generally. Long residential leases have had a varied history as regards statutory protection. They were not excluded from the early Rent Acts but in practice many were outside those Acts because they were at a low rent. Protection was then given by Part I of the Landlord and Tenant Act 1954 to tenants under long leases at a low rent. In 1957, protection under Part I was extended to all long leaseholders irrespective of the rent; this was as a result of the Rent Act 1957 which, at the same time, excluded *all* long leases from the Rent Act protection. The Leasehold Reform Act 1967 restored the pre–1957 position. The position now is that long leases at a low rent are

(*a*) outside the Rent Act because they are at a low rent; and
(*b*) within Part I of the 1954 Act.

All other long leases of residential properties at rents which are not low rents are within the Rent Acts (unless of course there is some other factor to exclude them).

2. Tenancies within Part I. In order to fall within the Landlord and Tenant Act 1954, Part I, a tenancy must be one to which s. 1 of the Act applies. By s. 2 of the Act a tenancy is one to which s. 1 applies if it satisfies the following three conditions:

(*a*) the tenancy must be a long one (*see* **3**);
(*b*) the rent must be a low rent (*see* **4**);
(*c*) the tenancy must fulfill "the qualifying condition" (*see* **5**).

3. A long tenancy. A long tenancy is one granted for a term of years certain exceeding 21 years: s. 2(4). Where a long tenancy comes to an end and the tenant becomes tenant under another tenancy at a low rent, the second tenancy is deemed to be a long one irrespective of its terms: s. 19(1).

EXAMPLE: T holds under two successive tenancies at low rents from 1950 to 1975 and from 1975 to 1990. The second tenancy is, by s. 19(1), deemed to be a long tenancy because it follows an earlier long tenancy at a low rent.

4. At a low rent. This expression means a tenancy where the rent payable is less than two-thirds of the rateable value of the property: Landlord and Tenant Act 1954, s. 2(5). The rateable value here is that which would be taken as the rateable value for the purposes of the Rent Act 1977, s. 5 (*see* XV, **19**). It must be remembered that in determining whether a long tenancy is at a low rent, there must be disregarded such part of the sums payable by the tenant as is expressed to be payable in respect of rates, services, repairs, maintenance or insurance: *see* s. 5(4) of the 1977 Act and s. 2(7) of the 1954 Act.

5. The qualifying condition. The qualifying condition is "that the circumstances (as respects the property comprised in the tenancy, the use of that property, and all other relevant matters) are such that on the coming to an end of the tenancy at that time the tenant would, if the tenancy had not been one at a low rent, be entitled by virtue of the Rent Act to retain possession of the whole or part of the property comprised in the tenancy": Landlord and Tenant Act 1954, s. 2(1).

This means that it is necessary to ask whether, if the tenancy were not at a low rent, it would be protected by the Rent Act 1977. There is required a consideration of the matters in XV, **5** *et seq*. The condition must be satisfied as at the "term date," that is to say as at the date of expiry of the term of the long tenancy.

If at any time in the last 12 months before the term date, it appears to the landlord that the qualifying condition is not fulfilled, he can apply to the court for an order declaring that the tenancy is not to be treated as one to which Part I applies: s. 2(2). If the court is satisfied that the tenancy is likely, immediately before the term date, to be a tenancy to which s. 1 does not apply, it must make such an order. The effect of such an order is that the tenant loses the protection of Part I as regards that tenancy.

6. Automatic continuance of tenancies. A tenancy which is current immediately before the term date and is then one to which Part I applies is automatically continued by the Act of 1954, s. 3 until it is ended in accordance with the provisions of Part I. This means that once the tenancy is continued beyond the term date it will carry on until ended by one of the specified methods of termination.

A distinction is made between the situation where the whole of the premises qualifies for protection and that where only a part so qualifies. The "premises qualifying for protection" means the premises of which, if the tenancy was not a long one at a low rent, the tenant could have retained possession as a statutory tenant under the Rent Act. Where the whole of the premises qualifies for protection, the tenancy continues on the same terms as before. When only a part qualifies for protection, the continuance is in respect of that part only and is at an apportioned rent and, if necessary, on modified terms.

METHODS OF TERMINATION

7. Termination by the tenant. The tenant may end a tenancy to which the Landlord and Tenant Act 1954, s. 1 applies in the following ways:

(a) by surrender: s. 17;

(b) by giving not less than one month's written notice to the immediate landlord to expire at the term date or later: s. 5.

8. Termination of tenancy by the landlord. The landlord may terminate a tenancy to which the Act of 1954, s. 1 applies by a notice given to the tenant. The notice must:

(a) be in the prescribed form (s. 4(1));

(b) specify the date at which the tenancy is to come to an end ("the date of termination"), and this must be the term date or a later date (s. 4(1));

(c) be given not more than twelve nor less than six months before the date of termination specified (s. 4(2));

(d) specify the premises the landlord believes to be, or to be likely to be, the premises qualifying for protection (s. 4(3)).

The notice will take one of two forms:

(a) a landlord's notice proposing a statutory tenancy (s. 4(3)(a): *see* **9**); or

(b) a landlord's notice to resume possession s. 4(3)(b): *see* **10**).

9. Landlord's notice proposing a statutory tenancy. A landlord will serve this form of notice when he wishes to bring up to date the terms upon which the tenant holds the premises but does not wish (or is unable) to recover possession. By virtue of the Act of 1954, s. 7(3), the notice must set out the landlord's proposals for the terms of the statutory tenancy:

    (*a*) the premises;

    (*b*) the rent, the amount and the manner of payment;

    (*c*) the responsibility for initial repairs (*see* below),

    (*d*) responsibility for repairs during the statutory tenancy; and

    (*e*) any other terms.

Following the service of the notice the parties will try to agree terms. If they cannot agree the landlord must apply to the county court to have them determined: Act of 1954, s. 7(1). The application must be made not less than two months after service of the notice and not less than two months before the date of termination: s. 7(2), (5). Failure to comply with this requirement renders the notice invalid.

10. Landlord's notice to resume possession. The landlord will serve this form of notice when he wishes to try to recover possession at the end of the long lease or at some time during its continuation under s. 3 (*see* **6**). The notice must:

    (*a*) be in the prescribed form (s. 4(1));

    (*b*) inform the tenant that, if he is not willing to give up possession at the date of termination, the landlord intends to apply to the court for possession on one or more of the grounds specified in s. 12 (s. 4(3)(b));

    (*c*) state the ground or grounds on which he proposes to apply (*ibid.*);

    (*d*) invite the tenant to notify the landlord in writing whether he is willing to give up possession at the date of termination (s. 4(4)).

11. Procedure following notice to resume possession. The effect of a notice to resume possession depends upon the tenant's response to it and whether the qualifying condition remains satisfied. The alternatives are:

    (*a*) if the tenant elects to retain possession within the two months, the landlord must apply to court for an order on the ground(s) in his notice: (Act of 1954, s. 13(1)(*a*));

    (*b*) if the tenant does not elect to retain possession but the qualifying condition is satisfied at the end of the two months, the landlord must apply to court (*ibid.* s. 13(1)(*b*));

(c) if the tenant does not elect to retain possession and the qualifying condition is not satisfied at the end of the two months, the landlord can recover possession without having to establish any of the specified grounds.

12. Application to court for possession. In cases (a) and (b) above the landlord must apply to the court within two months after the tenant elects to retain possession, or if he does not so elect, within four months of serving the notice: s. 13. The grounds upon which he can apply are those specified in the Landlord and Tenant Act 1954, Sch. 3, or, if the landlord is a local authority or other public body, upon a proposal to demolish or to reconstruct the whole or a substantial part of the premises: Act of 1954, s. 12(1).

13. The grounds in Schedule 3. Subject to the necessary modifications, the grounds in the Landlord and Tenant Act 1954, Sch. 3, correspond with Cases 1–9 of the Rent Act 1977, Sch. 15 (see XVII).

14. Making a possession order. On an application by the landlord relying on one of the grounds in the Act of 1954, Sch. 3, if the court is satisfied that the ground is established *and* that it is reasonable to make the order, the court must make the order: s. 13(1).

15. Position where landlord does not obtain order for possession. The rules governing this situation are as follows:

(a) if the landlord does not apply to court in the prescribed time his notice to resume possession will be of no more effect: s. 14(2);

(b) if the landlord makes his application but does not get an order, within one month of the final disposal of the matter he may serve a notice proposing a statutory tenancy and specifying as the date of termination a date not less than three months from the date of giving notice: s. 14(3). This is therefore a provision enabling the landlord to serve short notice proposing a statutory tenancy.

STATUTORY TENANCIES

16. Introduction. A statutory tenancy may arise in one of two ways:

(a) following a landlord's notice proposing a statutory tenancy; or

(b) following a landlord's unsuccessful application to court if he then serves notice under s. 14(3) (*see* **15**(*b*) above).

As has already been seen, the terms of the statutory tenancy will be agreed between the parties or, in default of agreement, determined by the court. Until the terms have been so agreed or determined, the long tenancy will continue until the date of termination or three months after the final disposal of the application by the court and any time for appealing has expired: Landlord and Tenant Act 1954, s. 64.

17. The application to the court to determine the terms. If the parties cannot agree the terms, the landlord must apply to court within a certain specified time to have the court determine the terms. By virtue of the Act of 1954, s. 7(2), the application must be made:

(a) during the currency of the notice proposing the statutory tenancy; and

(b) not during the first two months following service of the notice; and

(c) not during the last two months before the date of termination.

In the case of a short notice following a landlord's unsuccessful application to court, the period in which matters have to be agreed is adjusted. The terms must be agreed in the three months beginning with the service of the notice or application made to the court within that time.

18. Terms of the statutory tenancy: repairs. Under a long tenancy, the tenant will normally be responsible for all repairs. At the end of the term there may be considerable repairs necessary. Section 8 of the 1954 Act provides for the parties to agree or, in default the court to decide, terms for the carrying out of "initial repairs."

If the landlord is required to do initial repairs, he is entitled to payment from the tenant for doing them if they are required in consequence of failure by the tenant to fulfil his obligations under the former tenancy. The amount to which he is entitled is the cost reasonably incurred by the landlord in ascertaining what repairs are necessary and in carrying them out: s. 8(1).

A tenant can agree to carry out initial repairs, but the court cannot order him to do so unless he gives his consent: s. 9(3).

19. Rent. Until a rent is registered, the rent is the sum agreed between the parties or, in default of agreement, the rent payable under the former long tenancy. Either party may apply to the Rent Officer to have a rent registered. *See also* XVIII, **15** *et seq.*

20. The nature of the statutory tenancy. By virtue of the Act of 1954, s. 6, the statutory tenancy takes effect as a statutory tenancy arising under the Rent Act 1977 (*see* XVI).

MISCELLANEOUS PROVISIONS

21. Other provisions of Part I. Section 16 of the 1954 Act gives to tenants under long tenancies at a low rent special protection from forfeiture in addition to any rights to relief under the Law of Property Act 1925, s. 146. The special provisions are as follows.

(*a*) If a landlord seeks to forfeit the lease or seeks damages for breach of covenant when the tenancy has more than seven months to run, if the tenant applies for relief under s. 16, any order for possession or damages will have no effect except as to costs; the tenancy will then take effect as expiring in seven months.

(*b*) If a landlord seeks to forfeit the lease or seeks damages for breach of covenant when the tenancy has less than seven months to run and the tenant applies for relief, the court cannot make any order for possession or damages.

The effect of these provisions is that the landlord is prevented from forfeiting the lease *but* the operation of Part I is accelerated because in case (*a*) the tenancy is treated as having only seven months to run.

22. Exceptions to s. 16. The provisions of s. 16 do not apply to a failure to comply with any terms as to

(*a*) payment of rent or rates or insuring the premises,

(*b*) immoral or illegal user (Act of 1954, s. 16(4)).

23. Alternative relief. A tenant should be wary of applying for relief under s. 16 for he may be in a better position if he applies for relief from forfeiture under the general provisions (*see* VIII, **17, 26**). If a tenant applies under s. 16, the effect is to reduce his contractual term to seven months; if he obtains relief under the general law, his contractual term will continue unaffected and he will simply have to comply with the terms upon which relief was granted.

24. Contracting out. The provisions of Part I apply notwithstanding any agreement to the contrary. There can therefore be no contracting out of the Act.

25. Comparison with Part II. Part II of the 1954 Act applies to business tenancies. It will be seen, however, that there are several similarities between the two Parts. In particular:

(*a*) the notice procedure for determining the old tenancy and for agreeing or determining the terms of the new tenancy is similar;

(*b*) both Parts require strict compliance with the time limits and failure to comply with them may deprive the defaulting party of his statutory rights;

(*c*) the interim continuation provisions of s. 64 apply to both Parts.

PROGRESS TEST 20

1. L lets a flat to T:

    (*a*) for a term of 25 years at a low rent;
    (*b*) for a term of 22 years at a rack rent;
    (*c*) for a term of 10 years at a rack rent;
    (*d*) for a term of 5 years at a low rent.

By which Act is each lease protected? **(3, 4)**

2. What is a long tenancy? **(3)**

3. What is the test to determine if a long tenancy is at a low rent? **(4)**

4. What is the nature of the protection given to a long leaseholder at a low rent? **(4)**

5. What is the qualifying condition? When must it be satisfied? What is the effect if it is not satisfied within the last year before the end of the tenancy? **(5)**

6. How may a tenant end a tenancy protected by Part I of the Landlord and Tenant Act 1954? **(7)**

7. What is the effect of a notice proposing a statutory tenancy? What requirements must it satisfy? **(9)**

8. What steps must (*a*) the landlord, and (*b*) the tenant, take after the service of a notice proposing a statutory tenancy? **(9)**

9. Upon what grounds may a landlord seek to recover possession of a dwelling-house subject to Part I of the Landlord and Tenant Act 1954? **(13)**

10. What is a landlord's notice to resume possession? What requirements must it satisfy? **(10)**

11. What rent is payable by a tenant under a tenancy protected by Part I of the Landlord and Tenant Act 1954? **(19)**

12. What are initial repairs? Whose responsibility are they? **(18)**

13. In what ways do the interim continuation provisions of the Landlord and Tenant Act 1954, s. 64 affect a tenancy protected by Part I of that Act? **(16, 25)**

14. In what ways does Part I of the Landlord and Tenant Act 1954 affect the landlord's right to forfeit a lease for breach of covenant? **(22)**

15. What similarities are there between Parts I and II of the Landlord and Tenant Act 1954? **(25)**

CHAPTER XXI

The Leasehold Reform Act 1967

INTRODUCTION

1. Generally. The Leasehold Reform Act 1967 ("the 1967 Act") enables certain tenants of houses held on long leases at low rents to acquire the freehold of their house or an extended lease of it by the grant of an additional 50-year term. The 1967 Act came into operation on 1st January 1968. The process whereby a tenant may acquire the freehold is called enfranchisement.

The underlying principle of the 1967 Act is that it applies to long leases at a low (or ground) rent which would normally have been granted for a premium payable to the original landlord. In the case of such a lease the Act's approach is to treat the tenant as being the owner of the building, the landlord being left with the land, hence his entitlement to a ground rent only. Thus, when the compensation provisions in the Act are considered (*see* **17**) it will be seen that the landlord receives compensation assessed on the value of the site disregarding the buildings which are on it.

One of the main reasons for the legislation was that in the later part of the nineteenth century many 99-year leases were granted which have been falling in over the last 20 years or so. The Act was intended to alleviate hardship which might otherwise have been caused by the falling in of these leases and which Part I of the Landlord and Tenant Act 1954 was not able fully to deal with.

2. The scope of this chapter. The 1967 Act (as amended by the like-named Act of 1979) contains many complicated and detailed provisions for giving effect to the process of enfranchisement, for dealing with the different situations that may arise and for dealing with the interaction of the 1967 Act with other Acts such as Part I of the Landlord and Tenant Act 1954. This chapter does not attempt to deal with all these matters and simply gives a broad picture of the Act's operation.

STATUTORY CONDITIONS

3. The right to enfranchisement or extension. Section 1(1) provides
that a tenant of a house who satisfies certain conditions has a "right
to acquire on fair terms the freehold or an extended lease of the
house and premises." The conditions are:

(a) the tenant must be tenant of a leasehold house;

(b) his tenancy must be a long tenancy;

(c) the tenancy must be at a low rent;

(d) the rateable value of the house must be within specified
limits;

(e) the tenant must satisfy a residential condition.

4. The tenant of a leasehold house. The word house is defined by
s. 2(1) as including: "any building designed or adapted for living
in and reasonably so called, notwithstanding that the building is
not structurally detached, or was or is not solely designed or
adapted for living in, or is divided horizontally into flats or maison-
ettes; and

(a) where a building is divided horizontally, the flats or other
units into which it is so divided are not separate 'houses', though
the building as a whole may be; and

(b) where a building is divided vertically the building as a whole
is not a 'house' though any of the units into which it is divided
may be."

The effect of (a) is to exclude individual flats from the 1967
Act but an entire building divided into flats may be a house. The
effect of (b) is to exclude, say, a terrace of houses or a pair of
semi-detached houses although each property in the terrace or each
semi may be a house.

5. Premises with a mixed commercial and residential use. The House
of Lords has now decided that since Parliament clearly intended to
extend the benefit of the 1967 Act to tenants of premises which were
not exclusively designed or adapted for living in for residential purposes, it is only in exceptional circumstances that a judge will be
justified in holding that a building designed or adapted for occupation as a residence is not a house for the purposes of the 1967 Act:
Tandon v. *Trustees of Spurgeon's Homes* (1982). This means that
in all but the most exceptional circumstances, business premises
with integral residential premises will be within the 1967 Act.

6. House and premises. In parts of the 1967 Act reference is made to the "house and premises." For example, under s. 1(1), the tenant has the right to acquire the freehold or an extended lease of "the house and premises." The reference to premises is to be taken as referring to any garage, outhouse, garden, yard and appurtenances which at the relevant time are let to him with the house and are occupied with the house and used for the purposes of the house: s. 2(3).

7. A long tenancy. A long tenancy means one granted for a term of years certain exceeding 21 years: s. 3. The following points should be noted:

(*a*) A tenancy terminable before the end of such a term by notice given by or to the tenant or by re-entry or forfeiture or otherwise is, notwithstanding these matters, a long tenancy: s. 3(1).

(*b*) A tenancy granted so as to become terminable by notice after a death or marriage is not to be treated as a long tenancy if either:

(*i*) it was granted before 18th April 1980 or in pursuance of a contract entered into before that date; or

(*ii*) the notice is capable of being given at any time after the death or marriage of the tenant, the length of the notice is not more than three months and the terms of the tenancy preclude both its assignment and the sub-letting of the whole of the premises comprised in it.

(*c*) Where a tenant under a long tenancy at a low rent takes a new tenancy of the same property or part of it at the end of the long tenancy, the new tenancy is deemed to be a long one irrespective of its terms: s. 3(2).

(*d*) Where a tenant under a long tenancy takes another long tenancy of the same property or part of it at the end of the long one, the two long tenancies are treated as a single one running from the start of the first to the end of the second: s. 3(3).

(*e*) Where a tenancy is granted for 21 years or less, but there is a covenant for renewal, without payment of a premium, and the tenancy is or has been once more renewed so as to bring the total of the term to more than 21 years, the 1967 Act applies as it would if the term originally granted had been one exceeding 21 years: s. 3(4).

NOTE: It is important to remember that the term must *exceed* 21 years; this means that a term of 21 years will *not* be within the Act.

8. At a low rent. This requirement is designed to limit the leases to which the Act applies to those at a ground rent only. It does this by s. 4(1), which provides that a tenancy of any property is at a low rent at any time when the annual rent is less than two-thirds of the rateable value of the property on the appropriate day or, if later, the first day of the term. The "appropriate day" here means 23rd March 1965 or such later date as the house first appeared in the valuation list: s. 4(1)(a). "Rent" in this context means the rent reserved disregarding any part of the rent expressed to be payable for services to be provided or for repairs, maintenance or insurance to be effected by the landlord.

9. The proviso to s. 4(1). There is a proviso to s. 4(1) to the effect that, in the case of a tenancy created between the end of August 1939 and the beginning of April 1963, the tenancy will not be regarded as being one at a low rent if, at its commencement, the rent payable was more than two-thirds of the letting value of the property. This rule does not apply to building leases. The proviso is intended to benefit the landlord and to cover those cases where it might be said that the rateable value on the appropriate day was not a fair indication of the letting value of the house at the start of the tenancy. When any question arises on the operation of the proviso, s. 1(5) provides that it must be presumed in the tenant's favour that the proviso does not apply. This means that it will be for the landlord to bring evidence to prove that the letting value of the property was such that the tenancy should not be regarded as being at a low rent.

10. The time at which there must be a low rent. The requirement of a low rent must be satisfied for the three years prior to the claim and at the time the claim is made: Act of 1967, s. 1(1).

11. The rateable value of the house must be within specified limits. The following rules apply.

(a) The rateable value of the house and premises on the appropriate day (see **8**) must not have exceeded £200 (in Greater London, £400): s. 1(1)(a).

(b) Where the appropriate day is on or after 1st April 1973:

(i) in the case of a tenancy created on or before 18th February 1966, the rateable value must not have exceeded £750 (in Greater London, £1,500); and

(ii) in the case of a tenancy created after 18th February

1966, the rateable value must not have exceeded £500 (in Greater London, £1,000).

(c) If in relation to any house

(i) the appropriate day fell before 1st April 1973; and

(ii) the rateable value on that day exceeded £200 (in Greater London, £400); and

(iii) the tenancy was created on or before 18th February 1966; for the purposes of rule (a) above, it has effect as if for the sums of £200 (and £400) there were substituted £750 (and £1,500) and for the reference to the appropriate day there were substituted a reference to 1st April 1973.

12. Adjustment of rateable values. By s. 1(4A) of the 1967 Act a tenant may take action to have his property's rateable value adjusted for the purposes of the 1967 Act. This provision applies where the tenant or any previous tenant has made, or contributed to the cost of, any improvements to the premises, provided the improvement amounts to a structural alteration, extension of or addition to the premises. The procedure is for the tenant to serve notice requiring the landlord to agree to a reduction (for the purposes of the 1967 Act only). In default of agreement the county court may determine the matter. The effect of such a notional reduction may be to bring premises within the Act which would not otherwise be within it.

Pearlman v. *Harrow School* (1979). T held a long lease at a low rent of a house in London. He removed old style central heating and replaced it by a modern system which was connected to the walls and whose pipes ran through the walls, floors and ceilings to a tank in the roof. When installed the pipes could not be removed. The improvement led to an increase in the rateable value to £1,597 (outside the limits: *see* **11**). T applied to L for their agreement to a reduction under s. 1(4A) to £1,487 on the grounds that the central heating system was an improvement within these provisions. L did not agree and an application was made to the county court. On appeal to the Court of Appeal, it was HELD: That the central heating system, by affecting and being connected to the fabric of the house, was a structural alteration or addition to the house. This meant that the rateable value would be notionally reduced for the purposes of the 1967 Act and that T was entitled to enfranchise.

13. The residential condition. At the time of giving notice of his

claim, the tenant must have been occupying the house as his
residence for the last three years or for periods amounting to
three years in the last ten years: s. 1(1)(*b*) (as amended by the
Housing Act 1980, s. 141, Sch. 21). In each case whether this condition is satisfied will be a question of fact. Section 1(2) provides
that references to a "tenant occupying a house as his residence"
must be construed as applying where the tenant is, in right of the
tenancy, occupying it as his only or main residence, whether or not
he uses it also for other purposes. So a holiday home would not
come within the Act. It is also provided by s. 1(2)(*a*) that references
to "a person occupying" apply where he occupies it in part only.
So, where a tenant occupied a basement flat of a house and the
upper floors were sub-let as separate flats, it was HELD by the
Court of Appeal that the condition was satisfied: *Harris* v. *Swick
Securities* (1969).

NOTES: (1) Section 37(1) provides that no reference to "a person
occupying property as his residence" is to be taken to extend to
any occupation by a company or other artificial person. This
means that a company or other artificial person cannot claim the
benefit of the 1967 Act.

(2) Prior to 3rd October 1980 (the operative date of appropriate provisions of the Housing Act 1980) the period of required
residence was five years.

PROCEDURE FOR ENFRANCHISEMENT

14. Exercise of the right: the tenant's notice. A tenant may exercise his rights under the Act by serving on the landlord notice of
his desire to have the freehold or an extended lease of his house.
The notice must be in the prescribed form (*see* the Leasehold Reform (Notices) Regulations 1967, Sch. 3) and must contain particulars of his claim and the way in which he claims to satisfy the
conditions.

15. Landlord's counter-notice. Where a tenant gives notice of his
desire to have the freehold or an extended lease, the landlord must
within two months give the tenant notice in reply in the prescribed
form stating whether he admits the tenant's right and, if he does
not, the grounds on which it is not admitted.

16. Enfranchisement. Where a tenant has a right to acquire the
freehold and he gives to the landlord a written notice of his desire
to have it, except as is provided by the Act, the landlord is bound

to make to the tenant, and the tenant to accept, a grant of the house and premises in fee simple absolute: s. 8(1). Where notice is served the rights and obligations of the landlord and tenant arising from the notice enure for the benefit of and are enforceable against them as rights and obligations arising under a contract for a sale freely entered into between the landlord and the tenant: s. 5(1). This means that if either party fails to perform his part of the bargain the other will have the ordinary contractual rights and remedies (*see* I–III).

17. Purchase price. By virtue of s. 9(1) the price to be paid by the tenant for the freehold enfranchisement is the amount which at the date of the tenant's notice, the house and premises might be expected to realise if sold in the open market by a willing seller, with the tenant and members of his family who reside in the house not buying or seeking to buy, and on the following bases:

(*a*) that it is being sold subject to the tenancy but on the assumption that the Act confers no right to acquire the freehold but that the tenancy has been extended under the Act, unless it already has been extended: s. 9(1)(a);

(*b*) that it is being sold subject to the same rentcharges as in the sale to the tenant: s. 9(1)(b);

(*c*) that it is being sold subject to the same rights and burdens as in the sale to the tenant: s. 9(1)(c).

The aim of these provisions is to produce a price that will reflect the value of the site or ground alone. This is in accordance with the general philosophy behind the Act (*see* 1). If the parties are unable to agree the price, it will be determined by the Leasehold Valuation Tribunal.

In *Jones* v. *Wrotham Park Settled Estates* (1979), a landlord was able to obtain an artificially increased price by a complicated transaction involving the creation of an interest superior to the purchasing tenant's interest. The effect of the decision has been negated as regards such transactions made after 15th February 1979 by the terms of the Leasehold Reform Act 1979. Section 1(1) provides that as against a tenant in possession claiming under the Act of 1967, s. 8, the price payable on a conveyance for giving effect to that section may not be made less favourable by reference to any transaction since 15th February 1979 involving the creation or transfer of an interest superior to (whether or not preceding) his own, or any alteration since that date of the terms on which such an interest is held.

18. Purchase price; alternative method. By virtue of s. 9(1A), where the rateable value of the house and premises is above £1,000 in Greater London or £500 elsewhere, there is a different method of determining the price which is as follows. The price is to be the amount which at the relevant time the house and premises, if sold in the open market by a willing seller, might be expected to realise on the following bases:

(a) that the vendor is selling for an estate in fee simple, subject to the tenancy, but on the assumption that the 1967 Act conferred no right to acquire the freehold;

(b) that at the end of the tenancy the tenant has the right to remain in possession of the house and premises under the provisions of Part I of the Landlord and Tenant Act 1954;

(c) that the tenant has no liability to carry out any repairs, maintenance or redecorations under the terms of the tenancy or Part I of the Landlord and Tenant Act 1954;

(d) that the price be diminished by the extent to which the value of the house and premises has been increased by any improvement carried out by the tenant or his predecessors in title at their own expense;

(e) that (subject to (a) above) the vendor was selling subject, in respect of rentcharges, to the same annual charge as the conveyance to the tenant is to be subject to, but the purchaser would otherwise be effectively exonerated until the termination of the tenancy from any liability or charge in respect of tenant's incumbrances; and

(f) that (subject to (a) and (b) above) the vendor was selling with and subject to the rights and burdens with and subject to which the conveyance to the tenant is to be made.

19. The tenant's right to withdraw. On ascertaining the amount payable as the price for the house, the tenant may give written notice to the landlord that he is unable or unwilling to acquire the house at the price he must pay: s. 9(3). The effect is that the notice of desire to have the freehold ceases to have effect and the tenant cannot give any further notice for the following three years: *ibid.*

20. Extended lease. Where a tenant of a house has a right to an extended lease and gives to the landlord written notice of his desire to have it, then except as is provided by the Act, the landlord is bound to grant to the tenant and the tenant to accept in substitution for the existing lease a new lease of the house and premises for a term expiring 50 years after the term date of the existing tenancy: s. 14(1). By s. 5(1), where a tenant has given notice, the rights of the landlord and tenant arising from the notice enure for the benefit of and are enforceable against them to the same extent as rights and obligations arising under a contract for a lease freely entered into between the landlord and the tenant.

21. The rent under the new tenancy. There are detailed provisions for determining the rent payable under the new tenancy from what would have been the expiry of the old tenancy. In summary, the rent is to be an up-to-date ground rent—that is the letting value of the site for the use to which the house is put but without the buildings there. It is calculated by reference to the values prevailing on the date it is first to be paid, i.e. the expiry date of the old tenancy. This means that the rent will have to be calculated in the year preceding the expiry date. There is also provision for re-assessment of the ground rent after 25 years to bring it up to date with market trends: Act of 1967, s. 15(2).

22. Exclusion of further rights. When a tenancy has been extended under s. 14, the right to acquire the freehold can still be exercised but only by notice given not later than the expiry date of the old tenancy. Also there is no right to a further extension. At the end of an extended term the protection of the Landlord and Tenant Act 1954 will not be available to the tenant under the extended lease.

23. Landlord's overriding rights. There are two main situations where a landlord may have rights which exclude the tenant's rights under the Act. They are as follows.

(*a*) Where a tenancy has been extended under s. 14, the landlord may at any time not earlier than a year before the original term date of the tenancy (i.e. the date at which the old tenancy would have expired), apply to the court for an order that he may resume possession of the property on the ground that for purposes of redevelopment he proposes to demolish or reconstruct the whole or a substantial part of the house and premises. If the court is satisfied that the landlord has established this ground it must make an order and the tenant will be entitled to compensation: s. 17.

(*b*) Where the tenant has a right to acquire the freehold or an extended lease and has given notice of his desire but no effect has been given to it and the landlord purchased his interest, or it was created, before 18th February 1966, the landlord may apply to the court for an order that he may resume possession on the ground that it is required by him for the only or main residence of himself or an adult member of his family: s. 18. If the court is satisfied that the landlord has established this ground it must make an order for possession but the tenant is entitled to compensation.

MISCELLANEOUS MATTERS

24. Sub-tenants. There are special provisions in the 1967 Act, Sch. 1, which deal with the situation where the tenant entitled to enfranchise is a sub-tenant. The effect of these is that it is the person in possession who will be entitled to enfranchise, and the purchase money will be divided between the owners of intermediate tenancies and the freeholder.

The way the Act works is that one person, called the reversioner, acts for the owners of all interests above the tenant in possession. The owner of the first leasehold interest up the chain who has an expectation of possession of 30 years or more is the reversioner. If no leaseholder satisfies this test, it is the freeholder. The reversioner has the power to execute the conveyance of the freehold to the claimant.

25. Court proceedings. If any dispute arises between the parties there is provision for determination of such disputes by the courts. In summary, matters of valuation will generally be decided by a Leasehold Valuation Tribunal while matters of law will be decided by the county court.

The High Court (Chancery Division) has jurisdiction in relation to matters concerning schemes of management (*see* **26**) and the procedure where the landlord cannot be found (*see* **28**). Thus disputed claims to an entitlement to acquire the freehold or an extended lease will be adjudicated on by the county court. Issues concerning the price will be decided by a Leasehold Valuation Tribunal (*see* the Act of 1967, ss. 20, 21 and the Housing Act 1980, s. 142, Sched. 22).

The members of a Leasehold Valuation Tribunal are, in fact, the same persons as sit on the rent assessment committee, though their functions are different: *see* the Housing Act 1980, s. 142(2), and **29** below.

26. Schemes of management. Many large estates, such as the Grosvenor Estate in London, depend on leasehold covenants to maintain the high standard of the estate. These covenants give the landlord extensive control over the properties on the estate. The Act interferes with this by allowing enfranchisement which removes the control by covenants. Section 19 of the Act provides for a scheme of management which may enable the old landlord to retain some control over the properties formerly in the ownership of an estate. This applies to areas where all the houses are held under one head landlord. The Minister may certify that, in order to maintain adequate standards of appearance and amenity and regulate development in the area, in the event of tenants acquiring the landlord's interest in their houses, it is in the Minister's opinion likely to be in the general interest that the landlord should retain powers of management in respect of the houses. The next step is for the High Court, on an application made within one year of the giving of the certificate, to approve a scheme giving the landlord such powers and rights as are covered by s. 19 as the court thinks fair and practicable. The matters covered by s. 19 include:

(a) regulation of development, use or appearance of the properties;

(b) power to carry out repairs in or to any property;

(c) obligations on those interested in the properties to maintain them;

(d) inspection of the property.

If a scheme is approved its provisions are enforceable against persons who have acquired the freehold of their houses. By this means the general benefit of identical leasehold covenants—a sort of local law— can be preserved in the interests of all.

27. Enforcement of a scheme. A scheme when approved is to be registered under the Local Land Charges Act 1975 as a local land charge. It then binds those who later occupy or hold an interest in the property as if they had covenanted with the landlord to be bound by the scheme.

28. Missing landlords. By virtue of the 1967 Act, s. 27, where a tenant of a house has a right to acquire the freehold but is prevented from giving notice because the person to be served cannot be found or his identity cannot be ascertained, on an application to the High Court, the court may make an order the effect of which will be to vest the freehold in the tenant as if he had given notice. The procedure is that the tenant must show that all reasonable efforts have been made to find the landlord or to ascertain his identity. The court then will cause a conveyance to be executed and the tenant must pay into court the sum a surveyor selected by the court certifies to be a fair price for the freehold calculated in accordance with s. 9. The money in court will be held to the account of the missing person in case he should be found.

29. Leasehold Valuation Tribunal. Prior to the Housing Act 1980, the Lands Tribunal had jurisdiction to deal with disputes relating to prices, rents, values, etc. arising out of the 1967 Act. The 1980 Act transferred that jurisdiction to Leasehold Valuation Tribunals. They are actually rent assessment committees undertaking different functions. An appeal lies against the decision of a Leasehold Valuation Tribunal to the Lands Tribunal: Housing Act 1980, s. 142, Sch. 22, para. 2.

PROGRESS TEST 21

1. To what tenancies does the Leasehold Reform Act 1967 apply? **(3)**

2. What is a "house" for the purposes of the 1967 Act? **(4)**

3. What policy underlies the 1967 Act? **(1)**

4. Can a tenant enfranchise when he has a lease of mixed premises? **(5)**

5. What is a long tenancy for the purposes of the 1967 Act? **(7)**

6. What is the effect of the proviso to s. 4(1)? How does it operate in favour of the landlord? **(9)**

7. What are the rateable value limits for the purposes of the 1967 Act? How may they take account of structural alterations? **(11, 12)**

8. T has a house in the country where he spends his weekends and a flat in London where he spends his working week. Can T enfranchise either of his leases of these properties? **(13)**

9. How does a tenant exercise, and a landlord oppose, his right to enfranchise? **(14, 15)**

10. How is the purchase price for the freehold calculated under the 1967 Act? **(17, 18)**

11. Is a tenant bound to purchase the freehold once he has given notice? **(19)**

12. When is a tenant entitled to an extended lease under the 1967 Act? **(20)**

13. What is the rent payable under an extended lease? **(21)**

14. What is the effect upon the tenant's rights of the court ordering an extended lease?   **(22)**

15. When may a landlord resist a tenant's application to enfranchise?   **(23)**

16. Which courts or tribunals are involved in the resolution of disputes under the 1967 Act?   **(25)**

17. What is a scheme of management? How is it enforced? **(26, 27)**

18. T holds a long lease at a low rent of his house. He wishes to enfranchise but cannot locate his landlord. Advise T on what steps he may take to enfranchise.   **(28)**

PART FIVE

AGRICULTURAL TENANCIES

CHAPTER XXII

Agricultural Holdings

INTRODUCTION

1. Generally. Tenants of agricultural holdings have been the subject of a number of Acts since 1875. The earlier Acts were concerned with compensation. Now, tenants are given protection both as regards compensation and security of tenure. The principal Act today is the Agricultural Holdings Act 1948. In this and the following chapters these abbreviations are generally used:

(*a*) "the 1948 Act": Agricultural Holdings Act 1948;

(*b*) "the 1976 Act": Agriculture (Miscellaneous Provisions) Act 1976;

(*c*) "the 1977 Act": Agricultural Holdings (Notices to Quit) Act 1977;

(*d*) "the 1984 Act": Agricultural Holdings Act 1984;

(*e*) "the Minister": the Minister of Agriculture;

(*f*) "the Tribunal": the Agricultural Land Tribunal.

2. Outline. It is proposed to deal with this subject in the following way:

(*a*) definition of an agricultural holding (*see* **3–6**);

(*b*) the obligations and terms of tenancies of agricultural holdings (*see* **7–13**);

(*c*) compensation (*see* **XXIII**);

(*d*) security of tenure and contracting out (*see* **XXIV**).

DEFINITIONS

3. Agricultural holding. Section 1 of the 1948 Act defines an "agricultural holding" as "the aggregate of the land (whether agricultural land or not) comprised in a contract of tenancy which is a contract for an agricultural tenancy, not being a contract under which the said land is let to the tenant during his continuance in any office, appointment or employment held under the landlord." This definition comprises the following main elements:

(a) a contract of tenancy.

(b) which is a contract for an agricultural tenancy.

4. Contract of tenancy. The expression "contract of tenancy" is defined as a letting of land, or agreement for letting land, for a term of years or from year to year: Act of 1948, s. 94(1). This definition is extended by the operation of s. 2(1) which provides that where, by an agreement made after February 1948, any land is let, or a licence is granted to occupy land, for use as agricultural land for an interest less than a tenancy from year to year, in circumstances which otherwise would make the land an agricultural holding, then the agreement takes effect as if it were a tenancy from year to year. The effect of this provision is that tenancies less than from year to year and licences to use land as agricultural land are converted into tenancies from year to year and come within the meaning of the words "contract of tenancy."

5. A contract for an agricultural tenancy. A contract of tenancy relating to any land is a contract for an agricultural tenancy if, having regard to (a) the terms of the tenancy, (b) the actual or contemplated use of the land at the time of the conclusion of the contract and subsequently, and (c) any other relevant circumstances, the whole of the land comprised in the contract, subject to such exceptions only as do not substantially affect the character of the tenancy, is let for use as agricultural land: s. 1(1A) of the 1948 Act. In considering whether a contract which was not originally one for an agricultural tenancy has subsequently become one, there must be disregarded any use in breach of the terms of the tenancy unless the landlord has permitted, consented or acquiesced in it: s. 1(1B).

The expression "agricultural land" means land used for agriculture and which is so used for the purposes of a trade or business: s. 1(2). The word "agriculture" includes horticulture, fruit-growing, seed-growing, dairy farming and livestock breeding and keeping, the use of land as grazing land, meadow land, osier land, market gardens and nursery grounds, and the use of land for woodlands when that use is ancillary to the farming of land for other agricultural purposes: s. 94(1).

6. Grazing and mowing agreements. There is one exception to the sweeping effect of the Act of 1948, s. 2(1). By the proviso to that sub-section, lettings of land or licences to occupy land made only for the purpose of grazing or mowing during a specified part of the year are not converted into tenancies from year to year. So, for example, a grazing or mowing agreement for 364 days out of a year, or a lesser period out of a year, will not be converted. This is important because it means that these agreements are outside the protection of the Act.

THE PARTIES' OBLIGATIONS

7. At common law and by custom. By reason of the peculiar nature of agricultural lettings there have always been special rules concerning the parties' rights and obligations which do not apply to other lettings. In particular, at common law a tenant of a farm is under an implied obligation to use the farm in a husband-like manner in accordance with the "custom of the country." This means the customs which are prevalent throughout an area and which have existed for a reasonable period.

8. Provisions for securing written tenancy agreements. The parties' obligations will normally be regulated by the terms of the tenancy agreement. Where there is no written agreement, the 1948 Act contains provisions which, if the parties take advantage of them, will secure a written agreement. In particular, s. 5(1) provides that where there is not in force in respect of an agricultural holding any written agreement embodying the terms of the tenancy, or there is such an agreement but it lacks any of the matters specified in the 1948 Act, Sch. 1 (*see* **9**), the landlord or the tenant may require the other party to enter into such an agreement, and in default of agreement he may refer the terms of the tenancy to arbitration.

9. Matters for which provision is to be made in a written tenancy agreement. Schedule 1 to the 1948 Act prescribes the matters for which provision is to be made in a written agreement. The main matters covered are:

(*a*) the names of the parties;
(*b*) particulars of the holding;
(*c*) the term;
(*d*) the rent and when it is payable;
(*e*) liability for rates;
(*f*) a covenant by one party to maintain and repair fixed equipment.

10. Prescribed terms. By s. 6(1) of the 1948 Act there are incorporated into all contracts of tenancy of agricultural holdings (except in so far as liability for such matters is imposed by a written agreement on the other party) certain prescribed terms concerning the maintenance, repair and insurance of fixed equipment. The relevant regulations are the Agriculture (Maintenance, Repair and Insurance of Fixed Equipment) Regulations 1973. In summary, the effect of these regulations is to cast on the landlord the responsibility of repairing the structure of the various buildings, of insuring and re-instating them and of painting the exterior of the buildings every five years. Also, they cast on the tenant the responsibility of repairing the buildings in so far as the landlord is not bound to repair them, to paint the interior every seven years and to maintain the fences, hedges, walls, stiles, gates and similar items. Finally, they provide for the other party to do repairs and recover their cost when the party who is bound to do them fails to execute them.

11. Rent. The parties are free to agree the rent payable. This is, however, subject to s. 8 of the 1948 Act, which provides that either party may require the rent to be determined by arbitration. The arbitrator will determine the rent at which the holding might reasonably be expected to be let by a prudent and willing landlord to a prudent and willing tenant taking into account all relevant factors including the terms of the tenancy, the character and situation of the holding, the productive capacity of the holding and its related earning capacity and the current level of rents for comparable lettings, but disregarding any effect on rent of

(a) tenant's improvements or fixed equipment other than those executed or provided under an obligation imposed on the tenant by the terms of his contract of tenancy,

(b) landlord's improvements in so far as the landlord has received grants in respect of the execution thereof,

(c) the fact that the tenant who is a party to the arbitration is in occupation of the holding,

(d) any dilapidations, damage or deterioration caused or permitted by the tenant.

If the arbitrator considers that the existing rent is the rent properly payable, he will direct that the rent should continue unchanged.

12. Effect of determination of rent. Where the arbitrator determines a rent, or directs that the rent shall stay unchanged or the parties agree a rent, the position is as follows.

Once a rent has been fixed, whether by agreement or by arbitration, then (except in the case of a tenancy for a fixed term) that rent will continue for the next three years and cannot be varied for three years from either the start of the tenancy or the date of the last variation or the date of the last direction by the arbitrator that the rent should continue unchanged: Act of 1948, s. 8(8). In the case of a fixed term tenancy, the rent will stay the same for the duration of the term unless there is provision for its review in the terms of the tenancy.

13. Increase of rent for certain landlord's improvements. Section 9(1) of the 1948 Act provides that where a landlord has carried out certain improvements to the holding, he is entitled to an increase in the rent. The relevant improvements are those carried out

(*a*) at the request of, or in agreement with, the tenant; or

(*b*) in pursuance of a notice served by the landlord under the 1948 Act, s. 50(3) following the Tribunal giving its permission; or

(*c*) in compliance with a direction given by the Minister.

PROGRESS TEST 22

1. What is meant by an agricultural holding? **(3)**

2. Which are the main Acts governing the law relating to agricultural holdings? **(1)**

3. Which of the following constitutes "agriculture": (*a*) a fishery; (*b*) a market garden; (*c*) a forest? **(4)**

4. What contracts come within the expression "contract for an agricultural tenancy" as used in the Agricultural Holdings Act 1948? **(5)**

5. What are grazing and mowing agreements? **(6)**

6. How may a party to an oral tenancy of an agricultural holding secure a written agreement? **(8)**

7. What matters may be dealt with in such a written agreement? **(9)**

8. What are the "prescribed terms"? **(10)**

9. What rent is payable under a tenancy of an agricultural holding? **(11)**

CHAPTER XXIII

Compensation on the Termination of the Tenancy

1. Generally. At the end of a tenancy when the tenant quits, both parties may be entitled to compensation in respect of certain matters. The landlord may be entitled to it for:

(*a*) particular damage to the holding (*see* **2**);
(*b*) general damage to the holding (*see* **3**).

The tenant may be entitled to compensation for the following matters:

(*a*) disturbance (*see* **4–6**);
(*b*) improvements (*see* **7–9**);
(*c*) tenant right (*see* **10**);
(*d*) special system of farming (*see* **11**).

THE LANDLORD'S RIGHTS

2. Deterioration of a particular part of the holding. The landlord of an agricultural holding is entitled to recover compensation from a tenant of the holding, on the tenant's quitting the holding on the termination of the tenancy, in respect of the dilapidation or deterioration of, or damage to, any part of the holding or anything in or on the holding which is caused by non-fulfilment by the tenant of his responsibilities to farm in accordance with the rules of good husbandry: Agricultural Holdings Act 1948, s. 57(1). The amount of compensation payable is the cost, as at the date of quitting, of making good the dilapidations, deterioration or damage: provided that in no case shall the compensation exceed the amount, if any, by which the value of the landlord's reversion is diminished owing to the dilapidation, deterioration or damage: s. 57(2) and (4). In lieu of claiming compensation under s. 57(1), the landlord may claim compensation under the terms of the tenancy at the end of the tenancy: but again subject to the limitation that it shall not exceed the diminution in value of the landlord's reversion: s. 57(3) and (4). This provision therefore gives the land-lord a choice between his ordinary remedies under the tenancy and a special statutory claim.

3. General deterioration of the holding. Where, on the quitting of the holding by the tenant, on the termination of the tenancy, the landlord shows that the value of the holding generally has been reduced by non-fulfilment by the tenant of his responsibilities to farm in accordance with the rules of good husbandry, he is en-titled to recover from the tenant compensation equal to the de-crease in value of the holding attributable to the dilapidation, deterioration or damage: s. 58.

THE TENANT'S RIGHTS

4. Disturbance. Section 34 of the 1948 Act makes provision for the payment of disturbance compensation to a tenant. It is payable when either:

(*a*) the landlord gives notice to quit; or

(*b*) the tenant gives a counter-notice under the Agricultural Holdings (Notices to Quit) Act 1977, s. 9 (i.e. a notice by the tenant following notice to quit part given by the landlord);

and in consequence of the notice or counter-notice the tenant quits the holding.

Compensation is not, however, payable under s. 34 when the landlord serves notice to quit and relies on Cases C to G: *see* the proviso to s. 34(1) (*see* XXIV, **9** *et seq*.).

5. The amount of disturbance compensation. Section 34(2) of the 1948 Act provides that the amount of compensation payable is the amount of the loss or expense directly attributable to the quitting of the holding which is unavoidably incurred by the tenant upon or in connection with the sale or removal of his household goods, implements of husbandry, fixtures, farm produce or stock on or used in connection with the holding and any expenses reasonably incurred by him in the preparation of his claim. Alternatively, the tenant can claim as compensation an amount equal to one year's rent at the rate at which rent was payable immediately before the end of the tenancy without proof of loss or damage. If the tenant makes his claim under the first method, he is not entitled to compensation in excess of two years' rent of the holding. Where the tenant claims under the first method he must give the landlord a reasonable opportunity of making a valuation of the sale of his household goods etc. He must also give the landlord written notice of his intention to make a claim at least one month before the end of the tenancy.

6. Additional payments for disturbance. Where a tenant is entitled to compensation under s. 34 of the 1948 Act, the Agriculture (Miscellaneous Provisions) Act 1968, s. 9(1), provides that the tenant may be entitled to payment by the landlord of a "sum to assist in the re-organisation of the tenant's affairs." The sum is equal to four times the annual rent of the holding at the rate which was payable before the end of the tenancy. By virtue of s. 10 of the 1968 Act, however, no sum is payable where:

(*a*) the Tribunal has already consented to the operation of a notice to quit relying on Case A and the Tribunal has stated that it is satisfied as to any of the matters mentioned in s. 3(3) of the 1977 Act (*see* XXIV); or

(*b*) the Tribunal gives its consent to the operation of a notice in the same manner as (*a*) above;

(*c*) the Tribunal gives its consent to the operation of a notice to quit on the ground that greater hardship would be caused by withholding than by giving consent.

7. Compensation for improvements. This is payable by the landlord to the tenant on his quitting the holding on the termination of the tenancy. It replaces the old customary right to compensation, and falls into two parts:

(*a*) compensation for old improvements (*see* **8**);

(*b*) compensation for new improvements (*see* **9**).

8. Old improvements. Sections 36–45 of the 1948 Act deal with this. Old improvements are those specified in the 1948 Act, Sch. 2, Pts I and II, provided the improvements were begun before 1st March 1948.

The amount of compensation is an amount equal to the increase attributable to the improvement in the value of the holding having regard to its character and situation and the average requirements of tenants reasonably skilled in husbandry. Act of 1948, s. 37.

9. New improvements. These are improvements begun on or after 1st March 1948, provided they appear in the lists in Sch. 3 and Sch. 4 Part I.

THIRD SCHEDULE

Part I: Improvements to which consent of Landlord required

1. Making or planting of osier beds;
2. Making of water meadows or works of irrigation;
3. Making of watercress bed;
4. Planting of hops;
5. Planting of orchards or fruit bushes;
6. Warping or weiring of land;
7. Making of gardens.
7A. Provision of underground tanks.

Part II: Improvements to which consent of Landlord or approval of the Minister required

8. Erection, alteration or enlargement of buildings, and making or improvement of permanent yards;

8A. The erection or construction of loading platforms, ramps, hard standings for vehicles, or other similar facitities;

9. Construction of silos;
10. Claying of land;
11. Marling of land;
12. Making or improvement of roads or bridges;
13. Making or improvement of water courses, culverts, ponds, wells or reservoirs, or of works for the application of water power for agricultural or domestic purposes or of works for the supply, distribution, or use of water for such purposes;
14. Making or removal of permanent fences;
15. Reclaiming of waste land;
16. Making or improvement of embankments or sluices;
17. Erection of wirework for hop gardens;
18. Provision of permanent sheep-dipping accommodation;
19. Removal of bracken, gorse, tree roots, boulders or other like obstructions to cultivation;
20. Land drainage (other than mole drainage and works carried out to secure the efficient functioning thereof);
21. Provision or laying-on of electric light or power;
22. Provision of facilities for the storage or disposal of sewage or farm waste;
23. Repairs to fixed equipment, being equipment reasonably required for the proper farming of the holding, other than repairs which the tenant is under an obligation to carry out;

24. The grubbing up of orchards or fruit bushes;

25. Planting trees otherwise than as an orchard and bushes other than fruit bushes.

The measure of compensation for new improvements in the Sch. 3 list is an amount equal to the increase attributable to the improvement in the value of the agricultural holding as a holding: Act of 1948, s. 48.

FOURTH SCHEDULE: PART I

1. Mole drainage and works carried out to secure the efficient functioning thereof;

2. Protection of fruit trees against animals;

3. Chalking of land;

4. Clay burning;

5. Liming of land;

6. Application to land of purchased manure (including artificial manure);

7. Consumption on the holding of corn (whether produced on the holding or not) or of cake or other feeding stuff not produced on the holding by:

(*a*) horses, cattle, sheep or pigs;

(*b*) poultry folded on the land as part of a system of farming practised on the holding.

The measure of compensation for a new improvement in this list is the value thereof to an incoming tenant, calculated in accordance with the method prescribed by regulations made under the Act: Act of 1948, s. 51.

10. Tenant right. Part II of Sch. 4 specifies "other matters" for which a tenant is entitled to compensation. These are "tenant right" matters.

FOURTH SCHEDULE: PART II

8. Growing crops and severed or harvested crops and produce, being in either case crops or produce grown on the holding in the last year of the tenancy, but not including crops or produce which the tenant has a right to sell or remove from the holding;

9. Seeds sown and cultivations, fallows and acts of husbandry performed on the holding at the expense of the tenant (including the growing of herbage crops for commercial seed production);

10. Pasture laid down with clover, grass, lucerne, sainfoin or other seeds, being either:

(*a*) pasture laid down at the expense of the tenant otherwise than in compliance with an obligation imposed on him by an agreement in writing to lay it down to replace temporary pasture comprised in the holding when the tenant entered thereon which was not paid for by him; or

(*b*) pasture paid for by the tenant on entering on the holding.

11. Acclimatisation, hefting or settlement of hill sheep on high ground.

The measure of compensation is as for Part I (*see* **9**).

11. Special system of farming. Where the tenant of a holding shows that by the continuous adoption of a system of farming which has been more beneficial to the holding

(*a*) than the system of farming required by the contract of tenancy; or

(*b*) in so far as no system of farming is so required, than the system of farming normally practised on comparable holdings,

the value of the holding has been increased during the tenancy, he is entitled to compensation: Act of 1948, s. 56. It is payable by the landlord on the tenant quitting the holding on the termination of the tenancy. The amount of compensation is the increase in value.

Compensation is not payable under this provision unless:

(*a*) the tenant has, not later than one month before the end of the tenancy, given the landlord notice of his intention to claim compensation; and

(*b*) a record has been made of the condition of the fixed equipment on the holding and of the general condition of the holding.

If no notice is given or no record is made, no compensation is payable.

12. Compensation generally. It must be remembered that, save in the case of disturbance, compensation is only payable to the tenant on his quitting the holding on the termination of the tenancy. If these conditions are not both satisfied, no compensation will be payable. Any claim arising out of the Act, or any custom or agreement, or the terms of the tenancy shall be determined by arbitration (s. 71) in accordance with the provisions of the Sixth Schedule to the 1948 Act.

PROGRESS TEST 23

1. How do a landlord's statutory rights to compensation tie in with his contractual remedies under the tenancy? **(2)**

2. To what compensation is a landlord entitled at the end of a tenancy of an agricultural holding? **(3)**

3. What conditions must be satisfied if a tenant is to receive disturbance compensation? **(4, 5)**

4. How much compensation does a tenant get for disturbance? **(5)**

5. What additional payments may a tenant receive as disturbance compensation? **(6)**

6. Distinguish between old and new improvements. **(9)**

7. What is compensation for: (*a*) tenant right; (*b*) special system of farming? **(10, 11)**

CHAPTER XXIV

Security of Tenure

INTRODUCTION

1. Generally. The security of tenure provisions operate in the following ways. First, as has already been seen, the 1948 Act, s. 2(1) converts interests less than a tenancy from year to year into tenancies from year to year. Secondly, s. 3(1) of the same Act provides that tenancies for two years or more, instead of terminating on the expiration of the term for which they were granted, are to continue as tenancies from year to year. The effect of these two provisions is that almost all lettings or licences to use agricultural land will take effect as tenancies from year to year. The exceptions are:

(*a*) grazing and mowing agreements for a specified period of the year only (*see* XXII, **6**);

(*b*) tenancies for a fixed term which is more than one but less than two years; such a term will be outside s. 2(1) because it is not for an interest less than a tenancy from year to year and will also be outside s. 3(1) because it is less than two years: *Gladstone* v. *Bower* (1960);

(*c*) Section 3(1) has been modified by s. 3A which applies only to tenancies granted after 12th July 1984 and where the tenant dies during the term. If he dies one or more years before the expiry of the term, the tenancy does not continue by virtue of s. 3(1) but instead ends on the date of expiry. If he dies at any other time before the expiry of the term and no notice to quit has been given, the tenancy does not continue by virtue of s. 3(1) but instead continues for a further 12 months only from the expiry of the term;

(*d*) contracting out of s. 3(1) is now possible under s. 3B (*see* 32 post).

Finally, the third way in which the provisions operate is that the common law rules (*see* VII, **13**) concerning the termination of tenancies from year to year are altered by the Agricultural Holdings (Notices to Quit) Act 1977. The bulk of this chapter is concerned with that Act.

2. The Agricultural Holdings (Notices to Quit) Act 1977. Section 1(1) of this Act provides that a notice to quit an agricultural holding (notwithstanding any provision to the contrary in the contract of tenancy) will be invalid if it purports to end the tenancy before the expiration of 12 months from the end of the then current year of the tenancy. This therefore alters the common law rule that only six months' notice is needed to determine a yearly tenancy. Section 1(2) makes certain exceptions to s. 1(1), and these include the following:

(*a*) where the tenant is insolvent;

(*b*) where notice is given pursuant to a provision in the contract authorising the resumption of possession for some purpose other than the use of the land for agriculture;

(*c*) a notice given by a tenant to a sub-tenant.

In the case of these exceptions, the ordinary common law rules regarding the period of the notice apply. There are further exceptions added by the 1984 Act, where:

(*a*) in response to an award of an increased rent (*see* XXII, **11**), the tenant can give at least six months notice, to end on the anniversary of the tenancy;

(*b*) where a certificate of bad husbandry (*see* **9**) has been given, the Tribunal may specify a minimum period of not less than two months which need not expire on the anniversary.

3. Restrictions on the operation of notices to quit. Section 2 of the 1977 Act contains various restrictions on the operation of a notice to quit an agricultural holding given to the tenant. Where a notice is served on the tenant, he may within one month from the giving of it, serve on the landlord a written counter-notice requiring s. 2(1) to apply to the notice to quit. If the tenant does this the notice to quit will not have any effect unless the Tribunal gives consent to its operation under s. 2 of the 1977 Act.

4. Tribunal's consent under s. 2. Section 3(1) of the 1977 Act provides that the Tribunal must consent under s. 2 to the operation of a notice to quit an agricultural holding if, but only if, it is satisfied as to one or more of the matters in s. 3(3). Even if the Tribunal is satisfied under s. 3(1), however, s. 3(2) provides that the Tribunal must withhold consent under s. 2 if, in all the circumstances, it appears to it that a fair and reasonable landlord would not insist on possession. This gives the Tribunal an overriding discretion about whether the notice should take effect.

5. The grounds for consent. The grounds for consent are contained in the Act of 1977, s. 3(3), and are:

(*a*) that the carrying out of the purposes for which the landlord proposes to end the tenancy is desirable in the interests of good husbandry as respects the land to which the notice relates, treated as a separate unit; or

(*b*) that the carrying out of the purpose is desirable in the interests of sound management of the estate of which the land to which the notice relates forms a part, or

(*c*) that the carrying out of the purposes is desirable for the purposes of agricultural research, experiment or demonstration, or

(*d*) that greater hardship would be caused by withholding than by giving consent; or

(*e*) that the landlord proposes to end the tenancy for the purpose of the land being used for use other than agriculture and not falling within Case B of s. 2(3) (*see* **8**).

6. Exclusion of the requirement of consent to certain notices. The requirement of consent to a notice to quit is now excluded in eight cases: s. 2(2), (3). If the landlord serves notice to quit relying on any of these cases, he does not need the consent of the Tribunal. When the landlord gives the notice to quit, he must clearly state which of these cases, if any, he relies upon. These cases are considered in the following paragraphs.

7. Case A. This was abolished by the 1984 Act.

8. Case B. The notice to quit is given on the ground that the land is required for a use, other than agriculture

(*a*) for which planning permission has been granted; or

(*b*) for which such permission is not required;

and that fact is stated in the notice. This case covers the situation where the landlord requires the land for a non-agricultural use. It does not apply to a permission granted to the NCB relating to open-cast mining where there is a condition requiring restoration to agriculture or forestry.

9. Case C. Where not more than six months before the giving of the notice to quit the Tribunal granted a certificate under s. 2(4) that the tenant was not fulfilling his responsibilities to farm in accordance with the rules of good husbandry and that fact is stated in the notice.

10. Case D. At the date of giving of the notice to quit the tenant has failed to comply with a written notice served on him by the landlord requiring him either

(a) within two months of the service of the notice to pay any rent due in respect of the agricultural holding to which the notice to quit relates; or

(b) within a reasonable period specified in the notice to remedy any breach by him that was capable of being remedied of any term or condition of the tenancy which was not inconsistent with the fulfilment of his responsibilities to farm in accordance with the rules of good husbandry,

and it is stated in the notice to quit that it is given in accordance with these matters.

11. Case D: summary. Case D has two limbs to it. The first limb concerns failure by the tenant to comply with a notice calling on him to pay arrears of rent (*see* **12**). The second limb is where the tenant is in breach of his obligations and he fails to comply with a notice calling on him to remedy the breach; this form of notice is surrounded with restrictions on its operation (*see* **13**).

12. Case D: notice to pay rent. There is a prescribed form for this notice: see the Agricultural Holdings (Notice to Pay Rent or Remedy) Regulations 1984. If the tenant fails to comply with the notice requiring him to pay the rent the landlord will be entitled to give a notice to quit under Case D. The tenant cannot then give a counter-notice. By virtue of the Agricultural Holdings (Arbitration on Notices) Order 1978, art. 9, however, he can demand arbitration as to the reason stated in the notice to quit provided he does so within one month after service of the notice to quit.

13. Case D: notice to remedy. This part of Case D is subject to many restrictions which are only summarised here. Before looking at the restrictions it is first necessary to distinguish between two types of notice to remedy. First, there is a notice to do works of repair, maintenance or replacement ("a notice to do work"); secondly, there is a notice to remedy any other breach. It is now possible to summarise the procedure. There are the following stages:

(a) the landlord must first serve a valid notice to remedy and this must:

(i) be in the prescribed form: *see* **12** *above*;

(ii) specify the period (not less than six months in any case) within which the breach is to be remedied;

(*b*) if it is a notice to do work, the tenant may have the notice referred to arbitration, and dispute the validity of the notice, the reasonableness of the time, or his liability to do the work;

(*c*) the arbitrator may then make an award which affects the operation of the notice and while the arbitration is going on the time for doing the work is suspended;

(*d*) if the tenant fails to comply with the notice, at the end of the period specified for compliance, the landlord may serve notice to quit relying on Case D;

(*e*) within one month of the service of the notice to quit, the tenant may demand arbitration as to the reason stated in the notice to quit; arbitration is available whether the notice is a notice to do work or a notice to remedy some other breach; the operation of the notice to quit is suspended until the end of the arbitration;

(*f*) if the tenant fails in his challenge to the reason stated in the notice to remedy or does not challenge it, in the case of a notice to do work, he may serve a counter-notice under s. 4(2) of the 1977 Act;

(*g*) if the tenant does give such a counter-notice, the notice to quit will not operate unless the Tribunal consents to its operation.

14. Case E. At the date of the giving of the notice to quit the interest of the landlord in the holding to which the notice to quit relates had been materially prejudiced by the commission by the tenant of a breach, which was not capable of being remedied, of any term or condition of the tenancy that was not inconsistent with the fulfilment by the tenant of his responsibilities to farm in accordance with the rules of good husbandry, and it is stated in the notice that it is given by reason of the matters aforesaid.

15. Case F. At the date of the giving of the notice to quit the tenant was a person who had become insolvent, and the notice states that it is given by reason of those matters.

16. Case G. The notice to quit is given (*a*) following the death of a person who immediately before his death was the sole (or sole surviving) tenant under the contract of tenancy and (*b*) not later than the end of the period of three months beginning with the date of any relevant notice, and it is stated that it is given by reason of that person's death.

For the purpose of this case it is provided that "tenant" does not include an executor, administrator, trustee in bankruptcy or other person deriving title from a tenant by operation of law. The reference to the date of any relevant notice is a reference to the giving of notice by or on behalf of the executor or administrator of the tenant's estate informing the landlord of the tenant's death or notice of an application to the Tribunal for succession (*see* **17**), whichever is the earlier.

17. Restrictions on the operation of Case G. Certain restrictions on Case G are contained in the Agriculture (Miscellaneous Provisions) Act 1976, s. 19. In summary they are that the notice to quit will not have effect unless either:

(*a*) no application to become the tenant of the holding is made under s. 20 of the 1976 Act within three months after the death of the tenant; or

(*b*) an application or applications having been made, either:

(*i*) none of the applicants is determined by the Tribunal to be in their opinion a suitable person to become tenant; or

(*ii*) the Tribunal consents under s. 22 of the 1976 Act (*see* **22**).

18. Survivor's application for a tenancy. Section 20(1) of the 1976 Act provides that where the sole or sole surviving tenant of an agricultural holding dies and is survived by an eligible person (*see* **19**) or persons, then any eligible person may within the "relevant period" apply to the Tribunal for a direction entitling him to a tenancy of the holding. The relevant period is the period of three months beginning with the death of the tenant. The procedure is governed by the Agricultural Land Tribunals (Succession to Agricultural Tenancies) Order 1984.

NOTES: (1) An application under s. 20 may be made whether or not a notice to quit relying on Case G has been served.

(2) There can be up to two successions but no more: s. 18(4)(e) of the 1976 Act.

19. Eligible person. An eligible person is defined by the Agriculture (Miscellaneous Provisions) Act 1976, s. 18 as:

(*a*) the wife or husband of the deceased;

(*b*) a brother or sister of the deceased;

(*c*) a child of the deceased;

(*d*) any person who in the case of any marriage to which the deceased was a party, was treated by the deceased as a child of the family in relation to that marriage.

The person must also show that, in the seven years ending with the date of death, his only or principal source of livelihood throughout a continuous period of not less than six years, or two or more discontinuous periods amounting to not less than five years, derived from his (or in the case of a widow from her or the deceased's or both of their) agricultural work on the holding or on an agricultural unit of which the holding forms part and he is not an occupier of a commercial unit of agricultural land. In Sch. 3A to the 1976 Act there are complex provisions used to decide whether a claimant has another commercial unit under arrangements by which the occupancy is vested in another person.

20. Not fully eligible person. Section 21 of the 1976 Act enables the Tribunal, where it considers it to be fair and reasonable, to treat as eligible a person who is not fully eligible. It only applies, however, where the condition relating to principal source of livelihood, though not satisfied fully, is satisfied to a material extent.

21. The application. The following points should be noted regarding an application by a person under s. 20 of the 1976 Act.

(a) The applicant must satisfy the Tribunal that he is an eligible person; the Tribunal then determines whether he is in its opinion a suitable person to become the tenant: s. 20(2). In doing so it must give the landlord opportunity to be heard.

(b) If the applicants include a person validly designated by the deceased in his will as the person he wished to succeed him as tenant of the holding, the Tribunal must first determine whether that person is suitable and then only if he is not may it consider other applicants: s. 20(4).

(c) If the Tribunal decides that only one applicant is a suitable person it must make a direction entitling him to a tenancy of the holding: s. 20(5). This is, however, subject to the opportunity of the landlord to obtain the Tribunal's consent to the operation of a notice to quit under s. 22 (*see* **22**).

(d) If the Tribunal considers two or more applicants to be suitable then it must determine which is the more or most suitable person to be tenant: s. 20(6).

(e) In making its decision the Tribunal must:

(i) give the landlord a chance to state his views on the suitability of the applicants;

(ii) take into account the practical experience possessed by each applicant;

(iii) take into account the age, health and financial standing of the applicants;

(f) When the Tribunal has to choose between applicants it may direct, with the landlord's consent, that two, three or four applicants are to have a joint tenancy.

22. Opportunity for landlord to obtain Tribunal's consent. Before giving a direction entitling an applicant to a tenancy and where a notice to quit has been served on death, the Tribunal must give the landlord an opportunity to apply for consent to the operation of the notice: s. 22. In effect this gives the landlord a last chance to stop the succession of a new tenant.

23. Effect of a Tribunal's s. 20 direction. A direction by the Tribunal entitling an applicant or applicants to a tenancy of the holding entitles him or them to a tenancy of the holding from the relevant time on the same terms as those on which the holding was let immediately before it ceased to be let under the contract of tenancy under which it was let at the date of death; such a tenancy is deemed at that time to be granted by the landlord to and accepted by the applicant.

The "relevant time" here means the end of the 12 months immediately following the end of the year of the tenancy in which the deceased died. But if the application followed a notice to quit in reliance on Case G and the notice would have ended the tenancy at a time after the end of those 12 months, it means that time.

24. Arbitration on the successor's tenancy's terms. When a direction has been made under s. 20, the landlord or the tenant may, at any time within the "prescribed period" (which is the period between the giving of the direction and the end of the three months immediately following the relevant time) by written notice served on the other party demand a reference to arbitration of one or both of the questions:

(*a*) what variations in the terms of the tenancy to which the tenant is entitled are justified having regard to the circumstances of the holding and the length of time since the holding was first let on those terms;

(*b*) what rent should be or should have been properly payable in respect of the holding at the relevant time.

25. Exceptions to Case G. The preceding seven paragraphs have been concerned with applications for a new tenancy under s. 20 of the 1976 Act. It will be recalled (*see* **17**) that this consideration of s. 20 started from the consideration of Case G because applications under the section may restrict the operation of Case G (*see*

17). These restrictions outlined in **17** do not apply, however, in certain situations which include the following:

(*a*) if at the date of death the tenancy is the subject of a valid notice to quit to which s. 2(1) of the 1977 Act applies, being a notice given before that date and which the Tribunal consented to or where a counter-notice was not served in the month following the notice;

(*b*) if on the date of death the tenancy is the subject of a valid notice to quit given before that date and falling within cases A, C or F in s. 2(3) of the 1977 Act;

(*c*) if on the date of death the holding was held by the deceased under a tenancy for a fixed term of years of which more than 27 months was unexpired or a tenancy for a fixed term of more than one but less than two years or for an interest less than a tenancy from year to year.

25A. Tenancies granted after 12th July 1984. By virtue of s. 2 of the 1984 Act the succession provisions (*see* **17–25**) do not apply to tenancies granted after 12th July 1984 unless:

(*a*) the tenancy was granted pursuant to the succession provisions, or

(*b*) the parties agree that s. 2 of the 1984 Act shall not apply, or

(*c*) the tenancy was granted to a person who immediately before 12th July 1984 was a tenant of the same, or substantially the same, agricultural holding.

26. Case H. The notice to quit is given by the Minister of Agriculture and Fisheries and:

(*a*) the appropriate Minister certifies in writing that the notice to quit is given in order to enable him to use or to dispose of the land for the purposes of effecting any amalgamation or the reshaping of any agricultural unit; and

(*b*) the instrument under which the tenancy was granted contains an acknowledgement signed by the tenant that the tenancy is subject to the provisions of this Case.

26A. Case I. The holding is let as a smallholding by a smallholdings authority or the Minister and was so let after 12th July 1984 and (*a*) the tenant has attained the age of 65, (*b*) if the result of the notice would be to deprive the tenant of living accommodation, suitable alternative accommodation is available, and (*c*) the tenancy contains an acknowledgment signed by the tenant that this case applies to it, and it is stated in the notice to quit that it is given by reason of the above matters. Schedule 1A provides criteria for determining what is suitable alternative accommodation.

27. Miscellanea. This concludes the consideration of the Cases and notices to quit. There are various miscellaneous matters to be considered and which are dealt with in the following paragraphs. They are:

(a) notice to quit a part of the holding (**28–29**);
(b) the effect of a contract for sale by the landlord (**30**).
(c) contracting out (**31–2**);
(d) voluntary succession (**33**).

NOTICE TO QUIT PART

28. Notice to quit a part of the holding. Section 8 of the 1977 Act provides that a notice to quit part of a holding held on a tenancy from year to year given by the landlord will not be invalid on the ground that it relates to part only if it is given:

(a) for the purpose of adjusting the boundaries between agricultural units or parts of them; or
(b) with a view to the use of the land to which the notice relates for any of the following:

    (i) erection of farm labourers' cottages;
    (ii) provision for gardens of the same;
    (iii) provision of allotments;
    (iv) planting of trees;
    (v) opening of a deposit of coal or other minerals;
    (vi) making of a reservoir or water-course;
    (vii) making of a road, railway wharf or pier.

29. Tenant's right to treat notice to quit part as notice to quit the whole. Where a notice to quit part is given to the tenant of an agricultural holding and it is rendered valid by the 1977 Act, s. 8, it is provided by s. 9(2) that the tenant may within 28 days give notice to the landlord that he accepts it as a notice to quit the entire holding.

SALE BY LANDLORD

30. Agreement by landlord to sell holding while notice is current. Section 7 of the 1977 Act deals with the position where a landlord gives notice to quit and then contracts to sell his interest. In summary, the effect is that the landlord and tenant must agree in the three months prior to the making of the contract whether the notice operates. If they fail to agree, the landlord must give written notice to the tenant of the making of the contract and the tenant then has the right to elect whether the notice should continue in force.

CONTRACTING OUT

31. Contracting out. Section 2(1) of the 1977 Act, which provides that a notice to quit will not have effect unless the Tribunal consents to its operation, does not state whether the parties may contract out of it. If the parties could do so, the security of tenure provisions would be defeated and landlords granting new tenancies might insist that tenants contract out. It has now been held in *Johnson* v. *Moreton* (1978) that parties cannot contract out of s. 2(1), because such a term would be contrary to public policy, being an attempt to oust the jurisdiction of the Tribunal.

Johnson v. *Moreton* (1978). L granted to T a lease for ten years from 1st January 1967. T covenanted not to serve a counter-notice under s. 24(1) of the 1948 Act (the predecessor provision to s. 2(1) of the 1977 Act). In November 1975 L served a notice to quit on T who served a counter-notice. L treated the counter-notice as valid but served a second notice on T relying on Case E (i.e. claiming the landlord's interest was materially prejudiced by the breach of covenant). The breach of covenant relied upon was the service of the counter-notice. An arbitrator was appointed and a special case stated for the opinion of the court as to the validity of the notice relying on Case E. The House of Lords HELD: Despite the absence of any words prohibiting contracting out, it was not possible to do so. The covenant was therefore void, being contrary to public policy and L could not rely on it to prevent the tenant serving a counter-notice.

32. Statutory Intervention. Section 3B of the 1984 Act, added by the 1984 Act provides for contracting out where:

(*a*) the term is not less than two nor more than five years;

(*b*) before the grant the prospective landlord and tenant agreed that s. 3 should not apply;

(*c*) they jointly applied for and obtained the approval of the Minister; and

(*d*) the contract is in writing and contains a statement that s. 3 does not apply.

VOLUNTARY SUCCESSION

33. Voluntary Succession. Schedule 2 to the 1984 Act provides for a scheme of inter vivos voluntary succession which does not need the consent of the landlord. It applies only to tenancies granted before 12th July 1984. The effect is that where a tenant is 65 or over (or of a younger age if he can satisfy the Tribunal that he is incapable by reason of bodily or mental infirmity of farming in accordance with the rules of good husbandry) he can give notice to the landlord that he wishes a single eligible person to succeed him. The meaning of eligible is as in **19** above. If the parties cannot agree than the nominated successor must apply to the Tribunal within a month beginning with the day after the notice is given by the retiring tenant. The Tribunal then considers the applicant's eligibility and suitability and if greater hardship would be caused by making the direction rather than by refusing it. If a succession takes place, it counts as one of the two permitted successions: *see* **18**.

PROGRESS TEST 24

1. What is the effect of the decision in *Johnson* v. *Moreton*? **(31)**

2. What agreements do not take effect as tenancies from year to year under the 1948 Act? **(1)**

3. How does the 1977 Act alter the common law rules relating to notices to quit? **(1)**

4. When must a counter-notice to a notice to quit be served? What is the effect of such a counter-notice? **(3)**

5. What is the role of the Agricultural Land Tribunal in relation to notices to quit? **(3)**

6. On what grounds may consent be given to the operation of a notice to quit? **(5)**

7. What is an "eligible person" under the 1976 Act? How is a "not fully eligible person" to be treated as eligible? **(19, 20)**

8. What is Case A? How does it operate? **(7)**

9. L gives notice to quit to T, a tenant of an agricultural holding. The notice relies on Case C. Advise T. **(9)**

10. What is a "notice to pay rent" and a notice to remedy a breach? How does the procedure relating to each notice differ? **(13)**

11. Summarise the procedure where a landlord relies on Case D? **(13)**

12. What requirements must a notice to remedy satisfy?   **(13)**

13. What is Case E?   **(14)**

14. What restrictions are placed on a landlord serving notice to quit under Case G?   **(17)**

15. Who is the "tenant" for the purposes of Case G?   **(16)**

16. What exceptions apply to the restriction on the operation of Case G?   **(25)**

17. How may an eligible person apply for a tenancy under the 1976 Act?   **(21)**

18. What is Case H?   **(26)**

19. What is the effect of a notice to quit part of an agricultural holding?   **(28)**

CHAPTER XXV

The Rent (Agriculture) Act 1976

THE STATUTORY SCHEME

1. Introduction. The Rent (Agriculture) Act 1976 (referred to in parts of this chapter as the 1976 Act) affords security of tenure to certain agricultural workers housed by their employers. Prior to 1976 such workers were often outside the protection of the Rent Act either because they were licensees or because they paid no rent. The 1976 Act gives them protection analogous to that given to other residential tenants by the Rent Act. It also imposes a duty on housing authorities to re-house certain workers. The intention behind this latter provision is that new workers may then move into the houses occupied by old workers so that there may be some mobility of labour notwithstanding the security of tenure.

2. Summary of protection. The scheme of the 1976 Act is similar to that of the Rent Act 1977, and provides for a system of protected occupancies (the equivalent of protected tenancies) which on their termination become statutory tenancies which continue so long as the "tenant" occupies the dwelling-house as his residence. Possession of a dwelling-house cannot be recovered unless the landlord makes out one of the Cases in Sch. 4 to the 1976 Act. These cases are very similar to those in Sch. 15 to the 1977 Act (*see* XVII). There is one major difference: an occupier of agricultural land may apply to the relevant housing authority when he needs vacant possession of a house subject to a protected occupancy and he cannot provide alternative accommodation and the authority ought in the interests of efficient agriculture to provide the alternative accommodation. If those circumstances are satisfied the authority will come under a duty to re-house the protected occupier. This ties in with the grounds for possession because one of the grounds is that alternative accommodation is provided or arranged by the housing authority. There is also a system for regulating the rent payable under a protected occupancy or a statutory tenancy.

SCOPE OF PROTECTION

3. Protected occupiers and protected occupancies. The 1976 Act gives protection to what is called a "protected occupier." This is defined in the following way: section 2(1) provides that where a person has, in relation to a dwelling-house, a relevant licence or tenancy and the house is in qualifying ownership or has been in qualifying ownership at any time during the subsistence of the licence or tenancy (whether it was at the time a relevant licence or tenancy or not) he will be a protected occupier of the dwelling house if:

(*a*) he is a qualifying worker; or

(*b*) he has been a qualifying worker at any time during the subsistence of the licence or tenancy.

4. Elements. It will be seen that this is a complicated definition which introduces a number of new concepts. The essential elements are:

(*a*) there must be a relevant licence or tenancy (*see* **5, 6**);

(*b*) the property must be a dwelling-house in qualifying owner-ship (or one which has been in qualifying ownership at some time during the licence or tenancy) (*see* **8**); and

(*c*) the occupier must be a qualifying worker or have been a qualifying worker at some time during the licence or tenancy (*see* **7**).

5. Relevant licence. The 1976 Act, Sch. 2, para. 1, defines "relevant licence" as any licence under which a person has the exclusive occupation of a dwelling-house as a separate dwelling and which would be a protected tenancy

(*a*) if it was a tenancy; and

(*b*) if certain of the provisions in the Rent Act 1977 were modified.

The provisions of the Rent Act 1977 which have to be modified concern the exceptions to that Act. The main modifications are that:

(*a*) the exclusion from protection of tenancies at a low rent under the Rent Act 1977, s. 5, does not apply;

(*b*) the exclusion from protection of tenancies comprised in an agricultural holding and occupied by the person responsible for the control of the farming under the Rent Act 1977, s. 10, does not apply;

(c) for the Rent Act 1977, s. 7 there is substituted the following:

"a tenancy is not a protected tenancy if it is a bona fide term of the tenancy that the landlord provides the tenant with board or attendance; but board does not include meals provided in the course of employment."

The test for determining if an agreement gives rise to a relevant licence is therefore to ask if the agreement would give rise to a protected tenancy if the agreement was assumed to be a tenancy and the Rent Act 1977 was then applied with the above modifications.

6. Relevant tenancy. The 1976 Act, Sch. 2, para. 2 defines a "relevant tenancy" as a tenancy under which a dwelling-house is let as a separate dwelling and which

(a) is not a protected tenancy under the Rent Act 1977, but

(b) would be such a tenancy if certain of the provisions of the 1977 Act were modified.

The provisions which have to be modified are those already set out in 5 above.

7. Qualifying worker. The 1976 Act, Sch. 3, para. 1 provides that a person is a qualifying worker for the purposes of the Act at any time if, at that time, he has worked whole-time in agriculture, or has worked in agriculture as a permit worker, for not less than 91 out of the last 104 weeks.

NOTE: The Act contains detailed provisions in Sch. 3 to determine what constitutes whole-time and permit work, but the provisions are outside the scope of this book.

8. Dwelling-house in qualifying ownership. The 1976 Act, Sch. 3, para. 3 provides that a dwelling-house, in relation to which a person ("the occupier") has a licence or tenancy is in qualifying ownership at any time if, at that time, the occupier is employed in agriculture and the occupier's employer either:

(a) is the owner of the dwelling-house; or

(b) has made arrangements with the owner of the dwelling-house for it to be used as housing accommodation for persons employed by him in agriculture.

In this context "employer" means the person or one of the persons by whom the occupier is employed in agriculture, and "owner" in relation to the dwelling-house means the occupier's immediate landlord or, where the occupier is a licensee, the person who would be the occupier's immediate landlord if the licence were a tenancy.

9. Protected occupiers. A protected occupier may be either:

(a) a protected occupier in his own right (*see* **10**); or

(b) a protected occupier by succession (*see* **11**).

10. Protected occupiers in their own right. It has already been seen that under s. 2(1) a protected occupancy arises when the conditions in **5–8** above are satisfied. An occupier under such an occupancy is called a protected occupier in his own right. Section 2 extends the meaning of this expression to cover the following situations:

(a) where a person has a relevant licence or tenancy and the dwelling-house is in qualifying ownership, or has been at any time during the licence or tenancy, he is a protected occupier if and so long as he is incapable of working in agriculture because of a qualifying injury or disease;

(b) where a person has a relevant licence or tenancy then he will be a protected occupier if his licence or tenancy was granted in consideration of his giving up possession of another dwelling-house of which he was a protected occupier or statutory tenant.

NOTE: Qualifying injuries are defined in Sch. 3, para. 2, but they are outside the scope of this book.

11. Protected occupiers by succession. After the death of a protected occupier of the dwelling-house ("the original occupier") it is possible for him to be succeeded as a protected occupier by a member of his family: s. 3. The succession provisions operate in the following way:

(a) where the original occupier was a man (or woman) who died leaving a widow (or widower) who was living in the dwelling-house immediately before the death, after the death, if the widow (widower) has a relevant licence or tenancy in relation to the dwelling-house, she (he) will be a protected occupier of the dwelling-house;

(b) where the original occupier did not have a surviving spouse who was living in the dwelling-house immediately before the death, but one or more persons who were members of his family were residing with him at the time of and for six months prior to the death, if that person or any of them has a relevant licence or tenancy in relation to the dwelling-house, that person will be a protected occupier;

The expression "protected occupier by succession" is used in the Act to refer to a person who is a protected occupier by virtue of these provisions.

12. Statutory tenancies and tenants. Section 4 of the 1976 Act provides that where a person ceases to be a protected occupier of a dwelling-house on the termination of his licence or tenancy, if and so long as he occupies the dwelling-house as his residence, he will be the statutory tenant of it. (This provision is parallel to that in the 1977 Act concerning statutory tenancies.) There is also a provision in terms similar to s. 3 (*see* **11**) for determining the statutory tenant by succession where the original occupier dies.

13. Security of tenure. The 1976 Act operates in a way similar to the Rent Act 1977. Section 6(1) provides that a court may not make an order for possession of a dwelling-house subject to the protection of the 1976 Act except in the cases specified in Sch. 4 to the Act. Cases I–X of Sch. 4 are discretionary grounds and are similar to the discretionary grounds in the Rent Act 1977, Sch. 15. Cases XI–XIII (in Sch. 4, Part II) are those where the court must make an order for possession. In the discretionary cases the court has wide powers in making an order for possession to defer its operation or to make it subject to conditions: s. 7.

In the following paragraphs the Cases are set out; where they are the same as under the Rent Act 1977, reference should be made to XVII.

DISCRETIONARY GROUNDS FOR POSSESSION

14. Case I. Alternative accommodation provided other than by housing authority. This case applies where the court is satisfied that suitable alternative accommodation is available for the tenant or will be when the order for possession takes effect. The accommodation concerned here is accommodation provided otherwise than by the housing authority. There are detailed provisions as to when accommodation is suitable; they are parallel to those in the Rent Act 1977.

15. Case II. Alternative accommodation provided or arranged by the housing authority. This case applies where the housing authority has made a written offer to the tenant of alternative accommodation or given notice that another person has offered to re-house the tenant. The landlord must show that the tenant has accepted the offer or that he has not accepted it and the tenant does not satisfy the court that he acted reasonably in failing to accept the offer. The court must also be satisfied that the accommodation is suitable.

16. Cases III–X. These cases are the equivalent of some of the cases under the 1977 Act. In summary and with their Rent Act equivalent, they are as follows:

(*a*) *Case III*: Non-payment of rent or breach of obligation (Case 1);

(*b*) *Case IV*: Nuisance or annoyance, immoral or illegal use (Case 2);

(*c*) *Case V*: Deterioration in the condition of the dwelling-house (Case 3);

(*d*) *Case VI*: Deterioration in the condition of furniture (Case 4);

(*e*) *Case VII*: Notice to quit by the tenant (Case 5);

(*f*) *Case VIII*: Assigning, sub-letting or parting with possession of the dwelling-house or part of it without the consent of the landlord (Case 6 with certain differences);

(*g*) *Case IX*: Dwelling-house reasonably required by the landlord for occupation for himself, a son or daughter over the age of 18, or his father or mother, or the father or mother of his wife or her husband (Case 9);

(*h*) *Case X*: Excessive charge for sub-letting part of the dwelling-house (Case 10).

CASES WHERE THE COURT MUST ORDER POSSESSION

17. Case XI. This applies where an owner-occupier who occupied the house, prior to the grant of a tenancy, as his residence requires the dwelling-house as a residence for himself or anyone who resided with him when he last occupied the dwelling-house as his residence. This is equivalent to Case 11 under the Rent Act 1977.

18. Case XII. This applies where the person who granted the tenancy acquired the dwelling-house, or any interest in it with a view to occupying it as his residence at such time as he should retire from regular employment. This is equivalent to Case 12 under the Rent Act 1977.

19. Case XIII. This is where the dwelling-house is overcrowded within the meaning of the Housing Act 1957.

20. Effect of determination of superior tenancy. Section 9 provides for the protection of sub-tenants on the determination of a superior tenancy. The provisions are along the same lines as those in the Rent Act 1977, s. 137 (*see* XVII, **33**).

21. Terms and conditions of statutory tenancies. The Act of 1976, Sch. 5, contains provisions which regulate the terms and conditions under which a statutory tenant holds. The schedule refers to the licence or tenancy on the termination of which the statutory tenancy arises as the "original contract." In outline the provisions of Sch. 5 are:

(*a*) so long as he retains possession, the statutory tenant must observe and will be entitled to the benefit of all the terms of the original contract;

(*b*) if the original contract was a licence, the statutory tenancy will be a weekly tenancy;

(*c*) if the original contract was a licence, the statutory tenancy will include any term which would be implied if the contract had been a tenancy;

(*d*) the Housing Act 1961, s. 32, applies to the dwelling-house;

(*e*) the tenant must use the house only as a private dwelling-house, and must not assign, sub-let or part with possession of it;

(*f*) the tenant must give the landlord access for executing repairs;

(*g*) there is provision as to the payment of rates;

(*h*) there is provision as to the length of notice to quit to be served by the tenant on the landlord;

(*i*) there is provision for the variation of the terms of the statutory tenancy.

22. Agreed rents. The Act makes provision in s. 11 for agreed rents. There is no liability to pay rent under Sch. 5 (*see* **21**) until a rent is determined in accordance with the Act. Section 11(1) provides that the landlord and the statutory tenant may by agreement fix the rent payable under a statutory tenancy or may agree that no rent shall be payable. By s. 11(2) the rent so fixed must not exceed;

(*a*) where a rent is registered, the amount so registered;

(*b*) where a rent is not so registered, the amount of rent based on rateable value as defined in s. 12 which is called a provisional rent (*see* **23**).

The amount of any excess over these limits cannot be recovered from the tenant: s. 11(5).

23. Provisional rents. Section 12 of the 1976 Act applies where a rent is not registered by providing for a provisional rent which is a "rent based on rateable value." This means the weekly or other periodical equivalent of an annual sum equal to the prescribed multiple of the rateable value of the dwelling-house. The prescribed multiple is at present $1\frac{1}{2}$. Where a rent is not registered this is the lawfully recoverable rent. There is provision in s. 12 for increasing the rent up to the amount of the rent based on rateable value if the rent is currently less than that amount.

24. Registration of rent. Section 13 of the 1976 Act provides that there shall be a part of the register under Part IV of the 1977 Act in which rents may be registered for dwelling-houses which are subject to statutory tenancies. There are detailed provisions for increasing the rent up to the registered rent by notice of increase. There are also phasing provisions for increasing the rent in stages.

25. Protected occupancies and statutory tenancies: supplemental provisions. Part III of the 1976 Act contains various supplemental provisions. In summary they are as follows:

(*a*) s. 20 provides for the avoidance of any requirement that the rent be payable in advance or, if the rental period is more than six months, earlier than six months before the end of the rental period;

(*b*) s. 21 provides for the recovery of rent paid in excess of the recoverable rent;

(*c*) s. 22 provides for the rectification of rent in the light of the determination of the recoverable rent;

(*d*) s. 23 deals with the situation where the tenant shares accommodation with persons other than his landlord;

(*e*) s. 26 gives the county court jurisdiction to determine the question whether any person is a protected occupier or any question concerning the terms of a statutory tenancy.

26. Rehousing. It will be remembered that Case II (*see* **15**) provides that a landlord may recover possession when alternative accommodation is provided or arranged by the housing authority. Part IV of the Act provides a scheme whereby the housing authority may become under a duty to re-house. There are two stages to this process:

(*a*) the application to the housing authority concerned (*see* **27**);

(*b*) the creation of the duty of the housing authority (*see* **28**).

27. Applications to the housing authority. Section 27 provides that an application may be made by the occupier of land used for agriculture to the housing authority concerned on the grounds that

(*a*) vacant possession is or will be needed of a dwelling-house which is subject to a protected occupancy or a statutory tenancy, in order to house a person who is or is to be employed in agriculture by the applicant; and

(*b*) the applicant is unable to provide, by any reasonable means, suitable alternative accommodation for the occupier of the dwelling-house; and

(*c*) the authority ought, in the interests of efficient agriculture, to provide the suitable alternative accommodation.

28. The duty of the housing authority. On receipt of the application the authority must notify the occupier of the dwelling-house. Thereafter it may take the advice of an agricultural dwelling-house advisory committee (ADHAC) if it wishes. This will give advice on the case made by the applicant in the interests of efficient agriculture and regarding the urgency of the application. The authority must then notify its decision to the applicant and the occupier as to whether it is satisfied that the applicant's case is substantiated under s. 27. If it is so satisfied the notice must state the action it proposes to take; if not, it must give its reasons. If it is satisfied, the authority is under a duty to use its best endeavours to provide the suitable accommodation. The duty is enforceable at the suit of the applicant by an action against the authority for damages for breach of statutory duty. The duty does not, however, continue if, when the accommodation becomes available, the person for whom it is to be provided is employed by the applicant in the same capacity as that in which he was employed by the applicant when he made the application and will continue to be so employed if provided with the alternative accommodation.

Finally, there are detailed provisions in s. 28 for securing the notification to the authority of any material change of facts concerning the application. There are also criminal penalties for failure to comply with these provisions.

PROGRESS TEST 25

1. What is the scope of the 1976 Act? **(2)**

2. Explain the following terms: (*a*) protected occupier; (*b*) protected occupancy; (*c*) relevant licence; (*d*) qualifying worker. **(3, 5, 7)**

3. What conditions must be satisfied for a house to be in qualifying ownership. **(8)**

4. Distinguish between a protected occupier in his own right and one by succession. **(10, 11)**

5. What are the similarities between the 1976 Act and the Rent Act 1977? **(13)**

6. What are the discretionary grounds for recovering possession of a dwelling-house subject to the 1976 Act? **(14)**

7. What are the mandatory grounds for recovering possession? **(17)**

8. On what terms will a statutory tenant occupy his dwelling-house? **(21)**

9. Who is responsible for repairs in a statutory tenancy under the 1976 Act? **(21)**

10. How is a rent determined for a statutory tenancy under the 1976 Act? **(22)**

11. What is a provisional rent? **(23)**

12. Explain the provisions for registration of rents under the 1976 Act. **(24)**

13. What is Case 11? How does it fit into the scheme of protection under the 1976 Act? **(17)**

14. What is an ADHAC? What are its duties? **(28)**

PART SIX

THE HOUSING ACT 1980

CHAPTER XXVI

Secure Tenancies

INTRODUCTION

1. Generally. The effect of the Housing Act 1980 has been touched upon in dealing with the Rent Acts. In addition to making amendments to the Rent Act 1977, the Housing Act 1980 introduces three new types of tenancy which must be considered. They are:

    (*a*) secure tenancies;
    (*b*) protected shorthold tenancies (*see* XXVIII);
    (*c*) assured tenancies (*see* XXIX).

They are dealt with in that order in the Act and will be considered in that order in this book. The Act will generally be referred to in this chapter as the 1980 Act and reference to sections will generally be to that Act except when otherwise stated. The 1980 Act has been amended in a number of important respects by the Housing and Building Control Act 1984.

    The preamble to the 1980 Act states that it is "An Act to give security of tenure and the right to buy their homes to tenants of local authorities and other bodies". This aim is achieved by providing for a new form of protection called "secure tenancies." In this chapter the basic requirements and effects of the Act are considered. In the next chapter "the right to buy" is considered.

2. Definition of a secure tenancy. A secure tenancy is one under which a dwelling-house is let as a separate dwelling and in relation to which both "the landlord condition" and "the tenant condition" are satisfied: s. 28(1). In summary there must be:

    (*a*) a tenancy (*see* **3**);
    (*b*) of a dwelling-house (*see* **4**);
    (*c*) let as a separate dwelling (*see* **5**);

(*d*) satisfaction of the landlord condition (*see* **6**); and

(*e*) satisfaction of the tenant condition (*see* **7**).

Each of these requirements is considered in the following paragraphs. There are, of course, exceptions to the above which will be considered at **8–21** below.

3. There must be a tenancy. For the distinction between a tenancy and a licence *see* II, **12**. In certain circumstances a licence may be a secure tenancy. Section 48(1) provides that where a person who is not the tenant of a dwelling-house has a licence to occupy it and the circumstances are such that, if the licence were a tenancy, it would be a secure one, the licence is to be treated as a secure tenancy. Section 48(2), however, provides that s. 48(1) does not apply to a licence which was granted as a temporary expedient to a person who entered the dwelling-house or any other land as a trespasser.

4. A dwelling-house. The Housing Act 1980, s. 50(2)(*a*) provides that in this context a dwelling-house may be a house or part of a house. Section 50(2)(*b*) provides that land let together with a dwelling-house will be treated as part of the dwelling-house unless the land is agricultural land exceeding two acres.

5. Let as a separate dwelling. The law appears to be the same as for Rent Act 1977 cases: *see* XV, **7, 8**.

6. The landlord condition. The landlord condition is that the interest of the landlord must belong to one of the following:

(*a*) a local authority, defined as a district council, the Greater London Council, a London Borough Council, the Common Council of the City of London or the Council of the Isles of Scilly;

(*b*) a county council;

(*c*) the Commission for the New Towns;

(*d*) a development corporation;

(*e*) the Housing Corporation;

(*f*) a charitable housing trust;

(*g*) the Development Board for Rural Wales;

(*h*) a housing association which satisfies one of the conditions in XV, **31** (*c*) and (*d*);

(*i*) a housing co-operative approved by the Secretary of State: s. 28(2).

7. The tenant condition. The tenant condition is that the tenant is an individual and occupies the dwelling-house as his only or principal home; or, where the tenancy is a joint one, that each of the joint tenants is an individual and at least one of them occupies the dwelling-house as his only or principal home: s. 28(3).

EXCEPTIONS

8. Introduction. The Housing Act 1980, Sch. 3 deals with tenancies which are not secure ones. They are:

(a) long leases (*see* **9**);

(b) premises occupied under contract of employment (*see* **10**);

(c) police force and fire authority dwellings (*see* **11**);

(d) land acquired for development (*see* **12**);

(e) accommodation for homeless persons (*see* **13**);

(f) temporary accommodation for persons seeking employment (*see* **14**);

(g) short-term arrangements (*see* **15**);

(h) temporary accommodation during works (*see* **16**);

(i) agricultural holdings (*see* **17**);

(j) licensed premises (*see* **18**);

(k) student lettings (*see* **19**);

(l) tenancies protected by Part II of the Landlord and Tenant Act 1954 (*see* **20**);

(m) Almshouses (*see* **21**).

9. Long leases. A tenancy is not a secure one if it is a long tenancy. A long tenancy is one granted for a term certain exceeding 21 years, whether or not it is (or may become) terminable before the end of that term by notice given by the tenant or by re-entry or forfeiture.

10. Premises occupied under contract of employment. A tenancy is not a secure one if the tenant is an employee of the landlord or, if not such an employee, is an employee of anybody listed at **6** (a)–(c) and (f) above, or the governors of an aided school, and his contract of employment requires him to occupy the dwelling-house for the better performance of his duties.

11. Police force and fire authority dwellings. A tenancy is not a secure tenancy if the tenant is a member of a police force and the dwelling-house is provided for him free of rent and rates in pursuance of regulations made under s. 33 of the Police Act 1964.

A tenancy is not a secure tenancy if the tenant is an employee of a fire authority and (a) his contract of employment requires him to live in close proximity to a particular fire station and (b) the dwelling house was let to him by the authority in consequence of that requirement.

NOTE: After there has been a letting (after 26th August 1984) of a dwelling falling within **10** or **11** above, the landlord may let the dwelling for periods in aggregate amounting to not more than three years without creating a secure tenancy provided (*i*) the letting takes place within three years of the grant of a tenancy to which **10** or **11** applies and (*ii*) the landlord gives notice that this exception is to apply.

12. Land required for development. A tenancy is not a secure one if the dwelling-house is on land which has been acquired for development and the dwelling-house is used by the landlord, pending development of the land, for temporary housing accommodation.

13. Accommodation for homeless persons. A tenancy granted under certain provisions of the Housing (Homeless Persons) Act 1977, is not a secure one before the end of a period of 12 months after the authority notifies the tenant whether he is homeless.

14. Temporary accommodation for persons seeking employment. A tenancy of a dwelling-house in a district or London Borough granted to someone who was not immediately before the grant resident in the district or London Borough is not a secure one for a year if it was granted to meet the person's need for temporary accommodation within the district or London Borough in order to work there and for enabling him to find permanent accommodation there. Also, before the grant of the tenancy, the tenant must have obtained employment or an offer of employment in the district or London Borough or any district or London Borough which adjoins it and the landlord must have notified the tenant in writing that this exception applies.

15. Short-term arrangements. A tenancy is not a secure one if

(*a*) the dwelling-house has been leased to the landlord with vacant possession for use as temporary housing accommodation;

(*b*) the terms on which it has been leased include provision for the lessor to obtain vacant possession from the landlord on the expiry of a specified period or when required by the lessor;

(*c*) the lessor is not a body which is capable of granting secure tenancies; and

(*d*) the landlord has no interest in the dwelling-house other than under the lease in question or as mortgagee.

16. Temporary accommodation during work. A tenancy is not a secure one if

(a) the dwelling-house has been made available for occupation by the tenant or his predecessor in title while works are carried out on the dwelling-house which he previously occupied as his home; and

(b) the tenant (or his predecessor in title) was not a secure tenant of that other dwelling-house at the time when he ceased to occupy it as his home.

17. Agricultural holdings. A tenancy is not a secure one if the dwelling-house is comprised in an agricultural holding (within the meaning of the Agricultural Holdings Act 1948) and is occupied by the person responsible for the control (whether as tenant or as servant or agent of the tenant) of the farming of the holding.

18. Licensed premises. A tenancy is not a secure one if the dwelling-house consists of or comprises premises licensed for the sale of intoxicating liquor for consumption on the premises.

19. Student lettings. A tenancy of a dwelling-house is not a secure one before the expiry of the period of exemption if

(a) it was granted for the purpose of enabling the tenant to attend a designated course at an educational establishment; and

(b) before the grant of the tenancy the landlord notified him in writing of the circumstances in which this exception applies and that in its opinion the proposed tenancy would fall within this exception;

unless the tenant has before the expiry of that period been notified by the landlord that the tenancy is to be regarded as a secure tenancy.

A landlord's notice under (b) must specify the educational establishment which the person concerned proposes to attend.

In this context:

(a) "designated course" means any course of a kind designated in regulations made by the Secretary of State for the purposes of this paragraph;

(b) "educational establishment" means a university or establishment of further education; and

(c) "the period of exemption" means, in a case where the tenant attends a designated course at the educational establishment specified in the landlord's notice, the period ending six months after the tenant ceases to attend that (or any other) designated course at that educational establishment and, in any other case, the period ending six months after the grant of the tenancy.

20. Part II of the 1954 Act. A tenancy is not a secure one if it is one to which Part II of the Landlord and Tenant Act 1954 applies.

21. Almshouses. Certain licences to occupy an almshouse are not secure tenancies.

SECURITY OF TENURE

22. Security of tenure for secure tenants. The Act gives security of tenure to secure tenants by:

(*a*) restricting the ways in which the tenancy can come to an end (*see* **23**);

(*b*) allowing for succession on the death of a tenant (*see* **24, 25**); and

(*c*) providing that possession may only be recovered in certain limited cases (*see* **26** *et seq.*).

23. Restrictions on termination of a secure tenancy. The Act makes the following restrictions on the ways in which a tenancy may be determined:

(*a*) at the end of a tenancy for a term certain, there arises a periodic tenancy on the same terms as those of the first tenancy in so far as they are compatible with a periodic tenancy but not including any proviso for re-entry or forfeiture: s. 29(1),(2). The period of the tenancy will depend on the period for which rent was last payable under the first tenancy;

(*b*) a tenancy which is a weekly or other periodic one cannot be ended by the landlord except by obtaining a court order for possession of the dwelling-house;

(*c*) where there is a tenancy for a term certain with a proviso for re-entry or forfeiture the court cannot order possession in pursuance of that provision; the court may, however, make an order terminating the tenancy for a term certain (s. 32(2)) and there then arises a periodic tenancy under s. 29(1).

24. Succession on death of tenant. Where a secure tenancy is a periodic one and, on the death of the tenant, there is a person qualified to succeed him, the tenancy vests in that person by virtue of s. 30(1). A person is qualified to succeed if:

(a) he occupied the dwelling-house as his only or principal home at the time of the tenant's death; and either

(b) he is the tenant's spouse; or

(c) he is another member of the tenant's family and has resided with the tenant throughout the period of 12 months ending with the tenant's death.

Where there is more than one person qualified to succeed the tenant:

(a) the tenant's spouse is to be preferred to another member of the tenant's family; and

(b) of two or more other members, such one of them is to be preferred as may be agreed between them or, in default of agreement, be selected by the landlord: s. 30(3).

25. Exceptions to succession on death of tenant. The above provisions for succession do not apply where the tenant is a successor. A tenant is a successor if, inter alia:

(a) the tenancy was vested in him by virtue of s. 30;

(b) he was a joint tenant and has become the sole tenant;

(c) the tenancy is a periodic one which arose following the termination of a tenancy for a fixed term granted to another person or jointly to him and another person;

(d) he became the tenant on the tenancy being assigned to him or on its having vested in him on the death of the previous tenant: s. 31(1).

26. Recovery of possession in limited cases. There are two limitations on the landlord's right to possession. They are that the landlord

(a) must first serve a notice on the tenant (s. 33) (see **27**); and

(b) then establish one of the specified grounds for possession (s. 34) (see **28–31**).

27. Notice requiring possession. A court cannot entertain proceedings for possession against a secure tenant unless the landlord has served on the tenant a notice which complies with s. 33(1). The notice must:

(a) be in the form prescribed by the Secretary of State;

(b) specify the ground on which possession is sought;

(c) specify a date after which proceedings may be begun; in the case of a periodic tenancy the date must not be earlier than that on which the tenancy could have been brought to an end by notice to quit given on the same date as the notice under s. 30.

The notice remains in effect for only 12 months after the date specified in it and proceedings begun before the date or 12 months after the date are of no effect.

28. Grounds for possession. By virtue of the Housing Act 1980, s. 34(1), the court cannot make an order for possession of a dwelling-house let under a secure tenancy except on one or more of the grounds set out in Part I of Sch. 4. Further, the court cannot make an order unless the ground is specified in the notice given under s. 33(1).

29. Schedule 4, Part I. The specified grounds are as follows.

(a) *Ground 1.* Any rent lawfully due from the tenant has not been paid or any obligation of the tenancy has been broken or not performed.

(b) *Ground 2.* The tenant or any person residing in the dwelling-house has been guilty of conduct which is a nuisance or annoyance to neighbours, or has been convicted of using the dwelling-house or allowing it to be used for immoral or illegal purposes.

(c) *Ground 3.* The condition of the dwelling-house or of any of the common parts has deteriorated owing to acts of waste by, or the neglect or default of, the tenant or any person residing in the dwelling-house and, in the case of any act of waste by, or the neglect or default of, a person lodging with the tenant or a sub-tenant of his, the tenant has not taken such steps as he ought reasonably to have taken for the removal of the lodger or sub-tenant.

In this context "the common parts" means any part of a building comprising the dwelling-house, and any other premises which the tenant is entitled under the terms of the tenancy to use in common with the occupiers of other dwelling-houses let by the landlord.

(d) *Ground 4.* The condition of any relevant furniture has deteriorated owing to ill-treatment by the tenant or any person residing in the dwelling-house and, in the case of any ill-treatment by a person lodging with the tenant or a sub-tenant of his, the tenant has not taken such steps as he ought reasonably to have taken for the removal of the lodger or sub-tenant.

In this context "relevant furniture" means any furniture provided by the landlord for use under the tenancy or for use in any of the common parts (within the meaning given in ground 3).

(*e*)(*i*) *Ground 5*. The tenant is the person, or one of the persons, to whom the tenancy was granted and the landlord was induced to grant the tenancy by a false statement made knowingly or recklessly by the tenant.

(*ii*) *Ground 5A*. The tenancy was assigned to the tenant, or to a predecessor in title of his who is a member of his family and is residing in the dwelling, by an assignment made by virtue of s. 37A, and a premium was paid either in connection with that assignment or the assignment which the tenant or his predecessor himself made by virtue of that section. "Premium" means a fine or other like sum and any other pecuniary consideration in addition to rent.

(*iii*) *Ground 5B*. The dwelling forms part of, or is within the curtilage of, a building which is held mainly for purposes other than housing purposes and consists mainly of accommodation other than housing accommodation and (*a*) the dwelling was let to the tenant or a predecessor in title in consequence of the tenant or his predecessor being in the employment of the landlord or any of those bodies set out in **10** above, and (*b*) the tenant or any person residing in the dwelling has been guilty of conduct such that, having regard to the purpose for which the building is used, it would not be right for him to continue in occupation of the dwelling.

(*f*) *Ground 6*. The dwelling-house was made available for occupation by the tenant or his predecessor in title while works were carried out on the dwelling-house which he previously occupied as his only or principal home and

(*i*) he (or his predecessor in title) was a secure tenant of that other dwelling-house at the time when he ceased to occupy it as his home;

(*ii*) he (or his predecessor in title) accepted the tenancy of the dwelling-house of which possession is sought on the understanding that he would give up occupation when, on completion of the works, the other dwelling-house was again available for occupation by him under a secure tenancy; and

(*iii*) the works have been completed and the other dwelling-house is so available.

(*g*) *Ground 7*. The dwelling-house is overcrowded, within the meaning of the Housing Act 1957 in such circumstances as to render the occupier guilty of an offence.

(*h*) *Ground 8*. The landlord intends, within a reasonable time of obtaining possession of the dwelling-house

(*i*) to demolish or reconstruct the building or part of the building comprising the dwelling-house; or (*ii*) to carry out work on that building or on land let together with, and thus treated as part of, the dwelling-house; and cannot reasonably do so without obtaining possession of the dwelling-house.

(*i*) *Ground 9*. The landlord is a charity within the meaning of the Charities Act 1960 and the tenant's continued occupation of the dwelling-house would conflict with the objects of the charity.

(*j*) *Ground 9A*. The dwelling-house either forms part of a building, or is within the curtilage of, a building of the type described in Ground 5B above or is situated in a cemetery and (*a*) the landlord reasonably requires the dwelling-house as a residence for some person engaged in the employment of the landlord or of a body specified in **10** above or with whom, conditional on housing being provided, a contract for such employment has been entered into, and (*b*) the dwelling-house was let to the tenant or to a predecessor in title of his in consequence of the tenant or predecessor being in the employment of the landlord or of a body so specified and the tenant or predecessor has ceased to be in that employment.

(*k*) *Ground 10*. The dwelling-house has features which are substantially different from those of ordinary dwelling-houses and which are designed to make it suitable for occupation by a physically disabled person who requires accommodation of a kind provided by the dwelling-house and

(*i*) there is no longer such a person residing in the dwelling-house; and

(*ii*) the landlord requires it for occupation (whether alone or with other members of his family) by such a person.

(*l*) *Ground 11*. The landlord is a housing association trust which lets dwelling-houses only for occupation (alone or with others) by persons whose circumstances (other than merely financial circumstances) make it especially difficult for them to satisfy their need for housing; and

(*i*) either there is no longer such a person residing in the dwelling-house or the tenant has received from a local authority an offer of accommodation in premises which are to be let as a separate dwelling under a secure tenancy; and

(*ii*) the landlord requires the dwelling-house for occupation (whether alone or with other members of his family) by such a person.

(*m*) *Ground 12*. The dwelling-house is one of a group of dwelling-houses which it is the practice of the landlord to let for occupation by persons with special needs and (*i*) a social service or special facility is provided in close proximity to the group of dwelling-houses in order to assist persons with those special needs;

(*ii*) there is no longer a person with those special needs residing in the dwelling-house; and

(*iii*) the landlord requires the dwelling-house for occupation (whether alone or with other members of his family) by a person who has those special needs.

(*n*) *Ground 13*. The accommodation afforded by the dwelling-house is more extensive than is reasonably required by the tenant and

(*i*) the tenancy vested in the tenant, by virtue of the Housing Act 1980, s. 30, on the death of the previous tenant;

(*ii*) the tenant was qualified to succeed by virtue of the Housing Act 1980, s. 30(2)(b); and

(*iii*) notice of the proceedings for possession was served under the Housing Act 1980, s. 33, more than six months, but less than twelve months, after the date of the previous tenant's death.

30. Restrictions on court orders. By s. 34(2) the court is debarred from making an order under grounds 1–6 unless condition (*a*) below is satisfied; it cannot make an order under grounds 7–9 unless condition (*b*) is satisfied. It cannot make an order under Grounds 9A–13 unless both conditions are satisfied. The conditions are:

(*a*) that the court considers it reasonable to make an order;

(*b*) that the court is satisfied that suitable accommodation will be available for the tenant when the order takes effect.

The matters to be taken into account by the court in determining whether it is reasonable to make an order under Ground 13 include:

(*a*) the age of the tenant;

(*b*) the period for which the tenant has occupied the dwelling house; and

(*c*) any financial or other support given by the tenant to the previous tenant.

Sch. 4, Part II contains detailed provisions for determining whether suitable accommodation will be available for a tenant.

31. Suspended orders. The provisions of s. 87 apply to proceedings for the recovery of possession of a dwelling-house let on a secure tenancy, and give the county court a wide power to adjourn the proceedings or to postpone the date for possession or stay or suspend the execution of the order, or impose conditions on making such orders.

TERMS OF A SECURE TENANCY

32. Introduction. The terms of a secure tenancy will generally be those agreed between the parties. There are, however, some terms implied by statute. They relate to:

(*a*) sub-letting and lodgers (*see* **33**);

(*b*) assignment (*see* **34**);

(*c*) improvements (*see* **35**);

(*d*) variation of terms (*see* **36**);

(*e*) repairs (*see* **37**);

(*f*) heating charges (*see* **38**).

33. Sub-letting and lodgers. By virtue of s. 35(1) it is a term of every secure tenancy that the tenant may allow any persons to reside as lodgers in the dwelling-house.

By virtue of s. 35(2) it is a term of every secure tenancy that the tenant will not, without the written consent of the landlord, sub-let or part with the possession of part of the dwelling-house; consent is not to be unreasonably withheld and, if unreasonably withheld, will be treated as given.

34. Assignment. A secure tenancy which is either a periodic tenancy granted at any time or a tenancy for a fixed term granted after 5th November 1982 is not capable of being assigned unless (*a*) the assignment is made in pursuance of an order under the Matrimonial Causes Act 1973, s. 24, or (*b*) the assignment is made to a person eligible for succession (*see* **24** *above*) if the tenant had died immediately before the assignment, or (*c*) the assignment is made by virtue of s. 37A: *see* s. 37(1) and (2). A secure tenancy which is for a fixed term and was granted before 5th November 1982 ceases to be a secure tenancy if it is assigned unless the assignment falls within (*a*), (*b*) or (*c*) above: s. 37(1) and (3).

Section 37A(1) provides that it is a term of every secure tenancy that the tenant may, with the written consent of the landlord, assign the tenancy to any person who is a secure tenant who has the written consent of his landlord to assign his tenancy to the other tenant or some other person who is a secure tenant who has the written consent of his landlord to assign. In other words this provision enables secure tenants to exchange their tenancies. The landlord may only refuse his consent on the grounds set out in Sch. 4

which are outside the scope of this book. The landlord may give his consent conditionally subject to a condition requiring the tenant to pay any outstanding rent or remedy any breach of covenant.

If the tenant under a secure tenancy parts with the possession of the dwelling-house or sub-lets the whole of it (or sub-lets first part of it and then the remainder) the tenancy ceases to be secure: s. 37B(1). Where, on the death of the tenant, a secure tenancy is vested or otherwise disposed of in the course of the administration of his estate, the tenancy ceases to be a secure tenancy unless (*a*) the vesting is pursuant to the Matrimonial Causes Act 1973, s. 24, or (*b*) the vesting is to a person eligible for succession (*see* **24** *above*): s. 37B(2).

35. Improvements. This is dealt with in IV, **17**. In addition, s. 38 provides that where a secure tenant has made certain improvements, the landlord has a power (not a duty) to make such payment to the tenant as the landlord considers to be appropriate at or after the end of the tenancy.

36. Variation of terms. Section 40 provides that the terms of a secure tenancy may be varied in accordance with the provisions of the section but not otherwise; the variations may be effected by agreement or, in the case of rent or payments in respect of rates or services, by the landlord or the tenant in accordance with any provisions in the lease. If the tenancy is a periodic one, the variation may also be effected by the landlord by a notice of variation which must specify the variation effected by it and the date on which it takes effect and the period between the date of service and the date on which it takes effect must not be shorter than the rental period of the tenancy nor shorter than four weeks. Prior to serving a notice of variation the landlord must serve a preliminary notice on the tenant informing him of his intention to serve a notice of variation and must consider any comments made by the tenant in response to the preliminary notice: s. 40(5), (6). In relation to rent or the payment of rates and services, however, there is no need to serve a preliminary notice.

37. Provision of information about tenancies. By s. 41(1) every body which lets dwelling-houses under secure tenancies must within two years of 3rd October 1980 publish information about its secure tenancies to explain in simple terms the effect of, inter alia, the express terms of its secure tenancies and the effect of parts of the 1980 Act.

38. Repairs. Section 41A provides that the Secretary of State may make a scheme entitling secure tenants to carry out repairs which the landlords are obliged to carry out and to recover from the landlords such sums as may be determined under the scheme.

39. Heating charges. Under s. 41B the Secretary of State has power by regulations to require heating authorities (i.e. a landlord which operates its own generating station or other installation for producing heat and supplies heat produced by it to any premises) to adopt such methods of charging as ensure that the tenants pay no greater proportion of the cost of operating the installation and producing the heat than is reasonable.

PROGRESS TEST 26

1. What is the scope of the 1980 Act? **(1)**
2. What is a secure tenancy? **(2)**
3. What are the exceptions to secure tenancies? **(8)**
4. Explain how the 1980 Act gives security of tenure to secure tenants. **(22)**
5. How may a secure tenancy come to an end? **(23)**
6. What are the rules governing succession on the death of a secure tenant? **(24–26)**
7. How may the Landlord of a secure tenant recover possession against the tenant? **(26)**
8. What is ground 8? Is there an equivalent ground in the Rent Act 1977? **(29)**
9. What terms are implied in a secure tenancy? **(32)**
10. Under what duty as regards information is a landlord of a secure tenant? **(37)**

CHAPTER XXVII

Secure Tenants: The Right to Buy

1. Introduction. The Housing Act 1980 gives to certain public-sector tenants the right to buy their house or flat if they have lived there for at least two years. The price payable (*see* **10** *et seq.*) will be discounted so that the price payable by the tenant will be lower the longer he has lived in the house. A tenant who has a right to buy has a right to a mortgage (*see* **15** *et seq.*).

THE RIGHT TO BUY

2. Introduction. A secure tenant of a house has the right to acquire the freehold of it if the landlord owns the freehold or, if the landlord does not own the freehold to be granted a lease of it: s. 1(1). A secure tenant of a flat has the right to be granted a lease of it: s. 1(1). In addition, in either case the secure tenant has the right to leave the whole or part of the aggregate amount of the purchase price and certain costs outstanding on the security of a first mortgage of the dwelling-house or, if the landlord is a housing association, to have the whole or part of that amount advanced to him on that security by the Housing Corporation. The right to buy only arises after the secure tenant has enjoyed that status for not less than two years or for periods amounting together to not less than two years.

There are two special cases:

(*a*) in the case of a joint tenancy the condition need only be satisfied with respect to one tenant;

(*b*) where the secure tenant becomes a secure tenant on the death of his spouse under s. 30 (*see* **XXVI, 24**), any period during which the deceased spouse was a secure tenant is to be counted for determining the two years.

3. Exceptions to the right to buy. There are several cases when the right to buy does not arise. The main ones are:

(*a*) if the landlord is a housing trust which is a charity within the meaning of the Charities Act 1960: s. 2(1);

(*b*) if the landlord is a housing association which is either a charity within the meaning of the Charities Act 1960 or a society registered under the Industrial and Provident Societies Act 1965: s. 2(2);

(*c*) where the landlord does not have, in the case of a house, a lease for a term exceeding 21 years commencing with the relevant time and, in the case of a flat, a lease for a term of not less than 50 years commencing with that time;

(*d*) if the landlord is a local authority, a development corporation, an urban development corporation, the Commission for New Towns, a county council, an aided school or the Development Board for Rural Wales, and the dwelling-house either is in a cemetery or in the curtilage of a building held mainly for purposes other than housing and consists mainly of accommodation other than housing accommodation and the dwelling-house is let to the tenant in consequence of his employment by the landlord: Sch. 1, para. 1;

(*e*) the dwelling-house has features which are substantially different from those of ordinary dwelling-houses and which are designed to make it suitable for occupation by physically disabled persons and either (*i*) the dwelling house has had those features since it was constructed or, where it was provided by conversion, since it was so provided or (*ii*) the dwelling-house is one of a group of dwelling-houses which it is the practice of the landlord to let for occupation by physically disabled persons and a social service or special facilities are provided in close proximity to the group to assist those persons: Sch. 1, para. 3;

(*f*) the landlord or a predecessor has carried out, for the purpose of making the dwelling-house suitable for occupation by physically disabled persons one or more of (*i*) provision of not less than $7.5m^2$ of extra floor space, (*ii*) provision of an additional bathroom or shower-room, (*iii*) installation of a lift; Sch. 1, para. 3A;

(*g*) the dwelling-house is one of a group of dwelling-houses which it is the practice of the landlord to let for occupation by persons who suffer, or have suffered, from a mental disorder and a social service or special facilities are provided for assisting those persons: Sch. 1, para. 3B;

(*h*) the dwelling-house is one of a group of dwelling-houses which are particularly suitable, having regard to location, size, design, heating and other features, for occupation by persons of pensionable age and which it is the practice of the landlord to let for occupation by such persons or by them and physically disabled persons, and special facilities are provided to assist them; Sch. 1, para. 4;

(*i*) the Secretary of State has determined, on application by the landlord, that the right to buy is not to be capable of being exercised if the dwelling-house (*i*) is particularly suitable, having regard to its location, size, design and other features, for occupation by persons of pensionable age, and (*ii*) it was let to the tenant for occupation by such person or a physically disabled person, provided that the landlord must apply within 8 weeks of service of the notice exercising the right to buy: Sch. 1 para. 5.

NOTE: The above deals only with the main exceptions but there are other exceptions in s. 2 and Sch. 1.

4. Dwelling-house, house and flat. Section 5 contains provisions dealing with the inter-relation of these three words. The following rules emerge from s. 5:

(*a*) a dwelling-house is a house if it is a structure which can reasonably be called a house;

(*b*) where a building is divided horizontally, the units into which it is divided are *not* houses;

(*c*) where a building is divided vertically, the units into which it is divided *may* be houses;

(*d*) where a building is not structurally divided it is not a house if a material part of it lies above or below the remainder of the structure;

(*e*) any dwelling-house which is not a house is a flat.

In most cases it will be easy to decide if a unit is a house or a flat. Where there is doubt, the proper approach is to apply rules (*a*)–(*d*) above. If the result of applying the rules is that the unit is not a house then it will be a flat. There is treated as included in the dwelling-house any land which is or has been used for the purposes of the dwelling-house if (*a*) the tenant serves written notice exercising the right to acquire the land at any time before exercising the right to buy and (*b*) it is reasonable to include the land.

PROCEDURAL MATTERS

5. Procedure for exercising right to buy. In order to exercise the right to buy a secure tenant must serve a written notice claiming to exercise the right to buy: s. 5(1). Within four weeks of service the landlord must serve a written notice either admitting or denying the tenant's right and stating the reason why, in the opinion of the landlord, the tenant does not have the right to buy.

6. Purchase price. By s. 6(1), the price payable for a dwelling-house is the value of it at the date of service of the tenant's notice exercising the right to buy less the discount under s. 7.

7. The value of the dwelling-house. By s. 6(2) the value at the relevant time is taken to be the price which, at that time, the dwelling-house would realise if sold on the open market by a willing vendor on certain specified assumptions and disregarding:

(*a*) any improvements made by

(*i*) the secure tenant;

(*ii*) any person who under the same tenancy was a secure tenant before him; and

(*iii*) any member of the secure tenant's family who immediately before the secure tenancy was granted was a secure tenant of the same dwelling-house under another tenancy; and

(*b*) any failure by any of the above persons to keep the dwelling-house in good internal repair.

8. Assumptions on sale of freehold. By s. 6(3) the assumptions are that:

(*a*) the sale is of an estate in fee simple with vacant possession;

(*b*) neither the tenant nor a member of his family residing with him wanted to buy;

(*c*) the dwelling-house was to be conveyed with the same rights and subject to the same burdens as it would be in pursuance of the 1980 Act.

9. Assumptions on grant of a lease. By s. 6(4) the assumptions are that:

(*a*) the vendor was granting a lease for 125 years with vacant possession;

(*b*) neither the tenant nor a member of his family residing with him wanted to take the lease;

(*c*) the ground rent would not exceed £10 per annum; and

(*d*) the grant was to be made with the same rights and subject to the same burdens as it would be in pursuance of the 1980 Act.

10. Discount. A discount is available to those who are exercising the right to buy. The starting point is to calculate, in accordance with Part I of Schedule 1A, the period during which the secure tenant, the secure tenant's spouse or the secure tenant's deceased spouse, was a public sector tenant or the spouse of a public sector tenant. When that period has been calculated there are two basic rules to apply under s. 7(1):

(a) if the period is less than three years the discount is 32%;

(b) if it is three years or more, the discount is 32% plus 1% for each complete year by which the period exceeds two years, but not altogether exceeding 60%.

11. Limits on the discount. The discount cannot reduce the price below the amount which the Secretary of State determines to be the costs incurred in respect of the dwelling-house as is to be treated as incurred after 31st March 1974 or such later date as the Sceretary of State may specify by order: s. 7(2). Further, the discount cannot in any case reduce the price by more than such sum as the Secretary of State may by order prescribe: s. 7(4).

12. Repayment of discount on early disposal of freehold or leasehold. Where a discount is granted and there is a relevant disposal of the freehold or leasehold within five years of the initial sale, a proportion of the discount must be repaid to the landlord: s. 8. The repayment is the amount of the discount less 20% (thereof) for each complete year after the initial sale: s. 8(2). There are exceptions to this rule requiring repayment where, inter alia, the disposal is to a "qualifying person", i.e. one of the two joint owners, a spouse, or a member of the family residing in the house for twelve months ending with the disposal: s. 8(3A) and (3B).

13. Meaning of relevant disposal. A relevant disposal is (a) a further conveyance of the freehold or assignment of the lease or (b) a grant of a lease or sub-lease for more than 21 years otherwise than at a rack rent, whether the disposal is of the whole or part of the dwelling house: s. 8(3). For the purposes of (b) above, it is assumed that any option to renew or extend a lease or sub-lease is exercised and that any option to terminate a lease or sub-lease is not exercised.

14. Enforcement of recovery of discount. Any liability to repay a discount that may arise by reason of an early disposal takes effect as a charge in favour of the landlord on the dwelling-house having priority immediately after any legal charge securing any amount left outstanding by the tenant in exercising the right to buy or advanced to him by, inter alia, the Housing Corporation or any building society, for the purpose of enabling him to exercise the right to buy: s. 8(4), (5).

15. Right to a mortgage. It has already been stated that a secure tenant exercising the right to buy has a right to a mortgage. The amount which he is entitled to leave outstanding, or have advanced to him by the Housing Corporation, is the aggregate of:

(*a*) the purchase price;

(*b*) costs incurred by the landlord or the Housing Corporation and chargeable to the tenant under s. 26 (*see* **26**);

(*c*) any costs incurred by the tenant and defrayed on his behalf by the landlord or the Housing Corporation: s. 9(1).

16. Limits on the right to a mortgage. There are limits to the sum which can be advanced under s. 9(1). The rules are as follows:

(*a*) it must not exceed the amount to be taken into account, in accordance with regulations made under s. 9, as the tenant's available annual income multiplied by the appropriate factor under the regulations;

(*b*) where there is more than one person entitled to a mortgage, the limit is the aggregate of the amount calculated under (*a*) above.

NOTES: (1) Regulations have now been made; they are the Housing (Right to Buy) (Mortgage Limits) Regulations 1980 (S. I. 1980 No. 1423).

(2) By virtue of s. 9(5) the landlord may, if it considers fit and the tenant agrees, treat the tenant as entitled to leave outstanding on the security such amount exceeding the limit in (*a*) or (*b*) above but not exceeding the aggregate in s. 9(1) (*see* **15**) as the landlord may determine.

17. Notice of purchase price. Where a secure tenant has claimed to exercise the right to buy and that right has been established the landlord must as soon as practicable serve on the tenant a notice describing the dwelling-house and stating:

(*a*) the price, showing the value, the discount and improvements disregarded;

(*b*) the provisions of the conveyance or grant;

(*c*) that the tenant has the right to have the value determined by the District Valuer;

(*d*) that the tenant has the right to a mortgage;

(*e*) information regarding the right to claim a mortgage: Act of 1980, s. 10.

18. Determination of value by District Valuer. Any question arising as to the value of a dwelling-house will be determined by the

District Valuer: s. 11(1). A tenant can require the District Valuer to determine the value by written notice served on the landlord not later than three months after service of the notice under s. 10 (*see* **17**). The District Valuer must consider any representations made by the landlord or tenant. After the determination the landlord must serve a notice on the tenant stating the effect of the determination: s. 11(5).

19. Claim to a mortgage. A secure tenant cannot exercise his claim for a mortgage unless he does so by written notice served within three months beginning with the service on the tenant of

(*a*) if the tenant exercises his right under s. 11, the notice served under s. 11(5) (*see* **18**);

(*b*) otherwise, the notice served under s. 10 (*see* **17**).

As soon as practicable after the service of the tenant's notice, the landlord or the Housing Corporation must serve written notice on the tenant stating:

(*a*) the amount of the mortgage;

(*b*) how the mortgage is calculated;

(*c*) the terms of the mortgage.

20. Change of parties. In ss. 13, 14 there are provisions dealing with change of tenant and landlord. The rules to be derived from these sections are:

(*a*) where after a secure tenant has given a notice claiming the right to buy, another person becomes the secure tenant either

(*i*) under the same secure tenancy; or

(*ii*) under a periodic tenancy arising by virtue of s. 29 (*see* XXVI, **23**), on the coming to an end of the secure tenancy the new tenant is in the same position as if he had given the notice: s. 12(1);

(*b*) where, after a secure tenant has given a notice claiming the right to buy, the freehold passes to another body all parties are in the same position as if the other body had become the landlord before the notice was given.

21. Children succeeding parents. Section 15 contains provisions dealing with the case of children succeeding deceased parents as secure tenants of the dwelling-house. It gives the landlord a discretion to allow certain periods to count towards the periods required under s. 1(3) (the residential qualification: *see* **2**) and s. 7(5) (the discount: *see* **10**).

22. Completion. Section 16 contains provisions relating to the completion of the sale or lease. It enables the landlord to serve at least 56 days notice on the tenant requiring him, if all relevant matters have been agreed or determined, to complete the transaction within a specific period of not less than 56 days, or if any relevant matters are outstanding, to serve on the landlord within that period written notice specifying those matters, and, in any event, informing the tenant of the effect of the notice: s. 16(2). Under section 16(6), if the tenant does not comply with the above notice, the landlord may serve on him a further written notice requiring him to complete within a specific period of not less than 56 days, which period may be extended by the landlord under s. 16(6A). If the tenant does not comply with the notice under section 16(6), then the notice claiming the right to buy is deemed to be withdrawn at the end of the period specified therein or any extended period: s. 16(6B). Under s. 16(1) the landlord is under a duty to complete as soon as all matters relating to the grant of the freehold or the lease and the amount of the mortgage are agreed or determined; the duty is enforceable by the tenant by an injunction: s. 16(10).

23. Conveyance of freehold and grant of lease. There are detailed provisions in Sch. 2 to the Act dealing with the terms for the conveyance of the freehold and the grant of the lease. The conveyance and grant must conform with Sch. 2; the detailed provisions are outside the scope of this book.

24. Terms of mortgage deed. The mortgage must, unless otherwise agreed, conform with the following:

(*a*) it must provide for repayment of the amount secured in equal instalments of principal and interest combined;

(*b*) the period over which repayment is to be made must be 25 years or, at the option of the mortgagor, a shorter period, but shall be capable of being extended by the mortgagee; and

(*c*) it may contain such other terms as may be agreed between the mortgagor and the mortgagee or as may be determined by the county court to be reasonably required by the mortgagor or the mortgagee.

25. Dwelling-houses in National Parks and areas of outstanding natural beauty. Section 19 contains special provisions dealing with dwelling-houses in these areas.

26. Costs. Where a tenant exercises his right to a mortgage, the landlord or the Housing Corporation may charge to him the costs incurred by it in connection with the tenant's exercise of the right to a mortgage, subject to limits prescribed by the Secretary of State: s. 21(2). Save as aforesaid the tenant is not obliged to pay any part of the landlord's costs and any agreement to that effect is void: s. 21(1).

POWERS OF THE SECRETARY OF STATE

27. Secretary of State's power to intervene. Where it appears to the Secretary of State that tenants generally, or a tenant or tenants of a particular landlord, have or may have difficulty in exercising the right to buy effectively and expeditiously, he may, after giving the landlord notice of his intention to do so, use his powers under s. 23. Those powers are in wide terms and enable the Secretary of State to do all things as appear to him necessary or expedient to enable secure tenants to exercise the right to buy or the right to a mortgage. In summary the effect of ss. 23, 24 (which enables the Secretary of State to vest dwelling-houses in tenants by means of a vesting order) is that if a landlord creates difficulties in performing his duties under this Part of the 1980 Act, the Secretary of State can step in and perform all the functions of the local authority already described.

28. Further powers. The Secretary of State has power under s. 24A to direct that covenants or conditions may be contained in the conveyance or grant, notwithstanding that they are not consistent with Sch. 2 (*see* **23** *above*). Section 24B deals with the effect of such directions on the old covenants. Section 24C gives to the Secretary of State power to obtain information or documents necessary for the purposes of deciding whether to exercise his powers above under ss. 23, 24A or 24B.

29. Power to give assistance. Where, in relation to any proceedings or prospective proceedings, one party has claimed the right to buy, he may apply to the Secretary of State for assistance which includes giving advice, procuring or attempting to procure a settlement and arranging representation by a solicitor or counsel on the grounds that (*a*) the case raises a question of principle, or (*b*) it is unreasonable to expect the applicant to deal with the case without assistance, or (*c*) there are other special considerations.

30. Power to extend right to buy. The Secretary of State may by order extend the right to buy to cases where the landlord has a leasehold interest only but one or more of the superior interests is owned by a local authority, a county council, the Commission for the New Towns, a development corporation, the Housing Corporation, a housing association, an urban development corporation, or the Development Board for Rural Wales.

SHARED OWNERSHIP LEASES

31. Shared ownership leases. Sections 12 to 17 of the 1984 Act introduced the right to be granted a shared ownership lease in accordance with Sch. 3 to that Act. The right arises where: (*a*) the right to buy has been established; (*b*) the tenant has claimed the right to a mortgage and the amount which he is entitled to leave outstanding or have advanced to him is less than the limit under s. 9(1) (*see* **16** *above*); and (*c*) the tenant has, within three months of service on him of notice of the amount he is entitled to leave outstanding or have advanced to him, served notice on the landlord claiming to be entitled to defer completion and has deposited £100 with the landlord. When the right arises the tenant may serve on the landlord notice claiming to exercise the right to be granted a shared ownership lease and specifying the initial share which he proposes to acquire. Within four weeks thereafter the landlord must serve written notice in reply admitting the right or denying it and stating the reasons for the denial. If the tenant serves notice claiming a shared ownership lease, any notice under s. 16(2) or (6) (*see* **22** *above*) is deemed to be withdrawn.

The tenant's initial share must be at least 50 per cent and he may thereafter acquire additional shares in amounts of 12½ per cent. There are provisions in Sch. 3 to the 1984 Act dealing with the terms of a shared ownership lease. Where the dwelling house is a house and the landlord owns the freehold, when the tenant achieves 100 per cent ownership of the lease, he is entitled to require the freehold to be conveyed to him: Sch. 3, para. 3(5). It can be seen that this provides a means for tenants to acquire their dwelling house by instalments.

SERVICE CHARGES

32. Service charges. Section 18 and Sch. 4 of the 1984 Act contain provisions for regulating the service charge payable under a lease granted under the right to buy. The provisions impose limits on the recovery of the service charge and provide for the supply of information about the charge to the tenants.

DEFECTIVE HOUSES

33. Defective houses. Where the right to buy has been exercised and the house proves to be defective in some way, the owner *may* be entitled to assistance whether by way of a re-instatement grant or re-purchase: see the Housing Defects Act 1984. This only applies however to defects of design or construction by virtue of which the value of the dwelling has been substantially reduced. Further, it only applies to dwellings of a class (which may include only one dwelling) which the Secretary of State designates as defective.

PROGRESS TEST 27

1. When does the right to buy arise? **(1, 2)**
2. What are the exceptions to the right to buy? **(3)**
3. How may the right to buy be exercised? **(5)**
4. How is the purchase price calculated? **(6, 7)**
5. What is the amount of the discount? **(10, 11)**
6. When is the discount repayable? **(12, 13)**
7. What are the tenant's rights as regards mortgages? **(15)**
8. What limits are there to the right to a mortgage? **(16)**
9. If the parties cannot agree on the purchase price, how is it determined? **(18)**
10. How can the sale or lease of the house be completed? **(22)**

CHAPTER XXVIII

Protected Shorthold Tenancies

1. Introduction. In order to try to induce landlords or prospective landlords to let residential property, the Housing Act 1980 has introduced two types of protection under which the landlord may let his property and be sure of recovering possession. The two types are:

(*a*) protected shorthold tenancies: ss. 51–55;

(*b*) assured tenancies: ss. 56–58 (*see* XXIX).

The first type enables a landlord to recover possession but in Greater London the recoverable rent is only a registered rent. The second type enables the landlord to charge a market rent and recover possession.

2. Protected shorthold tenancies. It should be noted that a protected shorthold tenancy is still a protected tenancy (*see* XV). There is, however, a new Case added to the Rent Act 1977, Sch. 15, Part II (the mandatory grounds for possession) which enables the landlord to recover possession at the end of a shorthold letting: *see* Case 19 (at **6** below).

3. Conditions to be satisfied. In order for a tenancy to be a protected shorthold tenancy the following must be satisfied: s. 52:

(*a*) there must be a protected tenancy granted after 28th November 1980;

(*b*) the grant must be for a term certain of not less than one year nor more than five years;

(*c*) the tenancy must be incapable of being brought to an end by the landlord except in pursuance of a provision for re-entry or forfeiture for non-payment of rent or breach of any other obligation of the tenancy;

(*d*) before the grant the landlord must have given the tenant a valid notice in the prescribed form stating that the tenancy is to be a protected shorthold tenancy;

(*e*) in the case of a dwelling in Greater London, either:

(*i*) a fair rent is registered; or

(*ii*) a certificate of fair rent has been issued under s. 69 of the

1977 Act before the grant and an application for the registration of a rent is made not later than 28 days after the beginning of the term and is not withdrawn.

NOTES: (1) A tenancy of a dwelling-house is not a protected shorthold tenancy if it is granted to a person who, immediately before it was granted, was a protected or statutory tenant of that dwelling-house; s. 52(2).

(2) A protected shorthold tenancy will continue to be one if it is for a term certain as above followed, at the tenant's option, by a further term, or for a term certain as above and thereafter from year to year or some other period; s. 52(5).

4. Right of tenant to end protected shorthold tenancy. By s. 53(1) a protected shorthold tenancy can be brought to an end by the tenant giving written notice to the landlord. The period of the notice is:

(a) one month if the term certain is two years or less;

(b) three months if the term is more than two years.

5. Assignment or sub-letting. By virtue of s. 54(2) a protected shorthold tenancy is not capable of being assigned. By s. 54(1), where the tenant under a protected shorthold tenancy sub-lets the whole or part of the dwelling-house, the landlord becomes entitled as against the tenant to possession of the premises. He is also entitled to possession against the sub-tenant and the 1977 Act, s. 137 (*see* XVII, **36**) does not apply.

6. Case 19. Where the dwelling-house was let under a protected shorthold tenancy (or is treated under the Housing Act 1980, s. 55 as having been so let) and

(a) there either has been no grant of a further tenancy of the dwelling-house since the end of the protected shorthold tenancy or, if there was such a grant, it was to a person who immediately before the grant was in possession of the dwelling-house as a protected or statutory tenant; and

(b) the proceedings for possession were commenced after appropriate notice by the landlord to the tenant and not later than three months after the expiry of the notice.

A notice is appropriate for this Case if

(a) it is in writing and states that proceedings for possession under this Case may be brought after its expiry; and

(b) it expires not earlier than three months after it is served nor, if, when it is served, the tenancy is a periodic tenancy, before that periodic tenancy could be brought to an end by a notice to quit served by the landlord on the same day;

(c) it is served

(i) in the period of three months immediately preceding the date on which the protected shorthold tenancy comes to an end; or

(ii) if that date has passed, in the period of three months immediately preceding any anniversary of that date; and

(d) in a case where a previous notice has been served by the landlord on the tenant in respect of the dwelling-house, and that notice was an appropriate notice, it is served not earlier than three months after the expiry of the previous notice.

7. Power to dispense with conditions. In proceedings for possession under Case 19, if the court is of opinion that, although conditions (d) and (e) above are not satisfied, it is just and equitable to make an order for possession, it may treat the tenancy as a protected shorthold tenancy.

PROGRESS TEST 28

1. What conditions must be satisfied in order for there to be a shorthold tenancy? **(3)**

2. How may a shorthold tenancy be brought to an end? **(4)**

3. What is Case 19? Summarise the requirements of the case. **(6)**

4. What restrictions are there on assigning or sub-letting a dwelling-house subject to a shorthold tenancy? **(5)**

CHAPTER XXIX

Assured Tenancies

1. Introduction. The Housing Act 1980 introduces a new class of tenancy called "assured tenancies." The aim behind this new class is to encourage private individuals to build houses with a view to letting them instead of selling. Thus, it is hoped, a new stockpile of tenanted accommodation may be accumulated. Accordingly, an assured tenancy can only arise in respect of a dwelling-house erected after the passing of the 1980 Act, i.e. after 8th August 1980.

2. Assured tenancies. An assured tenancy is one which satisfies the following conditions:

(a) the interest of the landlord since the creation of the tenancy must have belonged to an "approved body";

(b) the dwelling-house must be, or form part of, a building which was erected (and on which construction work first began) after the passing of the 1980 Act (i.e. 8th August 1980);

(c) before the tenant first occupied the dwelling-house under the tenancy no part of it had been occupied by any person as his residence except under an assured tenancy: s. 56.

NOTES: (1) "Approved body" means a body or one of a description of bodies for the time being specified in an order made by the Secretary of State: s. 56(4).

(2) Section 56 does not apply if, before the grant of the tenancy, the landlord gives the tenant a valid notice in the prescribed form that the tenancy is to be a protected tenancy or a housing association tenancy and not an assured tenancy.

3. Effect of landlord ceasing to be an approved body. When the landlord under an assured tenancy ceases to be an approved body by reason of a variation in the bodies specified in an order under s. 56(4), in relation to that tenancy and any further tenancy granted by the landlord to the person who immediately before the grant was in possession of the dwelling-house as an assured tenant, the landlord is treated as continuing to be an approved body: s. 57(1). If, for any period, the reason for such cesser is other than above, then in determining whether condition **2**(*a*) above is satisfied, any period of less than three months will be disregarded.

4. Protection given to assured tenants. The protection given to assured tenants is that of Part II of the Landlord and Tenant Act 1954 (*see* X–XIV) subject to the exceptions and modifications specified in Sch. 5 to the 1980 Act.

5. Schedule 5. The main exceptions and modifications are:

(*a*) s. 23 does not apply (i.e. definition of business tenancy);

(*b*) s. 43 does not apply (i.e. exceptions from protection);

(*c*) "the holding" means the property comprised in the tenancy;

(*d*) for ground (*d*) of s. 30(1), there is substituted "the landlord has offered and is willing to provide or secure the provision of suitable alternative accommodation for the tenant."

There are other alterations for which reference should be made to Sch. 5.

6. Scheme of assured tenancies. It is generally agreed that of all landlord and tenant legislation, Part II of the Landlord and Tenant Act 1954 has worked most successfully balancing the interests of landlord and tenant in a fair way. The tenant pays a market rent; the landlord can recover possession if the tenant is bad or if the landlord requires possession for his own use or to re-construct. The aim behind the concept of an assured tenancy is to transfer the success of the business tenancy legislation to residential accommodation. A tenant will pay a market rent. The landlord will be able to recover possession as above. It remains to be seen what success, if any, assured tenancies may have.

PROGRESS TEST 29

1. What is an assured tenancy? **(2)**
2. What protection is given to a tenant under an assured tenancy? **(4)**
3. On what statutory code is the protection given to assured tenants based? What is the aim behind the creation of assured tenancies? **(1, 6)**

Specimen Lease

THIS LEASE made the .... day of .... One Thousand Nine Hundred and .... BETWEEN ....
....
..... (hereinafter called "the Lessor" which expression where the context admits includes the persons deriving title under the Lessor) of the one part and...
.... (hereinafter called "the Lessee" which expression where the context admits includes the persons deriving title under the Lessee) of the other part WITNESSETH and IT IS HEREBY DECLARED as follows:

1. IN consideration of the rent hereinafter reserved and of the covenants by the Lessee hereinafter contained the Lessor HEREBY DEMISES unto the Lessee ALL THAT building known as ....
....

EXCEPTED AND RESERVED unto the Lessor Full right of passage and running of water and soil from all neighbouring lands and houses of the Lessor through all drains channels and sewers in and under the premises and the right to build on any neighbouring land of the Lessor notwithstanding that the erection of the buildings may interfere with the access of light or air to the property hereby demised TO HOLD (except and reserved as aforesaid) unto the Lessee from 1st July 1972 for a term of years expiring on 24th September 1985 (determinable nevertheless as hereinafter mentioned) YIELDING AND PAYING therefor during the said term unto the Lessor the yearly rent of TWO THOUSAND FIVE HUNDRED POUNDS (£2,500) to be increased as hereinafter mentioned clear of all deductions (except as hereinafter mentioned) by equal quarterly payments on the usual quarter days in every year the first of such payments to be made in advance on the signing hereof for the rent to 29th September 1972 ALSO YIELDING AND PAYING (by way of further rent) the amount from time to time expended by the Lessor in effecting and maintaining the insurance of the premises against loss or damage by fire and other risks usually covered by a householders comprehensive policy in a sum not exceeding the full value thereof such further rent to be paid by the Lessee without any deduction on the quarter day for payment of rent which occurs next after the expenditure by the Lessor and for the hiring costs of the door telephone.

2. THE Lessee hereby covenants with the Lessor as follows:

(1) During the said term to pay the said yearly rents at the times and in manner aforesaid;

(2) To pay all rates taxes charges assessments and outgoings whether parliamentary parochial or otherwise of an annual or recurring nature which now are or which at any time hereafter shall be assessed or imposed upon the premises or any part thereof;

(3) At all times during the said term at the Lessee's own cost when and as often as need or occasion shall require well and substantially to repair amend renew uphold support maintain paint grain varnish paper whitewash and cleanse the interior of the premises and the fixtures and fittings and appurtenances belonging thereto save for the reinstatement caused by accidental fire or any other risk insured against by the Lessor;

(4) At the end or other sooner determination of the said term peaceably to surrender and yield up the premises the interior being so well and substantially maintained painted and cleansed as aforesaid unto the Lessor together with all fixtures which at any time during the said term shall have been affixed or shall belong to the premises (tenant's fixtures only excepted);

(5) That the Lessor or any persons authorised by the Lessor may twice in every year during the said term upon appointment previously made at all reasonable times in the daytime enter into and upon the premises to view and examine the state and condition thereof and of all defects decays or wants of reparation or amendment (which upon such view shall be found) give or leave notice in writing at or upon the premises for the Lessee to repair and amend the same;

(6) At the Lessee's own expense within three months from the giving or leaving of such notice well and sufficiently to repair and amend the same accordingly;

(7) That the Lessee will permit the Lessor and persons authorised by the Lessor at all reasonable hours in the daytime to enter into and upon the premises for the purpose of executing alterations or repairs to the adjoining premises or for carrying out upon the premises such repairs (if any) as either the Lessor or the Lessee may be liable to effect hereunder or for complying with any statutory obligation imposed on the owner or occupier of the

demised premises Provided That where the Lessee is liable to effect the repairs this power shall not be exercised until the Lessee has made default for 30 days after being required in writing to do the work and in that case shall be liable on demand to make good to the Lessor the costs of effecting the repairs with interest at £8 per cent p.a. from the date of the demand;

(8) Not during the said term to use exercise or carry on or permit or suffer to be used exercised or carried on in or upon the premises or any part thereof any noisy or offensive trade or business whatsoever but will use the premises only as and for a private dwelling-house;

(9) Not without the consent in writing of the Lessor to make any structural alteration in or addition to the premises or erect any new building thereon or carry out any operation or institute or continue any use of the premises for which planning permission is required without the consent of the Lessor such consent not to be unreasonably withheld;

(10) Not to assign charge underlet or part with the possession of the premises or any part thereof but in the event of an assignment or underletting being required by the Lessee the Lessor shall grant consent to an assignment or underletting of the whole in the case of a responsible and desirable person with proper references being put forward to the reasonable satisfaction of the Lessor;

(11) Within one month after any assignment charge or underlease of the premises or any part thereof shall have been executed or after the devolution of the said term or any derivative term to produce the disposition or evidence of the devolution to the Lessor's Solicitors for registration to whom a fee of £3 shall be paid for each registration;

(12) Not to do or permit to be done upon the demised premises or any part thereof any act or thing which may invalidate or render voidable any policies of insurance from time to time effected against loss or damage by fire and other risks of the premises or of any fixtures and chattels therein belonging to the Lessor or which may operate to increase the premiums payable in respect of any such policy;

(13) Not to do or permit to be done on the demised premises or any part thereof anything which may be or grow to be a nuisance damage inconvenience or annoyance to the Lessor or to the owners or occupiers of any adjacent premises;

(14) Not to allow any public meeting or sale by auction to be

held on the premises or permit to be placed on the premises any bill signboard placard hoarding or other outward mark;

(15) Within seven days of the receipt by the Lessee of any notice order or proposal made given or issued to the Lessee by a planning authority under or by virtue of any enactment relating to town and country planning to give full particulars thereof to the Lessor and without delay to take all reasonable or necessary steps to comply with any such notice or order so far as such compliance is the responsibility of the Lessee under the other covenants of this Lease;

(16) To permit the Lessor or the Lessor's agents from time to time during the last three months before the expiration or sooner determination of the said term to affix notices upon the premises advertising that they are to be sold, let or to be otherwise disposed of and also at all convenient times in the daytime (by agents or otherwise) to enter into with and show the premises to any person;

3. PROVIDED THAT if any part of the said rents shall be in arrear for twenty-one days (whether or not lawfully demanded) or if there shall be a breach of any of the covenants by the Lessee herein contained the Lessor may re-enter upon the premises and immediately thereupon the said term shall absolutely determine

4. IF the Retail Price Index issued by the Department of Trade and Industry for April 1974 shall show that there has been an increase in the cost of living over and above that for May 1971 the rent hereby reserved shall as from 1st May 1974 be increased in the same proportion and the rent with effect from each subsequent 1st May shall similarly be reviewed by reference to the increase (if any) in the cost of living as shown by the said Retail Price Indices for the immediately preceding month of April and the month of April in the previous year and any increased rent payable pursuant to this Clause in respect of the period from 1st May to 24th June in any year shall be paid not later than fourteen days after the Lessor shall have furnished to the Lessee evidence in writing of the relevant Retail Price Indices and the consequent recalculation of the rent;

5. THE Lessee shall have the right on giving not less than three months' notice in writing to the Lessor to terminate this Lease on the expiry of the fifth and tenth years of the said term the Lessor refunding to the Lessee the deposit referred to in Clause 6(4) hereof and paid by the Lessee in respect of any period after such termination.

6. THE Lessor hereby covenants with the Lessee as follows:

(1) That the Lessee paying the rent hereby reserved and performing and observing all the covenants by the Lessee herein contained shall and may quietly hold and enjoy the premises during the said term without any lawful interruption by the Lessor or any person rightfully claiming through under or in trust for that party;

(2) That the Lessor will during the subsistence of the term hereby granted insure and keep insured against loss or damage by fire and all other risks usually covered by a householder's comprehensive policy the premises hereby demised and the building of which they form part to the full value thereof and will apply all insurance money in or towards reinstating or making good any of the said buildings which may be destroyed or damaged by fire and make up any deficiency out of his own money and during such time as the premises shall be rendered uninhabitable due to fire no rental shall be payable hereunder or if partially rendered uninhabitable a proportion of rental only shall be payable such proportion to be decided by the Landlord's Surveyor;

(3) To observe and perform the covenants contained in the Headlease of the premises and to pay the annual rental and to maintain in good repair the structure roof and all external parts of the premises and the building of which it forms part as well as the electrical wiring and central heating system in the said premises and building;

(4) Provided the Lessee shall have complied with the covenant and obligation on his part hereinbefore contained to procure the refund at the end or sooner determination of the said term of the deposit of £300 paid by the Lessee on the execution hereof.

IN WITNESS whereof the parties hereto have hereunto set their hands and seals the day and year first before written

Signed sealed and delivered   *Signature* ....
by ....

in the presence of ....   (L.S.)

Examination Technique

Examination questions in landlord and tenant tend to be problems based on a combination of the facts of different reported cases. They aim to test the candidate's knowledge and application of principles of both the common law and statute.

A useful general approach to a landlord and tenant question is as follows. First, the matter should be considered by reference to basic common law principles (Chapter I–IX). Secondly, it must be considered whether any of the basic common law principles have been altered by statute. If so the modification must be applied to the problem.

The candidate may be assisted by the following general points on technique:

1. It need hardly be said that prior to the examination some work should be done. In particular, the candidate should familiarise himself with the contents of those books which appear on his syllabus. If it is not possible to remember the names of cases or provisions of each Act, the general principle to be derived from each case and provision must be understood and remembered.

2. Prior to the examination, the candidate should rough out some sort of timetable. This involves deciding how much time to set aside for (*a*) a first reading of the paper, (*b*) the planning of each answer, (*c*) the re-reading of each answer, and (*d*) final checking.

3. Once in the examination room it should be checked how many questions have to be answered. The style of paper changes from year to year and the number of questions can be altered.

4. The entire paper should be carefully read and a decision made about which questions, if any, can be answered. The candidate should select the four (or whatever number is required). The first answer should be sketched out in skeleton form so as to set a logical framework to the answer. It should then be written out.

5. The candidate should then proceed from question to question in accordance with 4 above and trying to keep to the timetable worked out beforehand.

6. In so far as it is possible, the answer should

(*a*) be written legibly;
(*b*) show a good command of grammar;
(*c*) be relevant to the question;
(*d*) follow in a logical order.

7. In relation to each case, the most important thing to remember is the principle to be derived from the case. Then there follow the facts, the case name, the court and the date, in that order. Case names should never be invented.

8. Time should be left at the end to read through and check the answers.

9. It is normally preferable to attempt problem questions before discussion questions.

Index